Law Addressing Diversity

Law Addressing Diversity

Pre-Modern Europe and India in Comparison (13th–18th Centuries)

Edited by
Thomas Ertl and Gijs Kruijtzer

DE GRUYTER
OLDENBOURG

Cover image: illustration to the German jurist Sebastian Brant's late fifteenth-century satire *Daß Narrenschyff ad Narragoniam* (The Ship of Fools). This is the first time that Lady Justice is depicted with a blindfold. Here this attribute seems to have a negative connotation (because of the jester putting it on), but over the following century it came to represent Justitia's blindness to the background of those before her in a positive sense. Woodcut probably by Albrecht Dürer, 1494.

ISBN 978-3-11-042718-9
e-ISBN (PDF) 978-3-11-042332-7
e-ISBN (EPUB) 978-3-11-042340-2

Library of Congress Cataloging-in-Publication Data
A CIP catalog record for this book has been applied for at the Library of Congress.

Bibliografische Information der Deutschen Nationalbibliothek
The Deutsche Nationalbibliothek lists this publication in the Deutsche Nationalbibliographie; detailed bibliographic data are available in the Internet at http://dnb.dnb.de.

Cover image courtesy Sächsische Landesbibliothek – Staats- und Universitätsbibliothek Dresden.
Typesetting: Dr. Rainer Ostermann, München
Printing: CPI books GmbH, Leck
♾ Printed on acid free paper
Printed in Germany

www.degruyter.com

Preface

The origin of this volume lies in the questions we were asking about diversity in medieval and early modern South Asia and Europe within the framework of the "Handling Diversity" project. This comparative project was based at the University of Vienna and funded by the WWTF, a fund for the promotion of science and scholarship in that city. There is little need to explain the concern of both scholars and governments today with the question of social diversity. Why South Asia and Europe make such interesting and comparable cases should become amply clear in the course of this volume.

Among the questions we were asking about how the diversity of administrative entities, peoples and cultures in both regions might be compared, were some about law. In the workshop "Law Addressing Diversity: Pre-Modern Europe and India in Comparison (12th to 17th Centuries)" which took place at the University of Vienna on 22–25 May 2014, we intended to look at laws that were created to manage the rights and duties of diverse groups within a social space, as well as the side-by-side existence of different laws for different people within one social space. We put questions to the participants such as: how was societal complexity perceived and categorised in legal texts, and which terms were used in this respect? How did legal practitioners evaluate their own role and position within their diverse societies and how did they perceive their ideological links across state boundaries and across the ages? To what extent was law a means of inventing or dismantling social identities and boundaries? Did people shop for justice by trying to tap into the various legal systems available? Was there a general tendency towards convergence or towards divergence, or were there opposing trends in different contexts such as empire, regional state or city state, or on different levels of society? To sum up: How did legal theory and practice cope with the challenge of social difference?

The workshop brought together a group of historians and legal historians to discuss specific topics or phenomena from a European as well as from an Indian perspective. In each panel we paired papers on the Indian context with others on the European context. Out of the discussion some *comparanda* emerged that we present in the Introduction. We believe that the discussions at the conference also enabled a convergence between the papers in the process of revising for this volume, yielding a "comparative surplus" that transcends the sum of the parts. We do, however, not strive for a coherent history of law addressing diversity, but instead hope to highlight certain junctions where law and diversity met, clashed, merged, influenced or hindered each other.

We would like to thank a number of people who contributed to the making of this volume. First of all the experts who anonymously peer reviewed each of

DOI 10.1515/9783110423327-202

the contributions, making many useful suggestions, as well as Paolo Sartori and Eirik Hovden for their input to the Introduction. With regards to the conference we thank, for their spirited contribution to the discussion, Cynthia Neville, Julie Billaud, Farhat Hasan, Sara M. Butler, Nadeera Rupesinghe, André Wink, Alexander Fischer, Indrani Chatterjee, Tilmann Kulke, Jovan Pešalj, Stephan Wendehorst, Ebba Koch, Najaf Haider, Aparna Balachandran, Ada-Maria Kuskowski, Thomas Frank, Anubhuti Maurya and Uros Zver. We also thank Katharina Ferstterer for her organising assistance. Finally we thank Lincoln Paine for style editing a few of the contributions, as well as Andreas Moitzi, Markus Mayer and Jennifer Privett for their work towards preparing the manuscript for publication. We also thank De Gruyter's Bettina Neuhoff for her support and patience.

Contents

Part III: **Transitions to modernity**

Thomas Ertl and Gijs Kruijtzer

Introduction

On the comparability of South Asia and Europe

In their critique of the historical use of the term "continent," and the distortions that come from comparing under that term entities of completely different size such as Europe and Asia, Martin Lewis and Kären Wigen arrive at a demotion of Europe to the status of "world region," on a par with other world regions such as Central Asia, East Asia, Southeast Asia, and so on. In particular, they make a case for calling Europe a subcontinent on the model of South Asia, for which the appellation "subcontinent" has been current for quite some time now (because it is for the most part circumscribed by the sea and long mountain ranges). South Asia is, in their view, the part of the world that is the most comparable to Europe:

> ...however Europe is defined, the European and Indian 'subcontinents' form roughly commensurable units of human geography. Both areas are of similar size and have historically maintained roughly comparable population levels. Both have been historically forged into cultural communities by the sharing of religious beliefs and institutions (Christianity and Hinduism, respectively), as well as by the common use of learned languages (Greek and Latin in Europe, Sanskrit and Persian in South Asia). Finally, both areas have been sufficiently integrated to generate linguistic convergence, whereby unrelated languages came to share certain structural features (although this phenomenon seems to be more strongly developed in South Asia than in Europe).[1]

Now while we may – and should, for the purpose of investigating "diversity" – regard the claim of Europe and South Asia as being "cultural communities" as an overstatement, we agree with the general thrust of this argument about the comparability of South Asia and Europe.[2] We may add to the list of parallels a number of developments that scholars have found over the past 35 years. Sheldon Pollock has pointed to the parallel rise from around the year 1000 of literatures that were not in the learned or "cosmopolitan" languages, but instead in the languages of place which both South Asia and Europe have so many.[3] Before that, in the 1980s

1 Martin W. Lewis, Karen E. Wigen, *The Myth of Continents: A Critique of Metageography,* Berkeley: University of California Press, 1997, 169–170.

2 The argument has also been well-received elsewhere, see Catherine B. Asher, Cynthia Talbot, *India before Europe,* Cambridge: Cambridge University Press, 2006, 8.

3 Sheldon Pollock, India in the Vernacular Millennium: Literary Culture and Polity, 1000–1500, *Daedalus* 127 (1998): 41–74.

DOI 10.1515/9783110423327-001

and 1990s, historians of early modern South Asia were preoccupied with discovering a "state formation" that was akin to the state formation that historians and sociologists had been talking about for Europe since Max Weber. Some historians, especially Chris Bayly and Sanjay Subrahmanyam, also traced a developing proto- or portfolio capitalism in South Asia in this period that was, however, cut short by the advent of colonialism around 1800.[4] In fact, it was for these reasons that the term early modern was then deemed more fitting for the period before 1800 than the labels medieval or Muslim. We believe that there is indeed much evidence for these parallels in vernacularisation, economic development, state formation and bureaucratization, which may to an extent be due to the increasing connectedness of Eurasia over our period through the exchanges generated by the renewed expansion of the Islamic world at the hands of Turkic conquerors, the rise of the Mongols, and European overseas expansion.[5]

Moreover, while the notion that Western Europe saw the formation of linguistically defined states in this period is well established, it is less well known that South Asia also saw many such formations. This is, we believe, because the focus of European theory formation has been very much with the nascent nation states of Western Europe, while South Asian historiography has had a strong focus on the dazzling imperial formations of the Indian subcontinent. Yet the dialectic of periods of imperial centralisation and periods of regionalization[6] that some historians have pointed to for South Asia can also be posited for Europe. In European history, important imperial moments in the west such as the Holy Roman Empire at the time of the crusades, the empire of Charles V, and the empire of Napoleon are often overlooked in preference for the ongoing process of nation state formation, while it is also only in recent years that the domestic implications of the overseas imperial projects of nascent Western European nation states have

4 Sanjay Subrahmanyam, *The Political Economy of Commerce: Southern India 1500–1650*, Cambridge: Cambridge University Press, 1990. Chris Bayly, *Rulers, Townsmen and Bazaars: North Indian Society in the Age of British Expansion, 1770–1870,* Cambridge: Cambridge University Press, 1983.

5 Compare Sanjay Subrahmanyam, Sixteenth-Century Millenarianism from the Tagus to the Ganges. In: *Explorations in Connected History: From the Tagus to the Ganges*, Sanjay Subrahmanyam (ed.), 102–137. Oxford: Oxford University Press, 2005, here 102–104, and the chapter on "Comparative and Connective Vernacularization" in Sheldon Pollock, *The Language of the Gods in the World of Men: Sanskrit, Culture, and Power in Premodern India,* Berkeley: University of California Press, 2006, 468–496.

6 Sugata Bose, Ayesha Jalal, *Modern South Asia: History, Culture, Political Economy,* London: Routledge, 1998, 6. Richard Eaton, *A Social History of the Deccan, 1300–1761, Eight Indian Lives.* The New Cambridge History of India, vol. 1 part 8, New York: Cambridge University Press, 2005, 9–32, 141–145.

come into focus. And then there is the impact on Eastern Europe of the Habsburg state after Charles V, the Ottoman state, and the czars of Russia. While the well-known imperial moments of South Asia were perhaps relatively more stable and long-lasting, we also want to point out some of the states arising over our period that were to a lesser or greater extent oriented towards a particular linguistic region. In the south, the twelfth century saw the rise of the Yadava, Kakatiya, Hoysala, and Pandya kingdoms, and the sixteenth century the rise of the Deccan sultanates, as well as of the Nayaka states and the survival of Kandy as the sole claimant to Sinhala loyalties. The seventeenth century saw the rise of the (exceptionally) well-studied Maratha state, while in the north the eighteenth century saw the rise of Bengal under the Nawabs, as well as the Sikh and Afghan states and Nepal.[7] In short, a comparison between South Asia and Europe does not have to begin and end in a contrast between the nascent nation states of France, England, Portugal, Spain, the Dutch Republic, Denmark and Sweden on the one hand and the empires of the Delhi Sultans, the Bahmanis, Vijayanagar and the Mughals on the other.

At the same time, however, we are aware that the location of such parallels as we have here identified has often been a one-way affair. That is, a phenomenon first identified in European history is then looked for in places outside Europe. As Dipesh Chakrabarty observes in his trenchant *Provincializing Europe*, more often than not, the way such a phenomenon appears in non-Europe (with special reference to India) is subsequently described in terms of a lack, absence, failure, incompleteness or inadequacy, as it is not found to have all the attributes that the phenomenon had or has in Europe. In light of Chakrabarty's critique, thinking the other way round is commendable but not easy to achieve, as Chakrabarty is also aware.[8]

---

7 Eaton 2005, 9–32, 141–145. Alan Strathern, *Kingship and Conversion in Sixteenth-Century Sri Lanka: Portuguese Imperialism in a Buddhist Land*, Cambridge: Cambridge University Press, 2007, 235–251. Chris Bayly, *Origins of Nationality in South Asia: Patriotism and Ethical Government in the Making of Modern India*, Oxford: Oxford University Press, 1998. Gijs Kruijtzer, *Xenophobia in Seventeenth-Century India*, Leiden: Leiden University Press, 2009, 265–284. P. B. Calkins, The Formation of a Regionally Oriented Ruling Group in Bengal: 1700–1740, *Journal of Asian Studies* 29 (1970): 799–806.

8 Dipesh Chakrabarty, *Provincializing Europe: Postcolonial Thought and Historical Difference*, Princeton: Princeton University Press, 2008, 32 and passim.

Law and diversity: Defining the problem

The trouble with the term "law," for our purposes, is twofold. First, the term is English and therefore comes with all the connotations that have accrued to it over the centuries in a small corner of Europe and subsequently in the colonies of that corner of Europe (which included India, but only at the end of the period we are looking at in this volume). As soon as one crosses the Channel into mainland Europe, one meets other terms that do not directly correspond to the term law. Oft-cited examples are the German terms *Gesetz* and *Recht*, the first with narrower and the latter with wider connotations than the English term law. Similar pairs are the Latin *lex/ius* and French *la loi/le droit*.[9] While both Latin and French were important languages in the British Isles during the period with which we are concerned, and *lex* and *loi* are etymological forerunners of law, the development of the connotations of the latter is in fact quite separate. On the fringes of Europe, practices and ideals that went under the name of sharia were met with, and these continued all the way into South Asia (which might, by the way, make a comparative investigation of how the notion of sharia shaped legal consciousness among non-Muslims in both subcontinents worthwhile)[10]. Of Arabic origin, the term sharia famously has much broader connotations than "law," which are perhaps best captured by a more literal translation of the term as "path." The term was sometimes contrasted to *'urf* (also Arabic) or custom, which was, however, also not devoid of connotations that we might render as "law." In South Asia there were also many other words in use in the period under consideration that can in some contexts be translated as law. Terms of Sanskrit origin as well cover much wider and much narrower ground than "law," notably in the words *dharma* and *acara*, the former translatable as obligation, duty, religion, or order and the latter sometimes translated as customary law, or lately as "*dharma* in practice."[11] Other terms in use in South Asia that may in certain contexts be translated as law include the *qanun* that harked back to the ancient kings of Iran, the *tura* or *yasa*

9 Compare Fernanda Pirie, *The Anthropology of Law*, Oxford: Oxford University Press, 2013, 4 and 18.

10 Compare Sheldon Pollock's careful consideration of the possible influence of the expansion of Islam on vernacularisation in both subcontinents in Pollock 2006, 488–494. For Europe, see Marcel A. Boisard, On the Probable Influence of Islam on Western Public and International Law, *International Journal of Middle East Studies* 11 (1980): 429–450.

11 Werner Menski, drawing on Donald Davis, in: Werner Menski, Sanskrit Law: Excavating Vedic Legal Pluralism, *SOAS School of Law Research Paper* No. 05–2010 (2010), http://ssrn.com/abstract=1621384, 5–6.

that the Mughal emperors brought from Central Asia, and *mamul, vahivat* and so on as further forms of custom.

While we believe that, in order to have a conversation, we should not shy away from translating non-English terms into English (with thorough but necessarily limited explanations of the qualifications and nuances), we encourage awareness that this volume is written in English, and that this language entails a cultural baggage that is tied to the province of Europe where it originated. As the legal historian Wael Hallaq notes in his important overview of the historical trajectory of sharia, the problem of translation is insoluble. Yet in the final instance, in order to avoid paralyzing his writing, Hallaq too settles for translating sharia as "Islamic law," as so many studies that he objects to have done before him.[12]

The second problem with the term law is that it has (at least) three uses in English itself. As Ronald Dworkin puts it, "we use 'law' in a sociological sense, as when we say that law began in primitive societies; an aspirational sense, as when we celebrate the rule of law; and a doctrinal sense we use to report what the law is on a particular subject."[13] Much confusion has come from efforts to use the definitions developed by doctrinal jurists (among whom Dworkin) for sociological, anthropological and historical purposes. It seems to be for this reason that two recent global comparisons of legal systems explicitly avoid defining the term "law" directly. In the introduction to the collected volume *Legal Pluralism and Empires, 1500–1850*, the editors suggest considering problems of "jurisdiction" instead. In *The Anthropology of Law*, Fernanda Pirie prefers working with the concept "legalism."[14]

The problem of definition is closely linked to the problem of locating law. Is it to be found in prescriptive pronouncements or in practices? While the approach that starts from the prescriptive has been widely criticized for essentialising "law" in general or legal systems such as sharia, "customary law," and so on, in particular,[15] empirical investigation of practices has been set aside as yielding detail that

12 Wael B. Hallaq, *Shari'a: Theory, Practice, Transformations*, Cambridge: Cambridge University Press, 2009, 1–3.

13 Ronald Dworkin, *Justice for Hedgehogs*, Cambridge, Mass.: Belknap Press of Harvard University Press, 2013, 402.

14 Lauren Benton, Richard J. Ross, Empires and Legal Pluralism: Jurisdiction, Sovereignty, and Political Imagination in the Early Modern World, in: *Legal Pluralism and Empires, 1500–1850*, Lauren Benton, Richard J. Ross (eds.), 1–17, New York: New York University Press, 2013, here 6. Pirie 2013, 1–25.

15 Compare Baudouin Dupret, What is Plural in the Law? A Praxiological Answer, *Égypte/Monde arabe*, Troisième série, 1 (2005), online version 2008: http://ema.revues.org/index1869.html, section 39 and passim. Hallaq 2009.

lacks interpretation or that cannot be much more than anecdotal.[16] As a way out, the comparative legal theorist Brian Tamanaha suggests calling law "whatever people identify and treat through their social practices as 'law' (or *droit*, *Recht* etc.)." Yet while that approach may perhaps resolve a problem with the analytical distinction between practice and theory, it cannot solve the problem of translation that inevitably comes up in a comparative study.[17]

For our comparative purposes, then, it is unavoidable to give some outlines of what we are thinking of when we investigate the phenomenon called law in English. We will do so by going over some aspects that have featured in previous definitions. As will be seen in the chapters of this volume, not all of these points apply everywhere in Europe and South Asia throughout our period,[18] but they have nonetheless provided a framework for the collaborative project:

1. Rules. It is quite clear to most observers of "law" that it involves rules, and the British legal positivist H.L.A. Hart put them at the centre of his definition of law. However, in the face of, for instance, English common law and sharia adjudication practices, both often relying heavily on the outcomes of previous cases and building on previous interpretations rather than on separately formulated rules, it is not so evident that rules should be the hallmark of a definition of law.[19] Recently, the Oxford Legalism group has brought rules back into focus by preferring to "law" the term "legalism," by which they mean "an appeal to rules that are distinct from practice, the explicit use of generalizing concepts, and a disposition to address in such terms the conduct of human life."[20] In this way Fernanda Pirie and Paul Dresch, anthropologists of the Oxford collective, mark a move away from a tradition in cultural anthropology that was marked by one of its founding fathers, Malinowski, who preferred to see law as defined "by function and not by form."[21] We believe that a historically sensitive approach needs to steer a course between the emphases on form and on function, between the theory and practice of adjudication and conflict resolution, and needs to take these multiple aspects into

---

16 Compare Scott J. Shapiro, *Legality*, Cambridge, Mass.: Harvard University Press, 2011, 21–22. Paul Dresch, Introduction: Legalism, Anthropology, and History: A View from Part of Anthropology, in: *Legalism: Anthropology and History*, Paul Dresch, Hannah Skoda (eds.), 9–15, Oxford: Oxford University Press, 2012, here 9–15.

17 This problem is recognised but not addressed by Tamanaha. Pirie 2013, 44–46.

18 It is precisely for this reason that Fernanda Pirie choses to describe law as a polythetic category. Compare Pirie 2013, 7–9.

19 Compare Pirie 2013, 7.

20 Dresch 2012, 1.

21 Cited in Dupret 2005, section 4.

account. "Systems" of rules should not be essentialised, but neither should an overemphasis on the diversity of practices keep us from, for instance, tracing the genealogy of specific rules through that diversity of practices. The significance of rules runs through all of the contributions to this volume, but particular attention to the formulation of rules by past actors is paid by Corinne Lefèvre and Blain Auer. Sanjog Rupakheti and Daniel Schönpflug highlight the process of revising the rules in the course of the relatively rapid world-wide changes around the turn of the nineteenth century.

2. Morality and Justice. The link between morality and law has been a bone of contention between doctrinal schools of legal positivism and legal realism of the English-speaking world over the past century.[22] For our socio-historical concerns, however, it is not so easy to work with the notion of morality, for exactly which past sensibilities would come under that term, and is it not (also) a western concept? Wael Hallaq celebrates what many western observers have described as Islamic law's failure to distinguish between law and morality, for that "lack" was, in his view, what lent sharia the authority to make do with less state coercion than western systems of law.[23] However, while it is clear that such notions as sharia and *dharma* drew on something that was wider than what is understood under many uses of the English word law, it also appears that in English usage the notion of justice has never been far from the notion of law (despite the efforts of legal positivists to separate the two). It is clear that we need to be sensitive to contemporary understandings of rights and duties as part of a range of values. Again these topics come up in all of the articles in this volume (see for instance the quotation at the top of Rupakheti's contribution), but particular attention to the making of moral communities through inclusion and exclusion is paid by Ali Anooshahr and Karl Haerter.
3. Institutions and Enforcement. In western doctrinal definitions of law developed over the past two hundred years, the state takes a central place as promulgator and enforcer. While to positivists state backing of rules is crucial in making those rules "law," even one of their main opponents, the realist Ronald Dworkin, concedes institutional enforcement a place in his delimitation of legal rights from other rights, as being "enforceable on demand in an adjudicative political institution such as a court."[24] Such doctrinal defini-

22 For two recent overviews from both sides of the doctrinal debate see: Shapiro 2011, and Dworkin 2013.

23 Hallaq 2009, 1–3.

24 Dworkin 2013, 404–405.

tions have had a great impact on the perception of South Asia's "lack" with respect to law. Recently, however, scholars investigating "Hindu" legal traditions and practices have arrived at a critique of the application of western doctrinal definitions of law to South Asian contexts. Donald Davis suggests that "in order to understand the practice of law in medieval India we must overcome the fact that we are culturally programmed to look for law's traces first in the institutions of the state."[25] Some scholars looking at Islamic law have arrived at a similar critique of western definitions, as the table-turning by Wael Hallaq noted above shows. While scholars of the Indic and Islamicate tradition are coming to an understanding of the promulgation of law without the backing of worldly power, examples of state promulgation without enforcement can be adduced from Germanic early medieval Europe. According to Patrick Wormald, ascendant Germanic monarchies created texts that looked like written codes as a matter of prestige, while what was enforced continued to be the word of the king or his officers, with hardly any reference to these codes.[26] The connection between the state, or more generally institutions backed by force, on the one hand, and the legal field on the other, was never straightforward in the medieval or early modern periods; nor is it perhaps today.[27] It seems, in any case, that as historians we need not make institutions and enforcement a necessary condition for "law" to be the case, but that we should draw the presence or absence of enforcement and institutions in legal phenomena into our comparison between world regions. All the articles in this volume touch on the institutional side of things, but we may draw particular attention here to the contributions by Sumit Guha and Mia Korpiola that trace the way institutions shaped laws and their location within states and communities.

Fortunately, the concept of "diversity" is more straightforward and less diffuse than that of "law." Nevertheless, the question came up at the conference as to what kinds of diversity we are talking about. The articles in this volume consider all the kinds of difference that historically came to the fore under any of the three aspects of "law" that we outlined above: in the drafting and application

---

25 Donald Davis, Centres of Law: Duties, Rights, and Jurisdictional Pluralism in Medieval India, in: *Legalism: Anthropology and History,* Paul Dresch, Hannah Skoda (eds.), 85–113, Oxford: Oxford University Press, 2012, here 88 (quotation) and passim. See also Menski 2010.

26 Pirie 2013, 7, 9, 176–180.

27 See Pierre Bourdieu, The Force of Law: Toward a Sociology of the Juridical Field, *The Hastings Law Journal* 38 (1987): 814–853.

of social rules, in questions of morality and justice, and in the face of institutions and enforcement. Differences that have historically been observed and lived under these aspects include gender, class, estate, caste, religion, and any kind of belonging by birth. Of course, it is also worthwhile to explore how what we would call "diversity" was conceptualized by contemporaries in such notions as that of *sulh-i kull* introduced by Mughal Emperor Akbar.

So, while we are starting from two concepts with a particular history in Europe, and specifically the Anglophone world, we hope that this volume will also enable us to think the other way by taking terms and concepts that were historically in use in South Asia and seeing how they would have fared in European contexts (or, for that matter, taking concepts from mainland Europe to the English sphere). For instance, as the Oxford anthropologist Morgan Clarke puts it, "*shari'a* discourse is good to think with" if we are to unsettle modern western conceptions of "morality," "ethics" and "law."[28] In the same way, other concepts in use in South Asia that seem to have something to do with the English concepts "law" and "diversity" can be brought into a dialogue of concepts between the two subcontinents that will never be entirely equal (because the starting point remains with the English terms) but that may balance out over time.

Law and diversity

While there are many points at which "law" and "diversity" may be seen to intersect, we believe that the problem before us has two main aspects: first, laws that were created to manage the rights and duties of diverse groups within a social space, and second, the side-by-side existence of different laws within one social space. Respectively, these aspects form the subjects of parts one and two of this volume. Neither aspect is of course straightforward, but it is the second aspect that has been the subject of especially intense debate over the past thirty years. Since the designation "legal pluralism" gained currency in the 1970s, many questions of how to approach what goes by this academic name and whether the term is useful at all have come up. A number of good summaries of the debate are available.[29] Much of the criticism revolves around the definition of law, and critics have found that too much or too little emphasis was being placed on any one of

28 Morgan Clarke, The Judge as a Tragic Hero: Judicial Ethics in Lebanon's Shari'a Courts, *American Ethnologist* 39 (2012): 106–121, here 106.
29 Dupret 2005. Benton, Ross 2013. Pirie 2013.

the aspects of "law" that we have identified above: rules, morality (as coming from below), or institutions (as imposed from above).

Rules were emphasized in a classic article by Sally Falk Moore that often comes up in discussions of legal pluralism, even though she did not mention that term and also avoided the term law. Moore proposed that every society or social structure is composed of many semi-autonomous fields that can "generate rules and coerce or induce compliance to them."[30] This notion of "semi-autonomous fields" may still be useful in describing, analyzing and comparing the intersection of law and diversity in the areas and period we are looking at here.

While many studies about legal pluralism were meant as a critique of the institutional, and especially the statist, perspective on law, identifying and often celebrating[31] many nonstate or bottom-up systems of arbitration and adjudication, the question is if and where we draw the line between law and other normative orders. In the words of Sally Merry, "where do we stop speaking of law and find ourselves simply describing social life?"[32] This is, however, what prominent players in the legal pluralism debate like Tamanaha and Griffiths now advocate: casting a very wide net. The challenge is to not let go of law as a category for a comparative conversation altogether.[33]

The question of whose viewpoint to take in establishing the presence of legal pluralism has been one of the major points of debate, and it remains of interest for our purposes. We should make clear where we think the plurality of law existed: was it recognized by the state?[34] Did contemporary nonstate actors orient to it?[35] Or does it exist only in our analysis? We believe that all three approaches are valid as long as they are explicit (which would again facilitate a comparison). In final instance, in order to compare the intersection of law and diversity in South Asia and Europe the use of English concepts such as "state" and "law" seems unavoidable, but these concepts should not be reified.[36]

---

30 Cited in Dupret 2005, section 17.

31 Mitra Sharafi has criticised the "spirit of aggressive celebration of…[the] romantic assumption that nonstate law was more egalitarian and less coercive than state law." Cited in Benton, Ross 2013, 2.

32 Sally Engle Merry, Legal Pluralism, *Law and Society Review* 22 (1988), 869–896, here 878–879.

33 Pirie 2013, 41 and 45.

34 John Griffiths calls this the "juristic" sense of legal pluralism best known from colonial situations but not exclusive to them, in: John Griffiths, What is Legal Pluralism?, *Journal of Legal Pluralism* 24 (1986): 1–55, here 5. See also Merry 1988, 871.

35 Baudouin Dupret writes, "the notion of legal pluralism does not exist as a sociological question unless people, participants, or members orient to it as such," in: Dupret 2005, section 51.

36 Paul D. Halliday warns against the paradoxical reification of the state that he finds in

Shared diversities

Although we should be careful to extend conclusions about one region to the whole of either subcontinent, as the contribution by Korpiola in particular makes clear, it seems safe to say that in the medieval and early modern period most states in both Europe or South Asia did not have one universal law that was equally valid for all their subjects. The authority to create, interpret and enforce was diffuse and there was a near ubiquitous plurality, which had not vanished by 1800, despite the increasing capabilities of states and empires of controlling their subjects and territories. The plurality of law was equalled by the diversity of the subjects living together in a given political entity, and the bodies of law diverged in form (written and unwritten), attributed origin (divine, natural or dharmic, royal, customary) and scope (universal, specific).

In both Europe and South Asia certain learned traditions of "law" continued to be elaborated in a dialectical relationship to royal or state ordinances on the one hand and custom on the other. For South Asia, the two learned traditions of *dharmashastra* and *fiqh* should be mentioned here. The genre of *dharmashastras*, written guides to the lives of people differing in family situation, gender and standing, yet part of one cosmic order, had been cared for and elaborated by Brahmins since antiquity. Numerous digests were produced from the start of our period onwards, some concerned with recognisably "legal" topics such as litigation and judicial procedure or inheritance, others with ritual or *dharma* in general. *Fiqh*, Islamic jurisprudence elaborated by ulema (plural of *'alim*, a certified scholar of theology and sharia), was introduced into the core areas of the subcontinent in the wake of the Turkish conquest of c. 1200. The Delhi Sultanate and Mughal Empire developed into centres of the Hanafi school in their own right through a number of compilations of *fatwas*, or *responsa*, published in the fourteenth and late seventeenth centuries. These two great traditions competed and intersected with royal *qanun*, as well as with various, largely unwritten, local or community-specific traditions designated as *'urf*, *vahivat*, *mamul*, *yasa*, and the like.

Europe, too, had various traditions perceived as great and minor.[37] Among the great traditions were the two in which one could obtain doctorates, canon

---

many analyses of legal pluralism, see: Paul D. Halliday, Laws' Histories: Pluralism, Pluralities, Diversity, in: *Legal Pluralism and Empires, 1500–1850*, Lauren Benton, Richard J. Ross (eds.), 261–277, New York: New York University Press, 2013, here 268.

37 Note that we are using the distinction between great and minor traditions here not for two currents within a phenomenon with one label (such as the distinction between great and minor

and Roman law. The custodian of canon law was the Roman Catholic Church and its greatest efflorescence took place around the start of our period in the work of the scholastics. The partial rediscovery of Roman law at Bologna just before the start of our period gave rise to a new class of jurists, and was closely tied to the emergence of universities throughout the subcontinent in our period, which also commenced at Bologna. Besides those two learned traditions, *halakha* was studied and elaborated among the Jewish diaspora and *fiqh* among the Muslim minorities as well as in the Muslim-ruled parts of Europe. The minor traditions were on the one hand the imperial, royal, estate or city ordinances, and on the other the many forms of Germanic tribal and regional custom. Regional customs were increasingly codified from the thirteenth century onwards, often in emulation of the Roman model (and initially also of *fiqh*).[38] Even some English jurists concerning themselves with the system of customary law that came to be known as common law seem to have embraced a Roman law approach, although the reception of Roman law was much more explicit on the continent, especially in the synthesis of great and minor traditions that was the *ius commune*.[39]

Moreover, the plurality of systems or sources of law was matched by a plurality of adjudicative bodies. In South Asia, adjudication and arbitration were exercised by kings of all varieties as well as by their regional representatives, figures of authority within particular communities such as Sufi shaikhs, Brahmins, leaders of corporate groups ("castes"), and, increasingly, by the *qazi* courts that could be more or less state sponsored, and finally, at the fringes, by the administrators of European establishments.[40] In most of Europe the royal or imperial "state" courts were also only one level of adjudication and arbitration amongst

traditions within Islam that has been criticised by Talal Asad), but for traditions that went under different labels, of which some where more highly regarded by contemporaries than others. For a definition of tradition, we refer to Talal Asad, *The Idea of an Anthropology of Islam,* Washington, D.C.: Center for Contemporary Arab Studies, Georgetown University, 1986, 14–15, and for his critique see 5–7.

38 Marcel Boisard details some elements of *fiqh* that may be traced in the Castilian *Siete Partidas*, one of the first texts in this wave of codifications of regional custom, in Boisard 1980, 235–236.

39 On English aspirations after Roman law and common law as customary law see Pirie 2013, 133–139, 155, 181–185. On the *ius commune* as an alternative great tradition for the Holy Roman Empire, see Karl Härter, The Early Modern Holy Roman Empire of the German Nation (1495–1806): A Multi-Layered Legal System, in: *Law and Empire: Ideas, Practices, Actors,* Jeroen Duindam, Jill Diana Harries, Caroline Humfress, Hurvitz Nimrod (eds.), 111–131. Leiden: Brill, 2013.

40 Davis 2012. Eaton 2005, 145–150. Farhat Hasan, *State and locality in Mughal India: power relations in western India, c. 1572 – 1730,* Cambridge: Cambridge University Press, 2004. Gagan D. S. Sood, Sovereign Justice in Precolonial Maritime Asia: The Case of the Mayor's Court of Bombay, 1726–1798, *Itinerario*, 37 (2013): 46–72.

a great variety of tribunals, though increasingly important. Lords or nobles long continued to claim jurisdiction over the inhabitants of their estates as well as their peers. Numerous aggregate bodies such as guilds, companies, universities, cities and the Roman Catholic Church as well as religious minority groups (Jews and Muslims in particular) claimed a measure of jurisdiction over their members. The practice of adjudication and arbitration was in both subcontinents determined not by the principle of one law for all but by a complex system of concurrent jurisdictions.

Thus it is clear that Europe and South Asia shared a diversity of legal traditions and of adjudicative practices beside a certain diversity of inhabitants that was to a greater or lesser extent recognized in those traditions and practices. In the face of these layers of plurality, describing the commonalities and differences between the two subcontinents is a challenge in itself, and it is with careful analytic description that this volume hopes to take the conversation forward. The conceptual framework of the volume puts a by now conventional research topic into the new perspective of a comparison of two parts of the world the comparability of which has only recently been recognized.

References

Asad, Talal, *The Idea of an Anthropology of Islam*, Washington, D.C.: Center for Contemporary Arab Studies, Georgetown University, 1986.

Asher, Catherine B., Talbot, Cynthia, *India before Europe*, Cambridge: Cambridge University Press, 2006.

Bayly, Chris, *Rulers, Townsmen and Bazaars: North Indian Society in the Age of British Expansion, 1770–1870*, Cambridge: Cambridge University Press, 1983.

Bayly, Chris, *Origins of Nationality in South Asia: Patriotism and Ethical Government in the Making of Modern India*, Oxford: Oxford University Press, 1998.

Benton, Lauren, Ross, Richard J., Empires and Legal Pluralism: Jurisdiction, Sovereignty, and Political Imagination in the Early Modern World, in: *Legal Pluralism and Empires, 1500–1850*, Lauren Benton, Richard J. Ross (eds.), 1–17, New York: New York University Press, 2013.

Boisard, Marcel A., On the Probable Influence of Islam on Western Public and International Law, *International Journal of Middle East Studies* 11 (1980): 429–450.

Bose, Sugata, Jalal, Ayesha, *Modern South Asia: History, Culture, Political Economy*, London: Routledge, 1998.

Bourdieu, Pierre, The Force of Law: Toward a Sociology of the Juridical Field, *The Hastings Law Journal* 38 (1987): 814–53.

Calkins, P. B., The Formation of a Regionally Oriented Ruling Group in Bengal: 1700–1740, *Journal of Asian Studies* 29 (1970): 799–806.

Chakrabarty, Dipesh, *Provincializing Europe: Postcolonial Thought and Historical Difference*, Princeton: Princeton University Press, 2008.
Clarke, Morgan, The Judge as a Tragic Hero: Judicial Ethics in Lebanon's Shari'a Courts, *American Ethnologist* 39 (2012): 106–121.
Davis, Donald, Centres of Law: Duties, Rights, and Jurisdictional Pluralism in Medieval India, in: *Legalism: Anthropology and History,* Paul Dresch, Hannah Skoda (eds.), 85–113, Oxford: Oxford University Press, 2012.
Dresch, Paul, Introduction: Legalism, Anthropology, and History: A View from Part of Anthropology, in: *Legalism: Anthropology and History,* Paul Dresch, Hannah Skoda (eds.), 9–15, Oxford: Oxford University Press, 2012.
Dupret, Baudouin, What is Plural in the Law? A Praxiological Answer, *Égypte/Monde arabe*, Troisième série, 1 (2005), online version 2008: http://ema.revues.org/index1869.html.
Dworkin, Ronald, *Justice for Hedgehogs,* Cambridge, Mass.: Belknap Press of Harvard University Press, 2013.
Eaton, Richard, *A Social History of the Deccan, 1300–1761, Eight Indian Lives*. The New Cambridge History of India, vol. 1.8, New York: Cambridge University Press, 2005.
Griffiths, John, What is Legal Pluralism?, *Journal of Legal Pluralism* 24 (1986): 1–55.
Hallaq, Wael B., *Shari'a: Theory, Practice, Transformations,* Cambridge: Cambridge University Press, 2009.
Halliday, Paul D., Laws' Histories: Pluralism, Pluralities, Diversity, in: *Legal Pluralism and Empires, 1500–1850,* Lauren Benton, Richard J. Ross (eds.), 261–277, New York: New York University Press, 2013.
Härter, Karl, The Early Modern Holy Roman Empire of the German Nation (1495–1806): A Multi-Layered Legal System, in: *Law and Empire: Ideas, Practices, Actors,* Jeroen Duindam, Jill Diana Harries, Caroline Humfress, Hurvitz Nimrod (eds.), 111–131. Leiden: Brill, 2013.
Hasan, Farhat, *State and Locality in Mughal India: Power Relations in Western India, c. 1572 – 1730,* Cambridge: Cambridge University Press, 2004.
Kruijtzer, Gijs, *Xenophobia in Seventeenth-Century India,* Leiden: Leiden University Press, 2009.
Lewis, Martin W., Wigen, Karen E., *The Myth of Continents: A Critique of Metageography,* Berkeley: University of California Press, 1997.
Menski, Werner, Sanskrit Law: Excavating Vedic Legal Pluralism, *SOAS School of Law Research Paper* No. 05–2010 (2010), http://ssrn.com/abstract=1621384.
Merry, Sally Engle, Legal Pluralism, *Law and Society Review* 22 (1988), 869–896.
Moore, Sally Falk, Law and Social Change: The Semi-Autonomous Social Field as an Appropriate Subject of Study, *Law & Society Review* 7:4 (1973): 719–46.
Pirie, Fernanda, *The Anthropology of Law,* Oxford: Oxford University Press, 2013.
Pollock, Sheldon, India in the Vernacular Millennium: Literary Culture and Polity, 1000–1500, *Daedalus* 127 (1998): 41–74.
Pollock, Sheldon, *The Language of the Gods in the World of Men: Sanskrit, Culture, and Power in Premodern India,* Berkeley: University of California Press, 2006.
Shapiro, Scott J., *Legality,* Cambridge, Mass.: Harvard University Press, 2011.
Sood, Gagan D. S., Sovereign Justice in Precolonial Maritime Asia: The Case of the Mayor's Court of Bombay, 1726–1798, *Itinerario*, 37 (2013): 46–72.
Strathern, Alan, *Kingship and Conversion in Sixteenth-Century Sri Lanka: Portuguese Imperialism in a Buddhist Land,* Cambridge: Cambridge University Press, 2007.

Subrahmanyam, Sanjay, *The Political Economy of Commerce: Southern India 1500–1650*, Cambridge: Cambridge University Press, 1990.

Subrahmanyam, Sanjay, Sixteenth-Century Millenarianism from the Tagus to the Ganges. In: *Explorations in Connected History: From the Tagus to the Ganges*, Sanjay Subrahmanyam (ed.), 102–137. Oxford: Oxford University Press, 2005.

Part I: State-formation and cultural and religious groups

Ali Anooshahr

Muslims among non-Muslims

Creating Islamic identity through law

This paper investigates the role of law in defining the Muslim community that dominated the ruling elite in north India in the medieval period. While perhaps the theme of the volume would recommend a study of the relationship between the law and the management of non-Muslims in medieval India, it would be worthwhile to also see how Muslims used law to define themselves. This approach is useful because the "Muslim community" as such was by no means a given and natural category, and that there must have been contending normative attempts at defining the limits of that community. Of course since the right to definition is also a right to power and a right to representation, it follows that those who had claimed this role had to contend with others who might have had different ideas about who spoke for the community and who had the right to define it.

To examine these problems, the most obvious choice would be to visit the legal texts of the medieval period (as other records are sparse). The most canonical of these was a large collection of legal opinions gathered together in a digest entitled *al-Fatawa-al-Tatarkhaniya* or "Tatar Khan's legal rulings", a text composed in the 1370's by a group of Muslim scholar/jurists at the behest of a major Delhi statesman called Tatar Khan, who significantly was not the king himself but a senior courtier.[1]

This happened during the reign of Firuz Shah Tughluq who ruled from Delhi from 1351–1388. The *fatawa* compilations belonged to a particular genre that had existed since the early Islamic period. Each compilation contained important rulings for various legal schools, arranged thematically (starting with prayer, ablution, fasting, all the way to inheritance, divorce, etc), and included one or more sample ruling per topic selected from older compendia or recent exemplary cases.

What would such a source reveal about the role of law in defining the Muslim community? After all, Islamic legal manuals have a number of problems that complicate their use as historical sources. First, legal manuals are not descriptive but prescriptive, in other words they do not necessary reflect legal practice but try to fashion it. Some modern scholars have even argued, rather extremely, that legal manuals are intentionally divorced from social reality. This trend of

1 'Alim b. 'Ala, *Al-Fatawa al-Tatarkhaniyah*, Sajjad Husayn (ed.), Karachi: 1990, henceforth *FT.*

DOI 10.1515/9783110423327-002

scholarship has stated that while it was possible for legal manuals like *al-Fatawa al-Tatarkhaniya* to perhaps incorporate new exemplary rulings not found in earlier collections, the authors of these texts would also issue their rulings for no other reasons than maintaining consistency within the particular legal school to which they belonged.[2] Another problem of these manuals is their reception in society. As Lefèvre and others in this volume argue, these texts are not at all hegemonic. What they express would not necessarily apply to all sectors of society. Nor would their users exclusively draw upon them. Judges interpreted these texts in a various ways, relying on local customs as often as textual digests.[3] The chapters by Farhat Hassan, Indrani Chatterjee, and Sara Butler have successfully utilized epigraphy, local charters, or court rulings that show the complexity and richness of law as applied in the local context.

So, how and why should we read al-*Fatawa al-Tatarkhaniya*? I have decided to read this text against the next major legal compendium composed in India in 1664 under the Mughal Emperor Aurangzeb. This book is called *al-Fatawa al-Hindiya* or the *'Alamgiriya*,[4] which is also discussed by Lefèvre and Hassan. I should note from the start that the current edition in circulation is not a thorough critical edition based on a study of all major manuscript recensions. My conclusions, derived from a preliminary comparison of this text with the *FT*, must therefore remain provisional pending an authoritative edition.

Why use the comparative method? Because in spite of the problems mentioned above, we still cannot say that these texts are created in a vacuum. They reflect in fact the idealized view of a small but very power juridical elite. Differences between legal manuals from different historical periods would at least bear witness to changing values and political conditions over time. So, by contrasting the preface of the first compendium (the *Tatarkhaniya*) with the second (the *'Alamgiriya*), we can find matters of interest to the 14th century that had been changed, challenged, or lost their interest in the 17th century. To test the validity of the resulting observations, I then read my findings against a contemporary court chronicle, the *Tarikh-i Firuzshahi* written in 1396 by Shams al-Din Siraj 'Afif.

---

2 Joseph Schacht, *An Introduction to Islamic Law*, Oxford: Clarendon Press, 1964, 75. For the argument in support of legal production for the sake of systematic consistency see Behnam Sadighi, *The Logic of Law Making in Islam: Women and Prayer in the Legal Tradition*, Cambridge: Cambridge University Press, 2013.

3 Richard Eaton, Introduction, in: *India's Islamic Traditions, 711–1750*, Richard Eaton (ed.), 1–36, Delhi: Oxford University Press, 2003, 23.

4 Shaykh Nizam, *Al-Fatawa al-Hindiyah fi Madhhab Imam al-A'zam Abi Hanifa al-Nu'man*, Beirut: 1991, henceforth *FA*.

A striking contrast could be observed right from the start. Initially a random comparison of similar chapters had showed that the Mughal manual shared numerous verbal parallels with the *Tatarkhaniya*. In other words it seemed quite likely that the authors of the *'Alamgiriya* had access to the earlier manual when composing their own. What was interesting however was that while the sultanate jurists would often cite numerous conflicting opinions about each legal issue (and cite their source for it), the Mughal authors removed the names of the cited jurists, eliminated the plurality of opinions, and only cited a single condensed version. This seemed to suggest that there was a reductive and unifying impulse at work in the 17th century text, absent from its medieval counterpart. I am of course assuming that the reductive and unifying impulse accurately reflects the agenda of the original compilers and not the short-hand of the lithograph editors.

This view was further confirmed when the prefaces of both texts were compared. There exists a glaring disparity between the two manuals. The preface of the *Tatarkhaniya* runs to nearly a 100 pages of the printed edition, but the *'Alamgiriya* only runs at two pages. An entire section was therefore missing from the Mughal text. The *'Alamgiriya* starts with a very terse prayer in the imperative mood, praising God as the sole agent in creating laws and as an autocrat and despot in enforcing them. The text reads, "Praise be to God, the one alone (*al-munfarid*) in laying down laws and regulations, the autocrat/despot (*al-mustabidd*) in elevating the distinction between what is permitted and what is forbidden, and who protects the jurists from those who are insubordinate in their knowledge or are obstinate".[5] This is a very harsh and terse beginning. Here God represents the idealization of the emperor Aurangzeb who is next praised for commissioning the text.

Nothing could be further from the vision expressed in the manual produced in the 14th century in which the rights of the jurists to issue legal rulings are argued for in detail. Let's go through the preface then and analyze the issues of sovereignty and authority over the Muslim community during the medieval period. In modern scholarship of the Delhi Sultanate, studies of contesting authorities usually focus on the competition between popular holy men and kings, a binary that perhaps reflects interest in aspects of oriental despotism within the scholarship (with an all-powerful king monopolizing power and then occasional rebellion).[6] Instead it would be worthwhile to focus on the complexity of the power relations within the various nexuses of "state power" in the medieval period in Delhi. Many of the conclusions and hypotheses offered below are in the preliminary stage of such an inquiry.

5 *FA*, I: 2.

6 James Mill, *History of British India*, Volume 2, London: Baldwin, Cradock, and Joy, 1840, 490.

In its long preface, *al-Fatawa al-Tatarkhaniya* expresses the plural voice of the jurists. The focus is on "us", plural and inclusive. The voice is that of the speakers as a whole. Their God is a kind and giving god, who protects them and provides for them. The authors proclaim, "We praise our Lord" for his "ample gifts". "We thank him" they say, "for leading us to the path of purity". They offer gratitude to God for "giving us the power to speak the words of fortune and joy" and for "repelling from us the heavy blows of villains".[7] Moreover God empowers his subjects not through physical or military might but through knowledge (*'ilm*). "He taught us knowledge", they write, "that will be our intercessor accompanying us on judgment day".[8] There are two points of interest here. One is that the best power of God is knowledge which is controlled by the jurists. The social and political significance of this statement is that in the absence of an anthropomorphic God, the truly powerful, i.e. those who can exert power over what happens to the people in this world *and* the next, are the jurists. We will see the further expansion and exposition of this position.

But it is important to highlight divine benevolence in this text, because again God is probably the abstraction and idealization of the living ruler. This is what the jurists expect from their ideal king: namely, to offer physical protection, show generosity through the bestowal of presents, leave undisturbed the speech of the jurists, empower the jurists for their knowledge, intercede mercifully at the moment of justice, and lead the community toward moral purity. This is quite a contrast with the royalist vision expressed during the Mughal period.

What constitutes the community? It is the people who follow tradition and consensus (*ahl-i sunna va jama'a*, or sunnis). The manual identifies membership through the following requirements. First, those who belong to the community pray communally five times a day. Second, they do not speak ill of the first three caliphs and other companions. Third, they do not lead armed rebellion against the ruling monarch. Fourth, they do not harbor doubt in their faith. Fifth, they will believe in divine providence whether it is good or bad. Sixth, they do not dispute God's religion. Seventh, they do not commit sin against monotheists. Eighth, they do not curse the soul of Muslims who have died. Ninth, they will pray behind an imam, be he pious or impious.[9]

What *al-Fatawa al-Tatarkhaniya* reveals is an early expression in India of the desire for the phenomenon of a legally-constituted religious community as prescribed by Medieval Indian jurists. What for them would make an ideal Muslim,

7 *FT*, I: 65.
8 *FT*, I: 65.
9 *FT*, I: 80.

in practice, is an individual's adherence to a body of laws and the authority of a jurist. In this sense, the vision of the authors of the *Tatarkhaniya* foreshadows the semantic development of the word *milla*, which is probably more familiar in its Persian form *millat* or the Ottoman form *millet*. This word initially meant law, semantically parallel with *sharia*. However in the Ottoman realm it was later used to denote a community that followed a particular legal system, for example the Greek Orthodox community led by the Patriarch in Istanbul which was subject to canon law in its day-to-day affairs. The same was applied to Ottoman Jews who were under the legal jurisdiction of the chief rabbi. Muslims also fell into the same category. The received wisdom tells us that the Ottomans managed religious diversity through communal autonomy but medieval Indian states did it through syncretism. However, the evidence of the *Fatawa* suggests the Indian case is indeed more similar to the Ottoman one than previously thought. Still though, the fact that Tughluq jurists did not seem to have a term for the Muslim community suggests perhaps more a vague, hazy sense of that community.

In this vision, the Muslim monarch would be a member of the community who mostly fulfills administrative and security functions—executive functions. This would mean that the position of the monarch is actually below the scholar/jurists. The preface of the *Tatarkhaniya* develops this idea further by drawing on canonical texts, the Quran and the hadith (the reports of the prophet Muhammad) to justify this claim. More on this below.

Moving along, following the delimitation of the community, the *Tatarkhaniya* then sets out to explain the importance of knowledge, the centrality of the jurists, and the significance of the community. The authors declare that everyone needs knowledge. But what is the best knowledge? They survey different forms of knowledge and evaluate them one by one. *Kalam* (dialectical argumentation), they argue, teaches the unity of God and his attributes. Exegesis and hadith serve as expository tools for understanding canonical texts and the traditions of the prophet. Sufism teaches various mystical paths. Then there are the unworthy sciences: astrology, casting spells, or magic. Poetry and Arab genealogy are a type of science that give no benefit nor cause any harm. Finally, Geometry and philosophy provide no knowledge for the afterlife and are studied by those who love this world more than the next.[10] Superior to all these sciences is jurisprudence as it benefits people both in this lifetime and the next: it determines completely what is allowed in human action, and it also protects humans from the hellfire.[11]

---

10 *FT*, I: 76, 79.
11 *FT*, I: 69 and I: 75.

We notice that the preeminence of jurisprudence is based on rational argumentation. Also, other sciences are at worst criticized but not branded as heretical or anything like that. In other words, the preeminence of jurisprudence does not require the suppression of other discourses. In fact the text harps on the elevated status of science/knowledge in general and scientists/scholars as a whole body. So, the argument runs, those who possess knowledge are also especially significant. The authors cite the Quran and the hadith to assert that jurists rank just below God and his angels, that God has elevated jurists over all Muslims, by 700 degrees no less, and that jurists are heirs to the prophets.[12]

The political implication of these claims was not lost to the authors. Medieval Islamic political theory derived sovereignty ultimately from God. However, Muslim thinkers argued that God then placed two types of individuals over people, prophets and kings (*rusul* and *muluk*).[13] The prophet Muhammad was the last person to embody both functions.[14] In the absence of living prophets, following the death of the prophet Muhammad, kings could use this theory to claim highest authority in society. What the jurists of the *Tatarkhaniya* were claiming was that they in fact stood for the prophet and as such held highest place in the Muslim community including even over kings.

This view was not shared by the court. The fourteenth century courtly chronicler, Shams al-Din Siraj ʿAfif, conceded the analogous role of the jurists and the prophet, but he saw the place of the ruler and the scholar/jurists as equal.[15] This is not the case in the *Fatawa*. Rather, the authors cite former Muslim authorities to claim, "Kings rule over people and jurists rule over kings".[16] These are competing claims then over the Muslim community. Are the jurists as a group alone the highest representatives or is the king also a successor to the prophet and hence parallel with the jurists?[17]

---

12 *FT*, I: 69–70.

13 ʿAbd al-Malik b. Muḥammad al-Thaʿalib, *Tarikh Ghurar al-Siyar*, H. Zotenberg (ed.), Paris, Imprimerie Nationale, 1900, 4. Ghiyas al-Din b. Humam al-Din Khvandamir, *Ma'asir al-Muluk bih Zamimah-i Khatimah-i Khulasat al-Akhbar va Qanun-i Humayuni*, M. H. Muhaddis (ed.), Tehran: 1993/4, 251–252. Patricia Crone, *God's Rule: Government and Islam*, New York: Columbia University Press, 2005, 11.

14 Sham Siraj ʿAfif, *Tarikh-i Firuzshahi*, Wilayat Husain (ed.), Calcutta: 1891, 3. Khvandamir 1993/4, 250.

15 ʿAfif 1891, 3–4.

16 *FT*, I: 70.

17 Blain H. Auer, *Symbols of Authority in Medieval South Asia: History, Religion and Muslim Legitimacy in the Delhi Sultanate*, London: I.B. Tauris, 2012, 52.

But if the jurists occupy a position between God and kings, then they should manifest divinity somehow. Numerous authorities are quoted to make precisely such a claim. The most striking example of these attributes is the power reflected in gazing upon the jurists. The text reads, "Whoever gazes upon a *'alim*'s face, it is as if he has gazed upon Muhammad's face; and whoever gazes upon Muhammad's face, it is as if he has gazed upon God; and whoever has gazed upon God, paradise belongs to him and his body will be protected from the fire [of hell]".[18]

The virtue of gazing upon the jurists is significant in two ways. The most obvious is that it divinizes the jurists. But the very act of beneficial gazing recalls the practice of imperial *darshan* adopted by the Mughal court beginning in the 16th century. We have numerous descriptions according to which the emperor would appear before an expectant public for their viewing. This act is thought to have been rooted in a Hindu ritual of apotheosis of solar monarchy. Alternatively it has been seen as a Sufi ritual common to Iran and India.[19] The citation of this authority however suggests that such practices were equally legitimate in the juridical/scholarly tradition as well.

Who has a right to be among the jurists then? Who can issue a *fatwa*? The question itself is significant. It implies the absence of a central body that could regulate the training and appointment of the *mufti* (the person who could issue a *fatwa*). Again the pluralistic aspect of this vision is worth noting. The authors specifically state that disagreement among the jurists/scholars is in fact a positive thing, a sign of God's mercy, as it brings reprieve to the people.[20] This is because plurality of legal opinions exonerates common Muslims from strictly adhering to a single unchanging set of demands. It is worth comparing this view with the "courtly" criticism. The court historian 'Afif criticized the jurists for their argumentative disagreement over all sorts of issues, which he saw as a sign of the egotism and unfairness of the jurists.[21] This criticism continues into the Mughal period.[22]

Of course while the *Fatawa* praises disagreement, legal decision making is not a free-for-all. The text says very clearly that the right to issue legal opinions

18 *FT*, I: 73.

19 A. Azfar Moin, *The Millenial Sovereign: Sacred Kingship and Sainthood in Islam*, New York: Columbia University Press, 2012, 130–170. Thomas de Bruijn, *Ruby in the Dust: Poetry and History in Padmavat by the South Asian Sufi Poet Muhammad Jayasi*, Leiden: Leiden University Press, 2012, 254–256.

20 *FT*, I: 80–83. 'Abd al-Qadir Badauni, *Najat al-Rashid*, S. Mu'in al-Haqq (ed.), Lahore: 1972, 111.

21 'Afif 1891, 8.

22 Qazvini, Asif Khan, Fath Allah Shirazi, Ahmad Tattavi, Mir Ghiyas al-Din Ali Qazvini, 'Abd-al-Qadir Badauni, Nizam al-Din Ahmad, Abu al-Fath Gilani, Hakeem Humam Gilani, *Tarikh-i Alfi*, Ghulamriza Tabataba'i, (ed.), Tehran: 2003, 4243.

is reserved for those who know the statutes contained in the Quran and hadith, who understand the rules of abrogation, and have mastery over the sayings of the companions of the prophet Muhammad.[23]

What is left out of these descriptions? The courtly view, as expressed by 'Afif makes extra demands of the jurists. For instance it requires of them the virtues of forgiveness towards sinful humanity. 'Afif equates this with royal forgiveness of criminals.[24] He also equates the leading of prayers by the jurists as battle against the devil, comparable to the holy wars of kings.[25] 'Afif cites a hadith according to which the prophet states, "Heaven is under the shadow of the sword" to back this claim.[26] The jurists apparently did not share the courtly view in this analogy as they cited another hadith that had stated "the ink of the jurists is superior to the blood of martyrs".[27]

In short, at the time when the *Fatawa* was written, we can observe a very interesting dynamic in the leadership of the Muslim community. The jurists and the monarch compete over it but are also interdependent. They disagree over the particulars but maintain consensus overall. This should not surprise us especially during the reign of Firuzshah. A series of events, as described by 'Afif, sheds further light on this matter.

For instance, we see the power of jurists already in play even before the accession of Firuzshah. According to 'Afif, Firuzshah was not the de facto successor of the previous king Muhammad Tughluq when the latter died in Sindh during a campaign against the Mongols in 1351. 'Afif states that a council attended by the *khans* (nobility), *muluk* (hereditary local kings serving the dynasty), and all the jurists and Sufi leaders in camp voted to bypass the dead king's nephew in Delhi and instead appoint his cousin Firuzshah to the throne in order to save the army from destruction.[28] In short we find the jurists with powers that are in harmony with the views in the legal manual coauthored by them. They meet as a group, they share the venue with other elites, they hold a lengthy discussion and deliberation ("*guft u shunud-i bishumar va andishah-i bishumar*"), they override dynastic prerogative, and finally act as a body and "elect" Firuz to be the ruler, and not just as monarch "*shahryar*", but leader of the Muslim community "*imam*".[29]

23 *FT*, I: 80–83.
24 'Afif 1891, 6–7.
25 'Afif 1891, 10.
26 'Afif 1891, 10.
27 *FT*, I: 73.
28 'Afif 1891, 43–44.
29 'Afif 1891, 43–44.

Now it is also worth noting, the consulting body, the assembly, is itself subdivided by 'Afif into two distinct bodies or parties (*firqah*): the (*muluk*) kings and people of religious path (*ahl-i suluk*.)[30] This is not a bicameral parliament in the modern sense, but it is a decision making body made up of members with separated functions: those engaged in the executive functions, and those engaged in the legislative/judiciary functions. Meanwhile the emperor obviously owes his accession to such a body with which, we might reasonably expect, he had to cooperate and compete.

A good example of mutual cooperation is provided by 'Afif in a passage describing the construction of two new cities and a number of villages by Firuzshah. 'Afif says that the monarch ordered various waterways and canals to be dug in order to channel water from the rivers to these new settlements. He then convened the judges (*qazis*), jurists, and the *shaykhs* (Sufi leaders) and asked them whether he had a right to the proceeds obtained by the farms watered with the canals he had excavated. The group discussed the matter and issued a *fatwa* that the king had the right to ten percent of the proceeds. The king began collecting his share and in return converted a number of barren property into farmland belonging to the royal purse with the income of which (3.6 million *tankas*)[31] he rewarded the consenting jurists as a body which counted 4,200 individuals.[32]

This is a clear example of mutual benefit between the jurists and the monarchy. At the same time, we find the king also competing with the jurists in a number of cases. For instance, 'Afif states that Firuzshah ordered the construction of a large percussive instrument to announce the hours of the day to the residents of Delhi. Now this may seem like an innocuous act. However, 'Afif shows how the king was in fact obtruding on the prerogative of the jurists by standardizing ambiguities about the times of prayer and fasting. For instance, he writes, during the shorter days of winter, if the air was dusty, people would not be able to know when the time had come for evening or afternoon prayers, or in the fasting month, they would not know the exact moment of breaking their fast. A good deal of disagreement existed among the jurists about this, and people apparently followed varying decisions. However, thanks to the king's time-telling device, everyone could pray or break their fast at the same time.[33] This of course expresses a unifying and standardizing desire by the crown to override the prized disagreements among the jurists.

---

30 'Afif 1891, 43–44.

31 Silver coins weighing about 10 grams.

32 'Afif 1891, 129–130.

33 'Afif 1891, 256–259.

In short, the *Fatawa Tatarkhaniya* must be understood in the context of rivalries and cooperations within the ruling elite. The *Fatawa* evinces a desire for the jurists to express their vision of what the ideal relationship between them and the king should be in matters relating to the leadership of the community. The events surrounding the date of the composition reflects an attempt by Firuzshah to be more respectful to [Islamic] law. And this is where the rare instance of imperial pressure on non-Muslims elites appears. ʿAfif tells us that in 1375 Firuzshah reviewed a number of unjust duties and taxes. Such duties included a tax collected by the officials after the *zakat* (a tax of about 2.5%) had been paid, and this apparently especially hurt cloth merchants. There were also property taxes on houses and shops, and a slaughtering fee on cow butchers. Last of all, merchants who dealt in sugar, salt, grains, and cloth were forced to use their horses to bring bricks into the king's new construction sites. As these men added their expenses to the price of their commodities, the cost on these items increased rapidly.[34] The jurists, we are told, convened by the request of the king and declared all these fees to be illegal (in contradiction to the sharia), and the king publically foreswore the resulting income which added up to three million *tanka*s.[35]

Perhaps there is little surprise that immediately [36] afterwards the king reformed and expanded the *jizya* (tax on non-Muslims). The general mood was set when "an idol worshipper" was arrested for spreading idolatry and worst of all for leading a Muslim woman into apostasy. The king held a trial and asked for a *fatwa* from the jurists who ruled that the accused should be asked to convert to Islam or be burnt at the stake. A public burning was staged, and soon thereafter the king asked the jurists whether he could begin collecting the *jizya* from the Brahmins who apparently had never had to pay it. The jurists ruled favorably. It is difficult to know how much was gained as a result of this. ʿAfif states that up until that point the *jizya* was levied at a graduated rate in three categories from Hindus other than the Brahmins: 40 *tanka*s for the wealthy, 20 for the middling sorts, and 10 for the poor. The king changed the rate and standardized it to 50 *tanka*s for every ten individuals. This new payment plan is significant in two ways. First, by spreading the burden out but increasing the number of payers, the king was very likely increasing his income in order to make up for loss of revenue caused by removal of "un-Islamic" taxes.[37] Second, by requiring payments per group, the king was reinforcing the vision for religio-legal group identity that had found

34 ʿAfif 1891, 375–376.
35 ʿAfif 1891, 379.
36 ʿAfif 1891, 380–381.
37 ʿAfif 1891, 383–384.

expression in the *fatawa* as well. This serves as a good example for the desire for mutually beneficial interdependence between the monarch and jurists, which then on occasion affects non-Muslims to prevent the apostasy of Muslims or more importantly shifting the burden of taxation away from merchants and poorer Hindus and toward priestly groups.

There are other such examples. Suffice it to say that the fourteenth century shows a period of collaboration and competition among two components of the ruling structure in the Delhi Sultanate: the executive/judicial (fulfilled by the emperor) and the judicial/legislative fulfilled by the jurists. Over the next centuries we see these institutional tensions play out more and more in favor of the monarch. Akbar the Mughal emperor will push back the power of the jurists and assume some of their powers for the monarch—often in the name of standardization and overcoming scholarly argumentativeness. The compilation of the legal digest under Aurangzeb in the 17th century may very well be a continuation of the assertion of imperial dominance in this tug of war. Aurangzeb perhaps yields more importance to Muslim jurists than Akbar, but never as much as Medieval Delhi monarchs. Even so, the compilation of the *'Alamgiri* did not create uniformity. To quote what Karl Härter said during the conference, "the monarch's attempt at standardization in fact creates diversity in the execution of the law". We do have evidence from the 19th century, where a Muslim jurist, the famous Shah 'Abd al-'Aziz Dihlavi (d. 1824), issued a ruling in a heresy case, and cited the *'Alamgiri* along with a number of other sources as support for his decision.[38] In other words, the *'Alamgiri* did not become the standard handbook that it purported to be. Rather it joined a series of authoritative sources of reference for Muslim jurists of the subcontinent.

References

'Abd al-Malik b. Muḥammad al-Tha'alib, *Tarikh Ghurar al-Siyar*, H. Zotenberg (ed.), Paris, Imprimerie Nationale, 1900.

'Abd al-Qadir Badauni, *Najat al-Rashid*, S. Mu'in al-Haqq (ed.), Lahore: 1972.

'Alim b. 'Ala, *Al-Fatawa al-Tatarkhaniyah*, Sajjad Husayn (ed.), Karachi: 1990.

Auer, Blain H., *Symbols of Authority in Medieval South Asia: History, Religion and Muslim Legitimacy in the Delhi Sultanate*, London: I.B. Tauris, 2012.

Crone, Patricia, *God's Rule: Government and Islam*, New York: Columbia University Press, 2005.

de Bruijn, Thomas, *Ruby in the Dust: Poetry and History in Padmavat by the South Asian Sufi Poet Muhammad Jayasi*, Leiden: Leiden University Press, 2012.

38 Manzurulhaq Siddiqi, *Ma'asir al-Ajdad*, Lahore: 1964, 506.

Eaton, Richard, Introduction, in: *India's Islamic Traditions, 711–1750*, Richard Eaton (ed.), 1–36, Delhi: Oxford University Press, 2003.
Ghiyas al-Din b. Humam al-Din Khvandamir, *Ma'asir al-Muluk bih Zamimah-i Khatimah-i Khulasat al-Akhbar va Qanun-i Humayuni*, M. H. Muhaddis (ed.), Tehran: 1993/4.
Mill, James, *History of British India*, Volume 2, London: Baldwin, Cradock, and Joy, 1840.
Moin, A. Azfar, *The Millenial Sovereign: Sacred Kingship and Sainthood in Islam*, New York: Columbia University Press, 2012.
Qazvini, Asif Khan, Fath Allah Shirazi, Ahmad Tattavi, Mir Ghiyas al-Din, 'Ali Qazvini, 'Abd al-Qadir Badauni, Nizam al-Din Ahmad, Abu al-Fath Gilani, Hakeem Humam Gilani, *Tarikh-i Alfi*, Ghulamriza Tabataba'i (ed.), Tehran: 2003.
Sadighi, Behnam, *The Logic of Law Making in Islam: Women and Prayer in the Legal Tradition*, Cambridge: Cambridge University Press, 2013.
Schacht, Joseph, *An Introduction to Islamic Law*, Oxford: Clarendon Press, 1964.
Sham Siraj 'Afif, *Tarikh-i Firuzshahi*, Wilayat Husain (ed.), Calcutta: 1891.
Shaykh Nizam, *Al-Fatawa al-Hindiyah fi Madhhab Imam al-A'zam Abi Hanifa al-Nu'man*, Beirut: 1991.
Siddiqi, Manzurulhaq, *Ma'asir al-Ajdad*, Lahore: 1964.

Blain Auer

Regulating diversity within the empire

The legal concept of *zimmi* and the collection of *jizya* under the Sultans of Delhi (1200–1400)

Introduction

One major point of discussion in the study of Islamicate South Asia has been the treatment of non-Muslim communities under Muslim rule.[1] Interpreters of Islamic law and Muslim rulers in the Islamic Earlier Middle Period (950–1250) developed various policies and laws to codify the relationship between non-Muslims and the ruling institutions. However, the nature of that historical relationship has been the subject of intense debates, particularly in relation to the politics of the pre- and post-independence period in India and Pakistan. In this article, I am interested in revising and redirecting the general discussion. In particular, I consider the period between 1200–1400 when Muslim rulers constructed an Islami-

1 For instance see the studies Khaliq Ahmad Nizami, *Royalty in Medieval India,* New Delhi: Munshiram Manoharlal Publishers, 1997, 153–167. Also see Khaliq Ahmad Nizami, *Religion and Politics in India during the Thirteenth Century,* New Delhi: Oxford University Press, 2002, 324–341. For a problematic monograph on the subject see Kanhaiya Lall Srivastava, *The Position of Hindus under the Delhi Sultanate 1206–1526,* New Delhi: Munshiram Manoharlal, 1980. For an early general and broad survey of these issues see Aziz Ahmad, *Studies in Islamic Culture in the Indian Environment,* Oxford: Clarendon Press, 1964, 71–118. See Riazul Islam, A Note on the Position of the Non-Muslim Subjects in the Sultanate of Delhi under the Khaljis and the Tughluqs, *Journal of the Pakistan Historical Society* 45, no. 3 (1997): 215–229. Also see Peter Jackson's chapter titled "The Sultans and their Hindu Subjects," in Peter Jackson, *The Delhi Sultanate: A Political and Military History,* Cambridge: Cambridge University Press, 1999, 278–295. On the treatment of Hindu and Shia communities see Iqtidar Husain Siddiqui, *Authority and Kingship under the Sultans of Delhi (Thirteenth–Fourteenth Centuries),* Delhi: Manohar, 2006, 157–159. Zafarul Islam discusses aspects of regulating social relations between Muslim and non-Muslim communities dealt within the law literature of the Delhi Sultanate. See Zafarul Islam, The *Fatāwā Fīruz Shāhī* as a Source for the Socio-Economic History of the Sultanate Period, *Islamic Culture* 60, no. 2 (1986): 97–117, here 105–107. Also see Zafarul Islam, Fīrūz Shāh Tughluq's Attitude towards Non-Muslims – A Reappraisal, *Islamic Culture* 64, no. 4 (1990): 65–79. For similar questions of how Muslim intellectuals conceptualized relationships with non-Muslim communities as they developed in the Mughal period see Muzaffar Alam, A Muslim State in a Non-Muslim Context, in: *Mirror for the Muslim Prince: Islam and the Theory of Statecraft*, Mehrzad Boroujerdi (ed.), 160–189, Syracuse: Syracuse University Press, 2013.

DOI 10.1515/9783110423327-003

cate polity in South Asia centered in Delhi but with social, cultural, and political networks that spanned the subcontinent. It was during this period that major legal texts were composed under the court patronage of Muslim rulers concerned with, at least in part, delineating the regulations of social interaction in certain contexts. The Delhi Sultanate legal tradition is testimony to the preservation, codification, and evolution of the sharia in this period. In that context there are at least two principle legal categories that governed the relationships between Muslim and non-Muslim communities, *zimmi* and *jizya*. *Zimmi* is a legal category applied to non-Muslims living within the Islamic polity. Those who fell within this category were given legal protections in exchange for acknowledgment and submission to Islamic rule along with the payment of *jizya*, a tax or tribute symbolic of the acceptance of Islamic rule. These categories pose some basic questions for scholars as they were discussed and debated in the Delhi Sultanate. What was the category of *zimmi* and how was it employed, both conceptually and in practice, by the sultans of Delhi? What was the purpose of *jizya* in the Delhi Sultanate?

In recent scholarship, some scholars have argued, outside of the context of South Asia, that sharia rules regarding the *jizya* and the status of *zimmi* were created to regulate diversity and minimize the risks of difference in imperial contexts of rule. Anver Emon argues that "imperial expansion had to be envisioned and framed in light of both the fact of diversity and an Islamic universalist ethos. The result was a pluralist approach to governance of which the *dhimmī* rules were symptoms. Indeed, helping to negotiate the tension between empire and universalism was one of the fundamental tasks the *dhimmī* rules fulfilled."[2] From a certain point of view the category of *zimmi* was part of a host of regulations aimed at controlling a diverse populace within an imperial framework. In a sense *zimmi* provided a space for accepting difference by creating a legal rubric that formalized certain categories of imperial subjects. Admittedly, individuals needed not, and in fact did not, rely solely on religious identification. However, many principles of regulating and managing diversity in the imperial framework operated on non-Muslim and Muslim categories alike. These abstract categories formed the basis of regulating the expression of acceptable and unacceptable difference. The important categories of difference not accepted within the imperial sphere were those of apostasy (*irtidad*), heresy (*alhad*), and an array of acts considered under the rules of rebellion (*akham al-baghy*).

There are three interlinking areas of discussion regarding the status of non-Muslims living under a Muslim ruler that can help clarify the question of

2 Anver M. Emon, *Religious Pluralism and Islamic Law: "Dhimmīs" and Others in the Empire of Law*, Oxford: Oxford University Press, 2012, 65.

diversity when considered together. First, what is the state of research and methodological problems that arise when responding to questions about the relationship between Muslim and non-Muslim communities within the Delhi Sultanate? Second, how can one approach the legal debates that address inter-confessional relationships under the Delhi sultans as expressed through the categories *zimmi* and *jizya*? Third, how can the limits and extent of the application of *zimmi* status and the degrees of implementation of the *jizya* on non-Muslim subjects under the laws of the Delhi Sultanate be explained on a historical basis? It should be noted that investigating the question of Muslim views of non-Muslim communities from a strictly legal and imperial perspective necessarily represents a narrow and controlled sphere of debates that circulated within the cadre of ulema, amirs, and courtiers at Delhi and other important urban centers of South Asia.[3]

The problem of tolerance and the treatment of non-Muslim Subjects

Before entering into a discussion of the topic of *jizya* and *zimmi* it is necessary to confront some conceptual and methodological problems current in scholarship that have predominated the study of non-Muslim subjects within the Delhi Sultanate. The first general misconception encountered is that some, if not many, scholars have viewed *jizya* and *zimmi* from a universal and essentialist Islamic perspective. That is to say that scholars felt that they could discern a unique Muslim attitude towards non-Muslims, a distinctive worldview that was shared and common across time and place, whether it be seventh and eighth century Sindh, thirteenth-century Delhi, or seventeenth-century Agra. However, the depth of discussion within Muslim intellectual circles on the subject, and the divergence of opinions, obviates against any single representative view of *jizya* and *zimmi* in

---

3 For a broader view Carl Ernst has published a series of articles exploring Hindu-Muslim encounters. See Carl W. Ernst, Admiring the Works of the Ancients: The Ellora Temples as Viewed by Indo-Muslim Authors, in: *Beyond Turk and Hindu: Rethinking Religious Identities in Islamicate South Asia*, David Gilmartin, Bruce B. Lawrence (eds.), 98–120, Gainesville, FL: University Press of Florida, 2000. Carl W. Ernst, Muslim Studies of Hinduism? A Reconsideration of Arabic and Persian Translations from Indian Languages, *Iranian Studies* 36, no. 2 (2003): 173–195. Carl W. Ernst, Situating Sufism and Yoga, *Journal of Royal Asiatic Society* 15, no. 1 (2005): 15–43. Carl W. Ernst, Accounts of Yogis in Arabic and Persian Historical and Travel Texts, *Jerusalem studies in Arabic and Islam* 33 (2007): 409–426. Carl W. Ernst, The Limits of Universalism in Islamic Thought: the Case of Indian Religions, *The Muslim World* 101, no. 1 (2011): 1–19.

any time and place. A bird's-eye view of legal history shows that over time, as Islamic dominion spread, interpretations of sharia changed to adapt to different contexts.[4] The fact of this variation in interpretation can be seen in the divergent perspectives from different schools of legal thinking on the status of non-Muslims. It should be kept in mind that while discussing the legal issues relating to the treatment of non-Muslim communities within the Delhi Sultanate, one is almost exclusively speaking of a Sunni-Hanafi perspective. This is a basic fact, but one that is often overlooked. It is significant because there are important differences between the Hanafi, Shafi'i, Hanbali and Maliki Islamic schools of law, within Sunni contexts.[5] Debate and diversity of opinion were recognized as an important part of the discursive tradition as practiced among the educated religious elite. Examples of differences between religious scholars of this period are numerous.

The Sunni-Hanafi perspective on these issues is self-evident in the sources utilized to reconstruct the legal history of this period. One major source is Fakhr-i Mudabbir (ca. 1157–1236) and his famous work of advice literature, the *Adab al-harb wa-l-shaja'a* (The etiquette of war and valour).[6] As a scholar of note who served under Ghaznavid, Ghurid, and Shamsi Sultans in the late 12th and early 13th centuries, he represents what can be considered a consensus Sunni-Hanafi perspective on the subject. Fakhr-i Mudabbir's discourse on the *jizya* and *zimmi* is one of the most extensive and comprehensive sources on the topic available. He covers the topic in chapter twenty-six in the *Adab al-harb* in a section that deals with the spoils of war and the imposition of the *jizya* on the infidel (*kafir*) and *zimmi*.[7] Another major source on the Sunni-Hanafi perspective is Ziya' al-din Barani (ca. 1285–1357). His ideas on the subject are found in his work of advice literature the *Fatawa-i Jahandari* (The edicts of world-rule) as well as in his history,

4 For an important work on changes in Hanafi Islamic law regarding tax policy in Ottoman and Mamluk contexts see Baber Johansen, *The Islamic Law on Land Tax and Rent: The Peasants' Loss of Property Rights as Interpreted in the Hanafite Legal Literature of the Mamluk and Ottoman Periods*, London: Croom Helm, 1988.

5 For some of these debates see Sunil Kumar, Politics, the Muslim Community and Hindu-Muslim Relations Reconsidered: North India in the Early Thirteenth Century, in *Rethinking a Millennium: Perspectives on Indian History from the Eighth of the Eighteenth Century, Essays for Harbans Mukhia*, Rajat Datta (ed.), 139–167, Delhi: Aakar, 2008, here 144–148.

6 The relevant problems of using the *Adab al-harb* as a historical source are dealt with in Sunil Kumar, The Value of the *Ādāb al-Mulūk* as a Historical Source: An Insight into the Ideals and Expectations of Islamic Society in the Middle Period (A.D. 945–1500), *Indian Economic and Social History Review* 22, no. 3 (1985): 307–327.

7 See Muhammad ibn Mansur (Fakhr-i Mudabbir) Mubarak Shah, *Adab al-harb wa-l-shaja'a*, Tehran: Intisharat-i Iqbal, 1967, 400–407. Nizami summarized Fakhr-i Mudabbir's position in Nizami 2002, 330.

the *Tarikh-i Firuzshahi*. There are also important legal texts produced in the period. The *Fatawa al-Tatarkhaniya* is a compilation of legal opinions drawn primarily from Hanafi authoritative sources such as the *Jamiʿ al-saghir* by Muhammad al-Shaybani (750–805), the *Sharh al-Tahawi* of Abu Jaʿfar al-Tahawi (d. 933), and the *al-Hidaya* of Burhan al-din al-Marghinani (d. 1197). It was organized by ʿAlim b. al-ʿAla' (d. 1384).[8] Legal opinions are arranged in a fashion that allows the reader to view the evolution of legal debates on particular subjects and see important differences of opinion with the Shafiʿi, Hanbali and Maliki legal traditions. The historian Shams al-din ʿAfif (b. 1356) stresses the fact that great pains were taken to include diverse legal opinions within the text.[9] Tatar Khan commissioned the work in 1375 during the reign of Firuz Shah (r. 1351–1388), following a pilgrimage to Mecca. He is also said to be responsible for an extensive Quran commentary titled *Tafsir-i Tatarkhani*. Another important legal compendium of the time is the *Fiqh-i Firuzshahi*.[10] This text was originally organized by Sadr al-din Kuhrami. It is also known as the *Fatawa-i Firuzshahi*, as it was completed under the supervision, or at least patronage, of Firuz Shah. It also provides further evidence to the legal understanding of the relationship between Hindu communities and the Muslim ruler.[11]

A second problematic area in approaches to the study of non-Muslim communities living within Islamic legal and political systems is that they tend to rely, implicitly or explicitly, on a basic concept of tolerance.[12] Studies of Islamic legal categories that discuss the status of non-Muslims in society are frequently undertaken to ascertain the degree that they were tolerated within the institutional framework. This was the case to an extreme degree in Kanhaiya Lall Srivastava's *The Position of the Hindus under the Delhi Sultanate 1206–1526*. Srivastava summarized his view of *jizya* and *zimmi* in a chapter on religious bigotry that he begins by saying, "with the foundations of Muslim rule in India the Hindus had lost their freedom of religious worship."[13] He viewed "Hindu-Muslim" relations as

---

8 For a study of the *fatawa* text see Zafarul Islam, *Fatāwā Literature of the Sultanate Period*, New Delhi: Kanishka Publishers, 2005, 88–107.

9 Shams Siraj ʿAfif, *Tarikh-i Firuzshahi*, Calcutta: Asiatic Society, 1888, 392.

10 For an overview of other important legal texts produced during the period see Zafarul Islam, The Contribution of the Tughluq Sultans to Islamic Jurisprudence, *Majallat al-Ta'rīkh al-Islāmī* 2, no. 3–4 (1997): 516–528.

11 Islam 1986, 104–07.

12 Emon provides an important critique of the tolerance approach citing a growth of studies. See Emon 2012, 3–7.

13 Srivastava 1980, 99. An earlier and equally strident version of this view can be found in a chapter title "Hindu Muslim Relations" in the edition Ramesh Chandra Majumdar (ed.), *The Delhi Sultanate*, Bombay: Bharatiya Vidya Bhavan, 1960; reprint, 1980, 617–625.

defined by conflict and shaped by the intolerance of Muslims towards non-Muslims.[14] Srivastava's study represents the perspective that the Delhi sultans were motivated by religious bigotry in their policymaking. In general, studies that use an arbitrary notion of tolerance judge one society or community as being more tolerant than another. Muzaffar Alam has argued that the history of South Asia has often been presented in a simplified and general way as either marked by deep enmity between Hindu and Muslim communities, or as predominated by amity.[15] These polar views are inadequate to explain the complexity of social and cultural relations between these communities which are deeply porous and heterogeneous. In fact, the tolerance/intolerance approach has led to some deeply contradictory views about regulating diversity. One can contrast the scholarship of two of the most important contributors on these debates to illustrate this point: K. A. Nizami and Yohannan Friedmann.

K. A. Nizami, a scholar who has written extensively on the subject, generally falls into an apologetic side of the spectrum where the attitude of Muslim rulers towards their non-Muslim subjects is described as tolerant. However, his tolerance position led Nizami into contradictory statements such as "Hindus enjoyed full religious freedom during the sultanate period" and on the same page "they had permission to repair their old temples, but could only build new temples away from the Muslim inhabited areas."[16] To support his view he relegates legal texts to the status of theory in preference for anecdotes taken from history writing. It is the case that some scholars give preference to either the legal or historical sources, finding it difficult to reconcile them with each other. For instance, in areas where he finds the views of Ziyaʾ al-din Barani intolerant, he dismisses them as an aberration arguing that "for the attitude of the *ʿulama* towards the Hindus we have no other source of information except Zia-u'd-din Barani. But he was so deeply prejudiced against Hindus that it is difficult to vouch for the truth of his statements."[17] Similarly, he finds it difficult to make sense of Fakhr-i Mudabbir's views on the subject. Fakhr-i Mudabbir lists those liable for *jizya* of the people of Persia (*ahl-i ʿajam*) as Christians (*tarsayan*), Jews, the Sabeans, Zoroastrians (*mugh*), and idol-worshippers (*but parast*).[18] However, Nizami tries to show that the imposition of *jizya* was not representative of the "actual posi-

14 A voice in this debate on the side of tolerance is Alyssa Gabbay, *Islamic Tolerance: Amīr Khusraw and Pluralism*, New York: Routledge, 2010.

15 See Muzaffar Alam, Competition and Co-existence: Indo-Islamic Interaction in Medieval North India, *Itinerario* 13, no. 1 (1989): 37–59.

16 See Nizami 1997, 156.

17 See Nizami 2002, 333.

18 Mubarak Shah 1967, 404.

tion" of Hindus. He dismisses Fakhr-i Mudabbir's legal viewpoint saying, "This is merely a statement of the theoretical position and, that too, a mere rehash of the statements of the *Hedayah*."[19] However, one could equally argue, and perhaps with more reason, that Fakhr-i Mudabbir's reliance upon the *Hidayah*, an influential Hanafi legal text rooted in longstanding interpretations of the Quran and hadith, represented a persisting norm concerning the legal view of *jizya*.

A second viewpoint distinct from the apologetic view represented by Nizami is a critical view that can be seen in the work of Yohannan Friedmann. In 2003, Friedmann published an extensive study on the treatment of non-Muslim subjects in a work titled *Tolerance and Coercion in Islam: Interfaith Relations in the Muslim Tradition*. Although not a study of the context of South Asia, it is a work that attempts to survey the important questions relating to the treatment of non-Muslim communities living within Islamic polities. Friedmann saw his work as a corrective of the kinds of apologetics represented in works like that of Nizami, though he cites other scholars. In his view, these kinds of works give readers the impression that "the Qur'ān never spoke about Islam as the only true religion, that it never said anything harsh about the non-Muslims, that classical Islamic tradition never imposed restrictions on non-Muslims' observance in *dār al-islām* [the Land of Islam] and never designated the Arabian peninsula as a region where Islam was the only faith to be tolerated."[20] While generally congratulated for his detailed analysis of sources discussing this issue, he faced criticism for his overall approach that focuses on Islamic practices that he viewed as uniquely intolerant and discriminatory.[21] Daniel Varisco noted in his review that, "this book opens the door on the bare bones of intolerance in Islamic textual sources and shines a bright critical light on it. My problem is not with the analysis as such but with the narrow focus that leaves other important parts of the story in the dark."[22] In another review Muhammad Qasim Zaman describes what he finds as a weakness in Friedmann's approach in that it "is guided by the assumption that it is the classical tradition that can be taken to represent the Muslim ethos in general."[23]

19 Nizami 2002, 331.

20 Yohanan Friedmann, *Tolerance and Coercion in Islam: Interfaith Relations in the Muslim Tradition*, Cambridge: Cambridge University Press, 2003, 6.

21 In a separate and much earlier article he deals with what he understands as a "sympathetic" Muslim view of non-Muslims in South Asia. See Yohanan Friedmann, Medieval Muslim Views of Indian Religions, *Journal of the American Oriental Society* 95, no. 2 Apr. – Jun. (1975): 214–221.

22 Daniel Martin Varisco, review of *Tolerance and Coercion in Islam: Interfaith Relations in the Muslim Tradition*, by Yohanan Friedmann, *Islamic Law & Society* 13, no. 2 (2006), 285–288, here 287.

23 Muhammad Qasim Zaman, review of *Tolerance and Coercion in Islam: Interfaith Relations in*

Zaman argued that it is important to distinguish between the legal status and the social status of religious minorities under Muslim rule. When one speaks strictly to the legal status it is in reference to an abstract principle of Islamic law. When one speaks in terms of social status it is the record of encounters and perceptions as well as economic and cultural relations between Muslims and non-Muslims. These factors may intersect, but not necessarily be coherent.

While Nizami and Friedmann have done much to bring together the relevant materials pertaining to the subject, they have hampered the development of an interpretive framework to understand them. They pit various kinds of evidence against others to prove the degree to which Islam is a tolerant or intolerant religion, the kind of debate that can be seen very much alive in the public and the media. However, the goal of proving Islam as tolerant or intolerant provides little insight into the historical causes of the intellectual and legal debates reflected in the texts themselves. Sunil Kumar has brought a methodological intervention into the debates on the broader question of "Hindu-Muslim" relations. He provides the historical background to how modern politics have played into the understanding of premodern issues, as well as questioning the underlying assumptions that enter into these types of debates. He summarizes the methodological problems posed by a reading of the Persian historical sources of the period saying, "With the state as the principal political actor in South Asia and the protection of the community of Muslims as its primary aim, it was always cast in an offensive or defensive engagement with non-Muslims. Modern positivist historiographical methodologies, especially if they belonged to secular traditions, had the greatest difficulty in dealing with these materials."[24]

These challenges, amongst others, have meant that the essential questions surrounding *jizya* and *zimmi* status remain little understood. Why did Muslim legal scholars and rulers institute distinct discriminatory laws for non-Muslims? How did these laws function within those societies? What were the underlying legal principles and debates? There is really no escaping the fact that sharia laws were discriminatory, in a strict sense that they recognized/established difference between Muslims and non-Muslims and instituted legal rules governing the behaviour of those categories of people. In terms of non-Muslim communities this has been noted primarily in the tax system with the imposition of the *jizya*. In some areas it refers to the standing of non-Muslim communities before the law. For instance, how do they serve as witnesses and the value of their testi-

---

the Muslim Tradition, by Yohanan Friedmann, *The Journal of Religion* 87, no. 3 (2007), 470–473, here 472.

24 Kumar 2008, 159.

mony in criminal cases? In other areas it relates to the question of the construction and maintenance of places of religious worship. There is also the question of the imposition of defining markings that publicly distinguish someone as a non-Muslim. While religious identity served as a marker of difference within the law, age and gender were also important categories of difference that necessitated special rules to govern the categories of men and women, the child and adult. While these differences as recognized within the law were given religious explanations, in the sense that they were said to have derived from a particular belief about God and the nature of prophesy, they were formed and shaped by socio-political contexts.

Legal and political history of the category of *zimmi* and *jizya*

What was the understanding of the categories of *zimmi* and *jizya* in the Delhi Sultanate? This question has posed significant challenges for historians developing a picture of non-Muslim communities based on historical and legal sources. The principle problem is that there is great diversity of opinion on fundamental aspects of these two categories. For instance, the understanding of which communities could be subject to the status of *zimmi* and from whom the *jizya* could be accepted is historically quite complex and evolved over time.[25] In early Islamic history, *jizya* was frequently used interchangeably with *kharaj*, a tax that gradually came to be understood more strictly in the sense of a land tax. For instance, Tsugitaka Sato notes that in the early Hanafi legal tradition it was "Abū Yūsuf (d. 182/798), a follower of Abū Ḥanīfa, [who] formed his tax theory on the principle that any land whose owner, Arab or non-Arab, became a Muslim should be considered ʿushr land [land taxed at ten percent], while lands taken over from non-Arabs and left in their possession should be categorised as kharādj land (69; Taxation in Islam, iii, 82)."[26] The early historical ambiguity and variation in legal definition is equally significant in the context of the Delhi Sultanate where the categories of *jizya* and *kharaj* were frequently used interchangeably and with

25 For a study that takes up the question of *jizya* in the Mughal period see Satish Chandra, Jizyah and the State in India during the 17th Century, *Journal of the Economic and Social History of the Orient/Journal de l'histoire economique et sociale de l'Orient* 12, no. 3 (1969), 322–340.

26 *Encyclopaedia of Islam*, second edition, P. Bearman, Th. Bianquis, C.E. Bosworth, E. van Donzel and W.P. Heinrichs (eds.), "ʿushr," (T. Sato).

varying connotations that range from a head tax, land tax, and tribute (of a ruler). Peter Jackson put forward a somewhat novel view believing that "the jizya did not exist as a distinct tax but was subsumed within the kharaj or land-tax."[27] This view was put forward earlier in another fashion by Peter Hardy who noted that, "djizya was not normally levied under the Dihlī Sultanate in the sense of a discriminatory religious tax."[28]

Jackson's and Hardy's views on the Delhi Sultanate are consistent with other historians' views concerning the history of *jizya* within Muslim communities considered globally and in different contexts.[29] Jackson does propose a possible distinction to be made between the Hindus living in rural areas who would be subject to *kharaj* as a land tax, while those living in the urban areas would be to subject to *jizya*, in the sense of a poll tax.[30] Relatedly, the *Fiqh-i Firuzshahi*, an important legal text of the period, indicates that "infidels" cultivating land classified as *kharaj*-land would be liable for *kharaj* just as Muslims.[31] This idea is further supported by 'Abd al-Hamid Muharrir Ghaznavi (b. ca. 1291) who contributed to our knowledge of taxes of the period. In his work *Dastur al-albab fi 'ilm al-hisab* [The foundation for understanding the knowledge of arithmetic], completed in 1364–65 during the reign of Firuz Shah, he notes that *zimmi* are liable for taxes on cultivated fields.[32] He also adds some clarity to the discussion of the relationship between *kharaj* and *jizya*. He states that the *jizya* is of two kinds, the *kharaj-i muqassima*, a percentage of the produce of the land that is equally applicable to Muslims, and the tax upon workingmen of a fixed rate dependent upon personal earnings.[33]

One of the principle concerns of Sunni jurists was who fit the category of *zimmi*. Early in Islamic history *zimmi* generally referred to Christian and Jewish communities as "People of the Book," that is sharing a tradition of revealed scripture. However, as Islamic empires expanded into regions comprising other religious communities the category of *zimmi* came to be applied to others, Zoroastrians for example, as was the case in Iraq and Iran. The expanding category of *zimmi* is particularly significant considering how Islamic law was used in the context of South Asia where the category was applied to groups considered "Hindu" or

27 Jackson 1999, 285.
28 *Encyclopaedia of Islam*, "djizya," (P. Hardy).
29 See *Encyclopaedia of Islam*, "djizya," (C. Cahen).
30 Jackson 1999, 285–86.
31 Sadr al-Din Kuhrami, Ya'qub Muzaffar, *Fiqh-i Firuzshahi*, BL I.O. Islamic 2987, fol. 410b.
32 See 'Abd al-Hamid Muharrir Ghaznavi, Dastur-ul-albab fi 'ilm-il-Hisab, *Medieval India Quarterly* (1954), 59–99, here 66. The work was initiated during the reign of Muhammad b. Tughluq and is available in manuscript from the Rampur Library.
33 Ghaznavi 1954, 67–68.

"Brahmin." It is difficult to say from available evidence how the category of *zimmi* was applied to non-Muslims during the earliest encounters with Arabs, from the time of the military activities of the Umayyad commander Muhammad b. Qasim in Sindh along the Indus River roughly in the years between 708–711. The evidence for the inclusion of Hindu communities within the category of *zimmi* is cited from al-Baladhuri, the late ninth-century historian writing in Arabic, "the idol temple is similar to the churches of the Christians, [to the synagogues] of the Jews, and to the fire-temples of the Zoroastrians" (*ma al-budd illa ka-kana'is al-nasara wa 'l-yahud wa-buyut niran al-majus*).[34]

A second source for this proposition is found in the *Chachnama* of ʿAli ibn Hamid Kufi, "[We] should treat the ascetic Brahmans with kindness and consideration, celebrate their festivals and ceremonies like their forefathers and pay the Brahmans the same alms they had been paying them in the past."[35] A principle problem in relying upon these sources is the date of their composition. Al-Baladhuri most likely composed his frequently cited *Futuh al-buldan,* the *History of the Conquests*, around 892 A.D., nearly two centuries after the activities of Muhammad b. Qasim. The *Chachnama* by al-Kufi is even more problematic as it is the Persian translation carried out around 1216–17 A.D. of an unattributed Arabic text. Dating this leads one to believe that it expresses a view of circumstances that existed at the beginning of the thirteenth century.[36]

On the subject of *zimmi* some scholars have assumed there was continuity in the application of the category, arguing that it was used in a coherent fashion from the time of earliest Muslim encounters with non-Muslims in South Asia. Nizami erroneously believed he had evidence that non-Muslims in Arab Sindh were considered "people resembling the *Ahl-i-Kitab*."[37] He extends this view to include the Delhi Sultanate. Nizami argues that "when Muhammad b. Qasim decided to realize the *jiziyah* from the Hindus, he placed them under the category of *mushabah-ahl-i kitab*. This position of the Hindus was accepted by all the

---

34 Hardy notes that Baladhuri refers to *kharaj* being imposed as a tribute. See *Encyclopaedia of Islam*, "Djizya," (P. Hardy). For the Arabic see Ahmad ibn Yahya Baladhuri, *Kitab futuh al-buldan*, Leiden: E. J. Brill, 1866, 439.

35 Quoted in Yohanan Friedmann, The Origins and Significance of the Chach Nāma, in: *Islam in Asia*, Yohanan Friedmann (ed.), 23–37, Jerusalem: Magnes Press, 1984, 31.

36 Peter Jackson made this point that echoes earlier statements by Peter Hardy. See Peter Hardy, Is the *Chach Nama* intelligible to the historian as political theory?, *Sind Quarterly* (1980): 16–22. Jackson 1999, 284. For a more recent and treatment of the text see Manan Ahmed, The Long Thirteenth Century of the Chachnama, *Indian Economic & Social History Review* 49, no. 4 (2012): 459–491.

37 Nizami 1997, 154.

Sultans of Delhi."[38] Here it is important to note the distinction made in Islamic law between groups considered *ahl al-kitab* and *ahl al-dhimma*. It was not necessary to be recognized as "People of the Book" to fit within the category of "Protected People." Yohanan Friedmann notes that "the *ahl al-kitāb* are not identical to the *ahl al-dhimma* ... and non-Arab polytheists, who are considered *ahl al-dhimma* according to the Ḥanafīs and Mālikīs, are not considered *ahl al-kitāb* by any school of Muslim jurists or by traditionalists."[39] This viewpoint can be discerned in the Sunni-Hanafi discussion of the category of *zimmi* taken up in the *Fatawa al-Tatarkhaniya*. There the compilers cite from the proof text taken from al-Marghinani who notes that the *jizya* can be accepted from the category of the "idolater of Persia" (*mushriki al-ʿajam*).[40] This position stands in contrast to the other Sunni schools of Islamic law. As noted earlier, Fakhr-i Mudabbir says that *jizya* is to be taken from these categories of the peoples of Persia: Jews, Christians, Sabeans, Zoroastrians, and idol worshipers (*but parast*).[41] Barani notes that it is only the Hanafi school that allows Hindus to pay the *jizya*. This position is likely based on the analogous situation in Hanafi law where *jizya* is accepted from the "idolater of Persia."[42] On this basis, it appears that it is possible to establish the case that on the whole Hindus were accorded the status of *zimmi* during the Delhi Sultanate.[43] Peter Jackson in his history of this period writes, "That the Indian polytheists who submitted to Islamic rule qualified, therefore, as 'protected peoples' seems to have won acceptance among a fairly wide spectrum of the educated Muslim community within the subcontinent."[44]

This all raises some very basic and essential questions. Whether the *jizya* was applied or not, what was the intended purpose of imposing a separate tax for non-Muslims within the sharia? Why not have non-Muslims pay the same tax as Muslims? One example described by Barani in the *Tarikh-i Firuzshahi* provides some potential answers to these questions. It is presented on the occasion of a discus-

---

38 Nizami 2002, 331.

39 *Encyclopaedia of the Qur'an*, Jane Dammen McAuliffe (ed.), "Dhimma," (Yohanan Friedmann).

40 ʿAlim ibn ʿAlaʾ, *al-Fatawa al-tatarkhaniyah fi al-fiqh al-hanafi*, Beirut: Dar al-Kutub al-ʿIlmiyah, 2005, 4:220.

41 Mubarak Shah 1967, 404.

42 Ziyaʾ al-din Barani, *Tarikh-i Firuzshahi*. Sayyid Ahmad Khan (ed.), Vol. 33, Bibliotheca Indica, Calcutta: Asiatic Society, 1862, 291. Also see Ziyaʾ al-din Barani, *Fatava-yi Jahandari*. Afsar Salīm Khān (ed.), 1st ed. Vol. 25, Intishārāt-i Idārah-yi Taḥqīqāt-i Pākistān. Lahore: Research Society of Pakistan, 1972, 18.

43 For an extensive list of sources on the topic see Jackson 1999, 282n33 and 34.

44 Jackson 1999, 283.

sion between the Qazi Mughis al-din Bayanah and the Sultan 'Ala' al-din Khalji (r. 1296–1316) who debates with the scholar the imposition of the *jizya* on Hindus. This passage is significant and deserves a full exposition to discuss it in more detail.[45]

> The first question the Sultan then asked Qazi Mughis al-din was, "According to the sharia, when is a Hindu designated as a payer of tribute (*kharaj-guzar*) or giver of tribute (*kharaj-dih*)?" The Qazi replied, "They are called payers of tribute, and when the revenue officer demands silver from them, they should, with all compliance (*linat*) and humility (*tawazu'*), and without question, tender gold with respect. If the revenue officer throws dirt into his mouth, they must without reluctance open their mouths wide to receive it. By doing so he is serving the revenue officer. The meaning of his compliance is his humiliation and the revenue officer throwing dirt into his mouth is the extreme obedience of the *zimmi*. The respect of Islam is a duty, and contempt of the religion is vain. God holds them in contempt, for he says, "Keep them under in subjection." To keep contempt for the Hindu is especially a religious requirement, because they are the most inveterate enemies of the Prophet, and because the Prophet has commanded us to slay them, plunder them, and make them captive, saying, "Convert them to Islam or kill them, enslave them and spoil their wealth and property." No one but the great scholar [Abu Hanifa], to whose school we belong, has accepted the *jizya* of the Hindus. According to the masters of the other schools of Islamic law it is not the tradition. In the opinion of the other religious scholars, for the Hindu it is "either fighting or Islam (*imma al-qatal wa imma al-islam*)."
>
> The Sultan laughed at the Qazi's response, and said, "I don't understand anything of what you said; but this I have discovered, that the Hindu headmen (*khutan*) and chiefs (*muqaddaman*) ride upon fine horses, wear fine clothes, shoot with Persian bows, make war upon each other, and go out hunting; but they do not pay a cent (*jital*) of the *kharaj-jizya* nor for their hearth and grazing land (*kurī wa charā'i*).[46] The headman's share is taken separately from the villages. They have assemblies and drink wine, and many of them pay no revenue at all, either upon demand or without demand. Neither do they show any deference to my officers. This has excited my anger, and I have said to myself, 'I will conquer other lands, but I have hundreds of leagues of country under my rule where proper obedience is not paid to my authority. How, then, will I make other lands submissive?' I have, therefore, taken measures, and have made my subjects obedient, so that at my command they scurry into holes like mice. Now you tell me that it is also in accordance with Islamic law that the Hindu must be made to suffer excessive orders." Then the Sultan said, "Oh scholar Mughis, you are a learned man, but you are not experienced. I am not well read, but I have a lot of experience. Be assured then that the Hindu will not become submissive and obedient until they are without wealth and means. I have, therefore, given orders that just sufficient shall

45 For the Persian text see Barani 1862, 290–292. I have edited the translation found in H. M. Elliot, John Dowson, *The History of India as Told by its Own Historians: The Muhammadan Period*, London: Trübner and Co., 1867, 3:183–185.

46 Qureshi identified this as a cattle and pasturage tax reading *kurrahi* or *kurrah* for *kurī*. *Kara'i* or grain house is a further possible etymology. See Ishtiaq Husain Qureshi, *The Administration of the Sultanate of Delhi* Lahore: Sh. Muhammad Ashraf, 1944.

> be left to them from year to year, of corn, milk, and curds, but that they shall not be allowed to accumulate excess wealth and means."

There are a number of elements of this discussion between the Sultan and the religious scholar that require comment. Clearly it is a discussion that focuses on the practicalities of revenue collection. The reference to the "Hindu" is used in the context of leaders of Hindu communities. Barani indicates that Hindu leaders largely operated independently of the Sultanate's revenue collection system. The subtext is the efforts of the Sultan to gain control of the wealth of the Hindu leaders, without consideration to theological justifications or religious explanations for those efforts.[47] If the goal was to collect *kharaj* and *jizya* from the Hindu leaders it would appear from the sultan's perspective in the text to be taken in the sense of a tribute, and not poll-tax, as it is sometimes understood.[48] Thus, ʿAlaʾ al-din Khalji's critique of the Qazi's views comes from a governance perspective with an element of pragmatics and realpolitik. The political elite were not the only section of the Muslim polity to criticize the dogmatic Sunni perspective. As regards *zimmi* status and debates about the place of non-Muslims inside the empire there was also a literature about "transcending religious and sectarian differences."[49] Certain kinds of conservative and traditional Islamic attitudes exemplified in the ignorance and hypocrisy of the Muslim judge were satirized and criticized. There was a language that downplayed differences between the "infidel" and "believer" and universalized a concept of divinity in the language of love (*ʿishq*), drawing away from the specific sectarianism of Allah and idol. However, considered at face value, the arguments of Qazi Mughis al-din present a definite theological view that must be taken into consideration. When Sultan ʿAlaʾ al-din questions Qazi Mughis al-din, the later makes recourse to Quranic proof texts to validate his position. The first reference appears when the scholar responded, "The respect of Islam is a duty, and contempt of the religion is vain. God holds them in contempt, for he says, 'Keep them under subjection' (*an yadin wa hum saghirun*)."[50] The *locus classicus* cited here is Quran 9:29 and it has produced a large body of commentary.[51]

---

47 Further indications of the efforts to constrain the economic wealth of the Hindu community are given by Baranī. Elliot, Dowson 1867, 3:182.

48 The principles for the payment of this tribute are explained in Ghaznavi 1954, 68.

49 Muzaffar Alam gives some examples of this kind of writing taken from Amir Khusraw and Amir Hasan Sijzi. See Muzaffar Alam, *The Languages of Political Islam: India 1200–1800*, Chicago: University of Chicago Press, 2004, 119–121.

50 Barani 1862, 290.

51 For cases of this in Mamluk Egypt with references to interpretation of this verse see Kristen Stilt, *Islamic Law in Action: Authority, Discretion, and Everyday Experiences in Mamluk Egypt*, Ox-

Some scholars have tried to portray the views expressed by Qazi Mughis al-din as merely a reflection of the historian Barani's distorted opinion and that they represent an exception in Quranic interpretation with regard to the status of non-Muslims.[52] However, whether or not Barani faithfully recorded the views of another Muslim scholar, he expressed a viewpoint clearly proposed by other important medieval Muslim thinkers. For instance, Fakhr al-din Razi (1149–1209), the noted late twelfth-century Quran scholar and theologian, shared this same opinion. In Fakhr al-din's commentary on Quran 9:29 he expresses the opinion that *jizya* is a time bound contract that allows the opportunity for non-Muslims to reflect on the merits of Islam. The text of Quran 9:29 has also been taken in a broader sense as expressed in the *al-Muwatta'* of Malik b. Anas, "the Muslim tax was levied on Muslims as of means of purifying them [*taṭhīran lahum*] ... and the *jizya* was levied on the People of the Book as a means of subordinating them [*ṣaghāran lahum*, i.e. to Muslim rule]."[53] Thus *jizya* has two functions, one as acknowledgement of the authority of Islam, and two, as humiliation with the intended purpose of creating the incentive for conversion.[54] The relationship between *jizya* and conversion is referenced in at least one important case. Sultan Firuz Shah claims that members of the *zimmi* community converted to Islam, knowing that they would be exempted from the *jizya*, with a proclamation of their faith in a single God and the Prophet Muhammad.[55] Razi's views certainly give meaning to the occasions when Fakhr-i Mudabbir and Ziya' al-din Barani advo-

ford: Oxford University Press, 2011, 122 and 122n47. Also see M. J. Kister, "An Yadin,' An Attempt at Interpretation, *Arabica* (1964): 272–278. And Uri Rubin, Quran and *Tafsīr*, The Case of "an yadin', *Der Islam* 70, no. 1 (1993): 133–144. Haleem shows the breadth of interpretation within the exegetical tradition concerning this verse. See Muhammad Abdel Haleem, The Jizya Verse (Q. 9:29): Tax Enforcement on Non-Muslims in the First Muslim State, *Journal of Qur'anic Studies* 14, no. 2 (2012): 72–89.

52 Nizami dismissed this historical anecdote as a product of "Barani's rigid and fanatical thinking." See Nizami 1997, 157. A response to Nizami's assessment of Barani can be found in Raziuddin Aquil, On Islam and Kufr in the Delhi Sultanate: Towards a Re-interpretation of Ziya' al-Din Barani's *Fatawa-i Jahandari*, in: *Rethinking a Millennium: Perspectives on Indian History from the Eighth of the Eighteenth Century, Essays for Harbans Mukhia*, Rajat Datta (ed.), 168–197, Delhi: Aakar, 2008.

53 *Encyclopaedia of the Qur'an*, "Poll Tax," (Paul Heck).

54 The reasoning behind this form of humiliation is given by Fakhr al-din Razi in Jane Dammen McAuliffe, Fakhr al-Dīn Rāzī on *āyat al-jizyah* and *āyat al-sayf*, in: *Conversion and Continuity: Indigenous Christian Communities in Islamic Lands, Eighth to Eighteenth Centuries*, Michael Gervers, Ramzi Jibran Bikhazi (eds.), 103–119, Toronto: Pontifical Institute of Mediaeval Studies, 1990, here 108–111.

55 Reference to conversion and the *jizya* in Firuz Shah Tughluq, *The Futuhat-i Firuz Shahi*, trans. Azra Alavi, Delhi: Idarah-i Adabiyat-i Delli, 1996, 31–32.

cate the use of various forms of humiliation without indicating their fundamental intention.[56] In their theological perspective one understands *jizya* as motivated less by economic interests than by principles of subordination, humiliation, and obedience.[57]

There is another source, the *Sahifat-i Na't-i Muhammadi*, also written by Barani, that reveals something of the legal discourses concerning *jizya* and *zimmi*.[58] In an incident said to have occurred during the reign of Shams al-din Iltutmish (r. 1211–1236), a group of scholars gathered to debate the question of whether or not Hindus (*hunud*) should be afforded the status of *zimmi*, or simply put the proposition "either fighting or Islam" (*imma al-qatal wa imma al-islam*). They are said to subscribe to the Shafiʿi legal position where Hindus are not considered eligible for *zimmi* status. The outcome is that they wish to pressure the Sultan into adopting this policy. The Sultan's response is given through his vizier Nizam al-Mulk Junaydi who relates that it was absolutely impossible to implement such a policy under the conditions found in North India where Hindus were in such a vast majority. There are some interesting elements in the subtext of this historical anecdote. In discussing the tax to be imposed the term *kharaj* is used along with *kharaj wa jizya*. The text does not indicate if the tax was imposed, or not. However, the use of the term *kharaj* implies a fluid concept of this tax, in a more general sense, than as a discriminatory tax for non-Muslims.

While Barani depicts this as a unified group of Sunni ulema approaching the Sultan, it can as well be imagined that they represented a faction of scholars who did not necessarily represent a majoritarian point of view on the subject. In fact, there are other indications that support this idea. The historical frame of reference for this discussion is interesting as Barani said it follows from the invasions of Chingiz Khan "the cursed," an event that forced the migration of Muslim scholars from Central Asia to the kingdom of Shams al-din Iltutmish. Therefore, one could suppose that immigrant scholars representing a Shafiʿi perspective instigated the debate, refugees from a violent conflict perceived to be a battle of infidelity against Islam. The anecdote also demonstrates the kind of legal diversity of

56 Barani mentions Razi and indicates his respect for him. See Barani 1862, 353.

57 See chapters 3–4 of Emon 2012. Aziz Ahmad briefly mentions this as an aspect of the *zimmi* category in his reading of Fakhr-i Mudabbir saying the "*dhimmī* element which is to be demonstrably and conspicuously placed in a position of discriminated inferiority." See Aziz Ahmad, Trends in the Political Thought of Medieval Muslim India, *Studia Islamica* 17 (1962): 121–130, here 123.

58 Nurul Hasan, Sahifa-i Na't-i Muhammadi of Zia-ud-Din Barani, *Medieval India Quarterly* 1, no. 3 & 4 (1954), 100–105, here 101–103 and Persian text 104–105. This anecdote has been a central point of debate on the treatment of Hindus in the Delhi Sultanate and has been commented upon by numerous scholars. See Jackson 1999, 290.

opinions that were common in scholarly circles. Barani self-identified as belonging to the Hanafi school of Islamic law, but here appears to adopt a Shafiʿi legal perspective on the issue of *zimmi*.[59] His view does not appear to have been particularly suited or popular in his time, but it perhaps represents a growing influence of this legal position. Thus, these debates can be thought of as being stimulated by Mongol conquests to the north-west of Delhi and the influx of a group of religious scholars representing a legal tradition more developed in Central Asia.

In the *Fatawa-i Jahandari*, Barani returns to the subject of *jizya* and *zimmi*. To provide evidence for his position on the need to increase pressure on Hindus subject to Muslim rule he cites the hadith, "I have been ordered to fight the people until they say 'There is no god but God.' And if they say that then they will have gained protection from me by what is a right in Islam."[60] It is also in this passage that Barani situates his discussion of *jizya* and infidelity along with other forms of religious difference that he viewed as a threat to Islam, groups such as bad religionists (*bad mazhaban*) and philosophers who also represented a confessional identity.[61] These also included various Shia groups, charismatic religious leaders who made claims to divinity, others claiming to be the Mahdi, a messianic figure whose appearance signals the end of times, and in general, individuals considered as heretics and apostates by the Sultan, or the dominant Sunni religious elite. Considered in this manner, it does not come as a surprise that some religious scholars criticized rulers who did not view their subjects through the confessional lens. The greatest threat to the organization and maintenance of the Sultanate was perceived to rise from those who rejected the faith and the highest form of punishment, capital punishment, was reserved for them. Cases of apostasy in the Delhi Sultanate are almost always framed within the discussion of rebellion. *Fitna*, or strife within the Muslim community was a major preoccupation of Sunni scholars writing on governance, and it is the feared result of religious difference.[62]

---

59 This important point was noted much earlier by Aziz Ahmad. See Aziz Ahmad 1962, 124. However, later scholars did not take up this issue and ascribed Barani's view on *jizya* to intolerance.
60 Barani 1972, 166. Ziyaʾ al-din Barani, *The Political Theory of the Delhi Sultanate (including a translation of Ziauddin Barani's Fatawa-i Jahandari, circa, 1358–9 A.D.)*, trans. Afsar Umar Salim Khan, Allahabad: Kitab Mahal, 1961, 46. The text of the hadith is incomplete and inaccurate. For a widely read version of this hadith circulating in the 13th century see Muhyi al-din al-Nawawi, *an-Nawawī's Forty Hadith: An Anthology of the Sayings of the Prophet Muhammad*, trans. Ezzeddin Ibrahim, Denys Johnson-Davies, Cambridge: Islamic Texts Society, 1997, 46–47.
61 Barani 1972, 168. Barani 1961, 48.
62 See the important discussion of *fitna* during the reign of Muhammad b. Tughluq in Blain Auer, Concepts of Justice and the Catalogue of Punishments under the Sultans of Delhi (7th–8th/13th–14th Centuries), in: *Public Violence in Islamic Societies: Power, Discipline, and the*

Islamic rule, from this perspective, is viewed from a narrow sectarian point of view. The fact that Barani exhorts Muslim rulers to eschew the *jizya* in the effort to combat infidelity, or in his words "to strive day and night for the degradation of infidelity," is significant.[63] It is again further evidence that the tax was only in place in a general sense, if at all. This is indicated in another passage in which Barani refers to the taxes in kingdoms with non-Muslim rulers as *jizya* and *kharaj*, without making a clear distinction between the two. He writes, "The infidel kings (*rāyān-i kufr*) take the *jizya* and *kharaj* from the polytheist and infidel Hindus (*hinduan-i mushrik wa kafir*)."[64] This perhaps even indicates that when the *jizya* and *kharaj* were applied it was done so in a manner consistent with tax policies in other kingdoms in South Asia. However, this would have to be demonstrated with a comparative study of other tax systems in use during this time. Nevertheless, this background provides more comprehensibility to the debates about *jizya* and *zimmi* than explanations that identified them as aberrations of the legal norm. The anecdotal discussion between the Sultan and the Qazi gives credence to the view that rulers, for a variety of reasons, eschewed imposing the letter of the law when it concerned *jizya*.

Shifting sands in the policy towards non-Muslims in the Delhi Sultanate

From the previous evidence it can be clearly stated that the tax or tribute of *jizya* was not consistently or uniformly applied in the Delhi Sultanate, and its meaning evolved and changed over time. At times it referred to a poll-tax, at times a land tax, and at other times a collective tribute. It is true that viewed historically it is difficult to say that the Hanafi legal view on the question of *jizya*, described in detail in texts from the period, was adhered to. On the other hand, there is certainly evidence that at least some Muslim rulers of the Delhi Sultanate took that legal theory seriously and attempted to implement it through government actions. Those examples cannot be dismissed as aberrations or interpreted as norms. Rather, they are signs of shifting understandings and interpretations of legal frameworks. This brings us to the clear case were the *jizya* was imposed and

---

Construction of the Public Sphere, 7th–19th Centuries CE, Maribel Fierro, Christian Lange (eds.), 238–255, Edinburgh: Edinburgh University Press, 2009, here 241–244.

63 Barani 1972, 169. Barani 1961, 47.

64 Barani 1972, 166. Barani 1961, 46.

leads us to strive for a more complex understanding of the historical context that made those changes in policy possible.

A major shift in the regulation of difference of non-Muslim communities occurred in the late fourteenth century. The historical change came under Firuz Shah, one of the most expansive and sustained reigns of a Muslim sultan to rule from Delhi before the invasion of Amir Timur. One might describe the situation up to Firuz Shah as one characterized by a *laissez-faire* attitude of sultans who chose not to regulate in a discriminate manner non-Muslims within the kingdom.[65] However, it was during his reign that we find the first "incontrovertible evidence of the *jizya* as a discriminatory tax on individual non-Muslims."[66] One primary source for this view is the *Tarikh-i Firuzshahi* written by Shams al-din 'Afif. 'Afif goes to great pains to make it clear that Firuz Shah worked hard to establish his rule on the principles of the sharia. He argues this was carried out by establishing the *jizya* with reference the *zunnardarān*, literally the "corded-ones," a term used here to refer to Brahmins, but was also used in other contexts to refer to the Eastern Christians, Jews, and Zoroastrians.[67] The historian creates the impression that it was confined to a class of Brahmin religious scholars, and not to a general populace. Furthermore, the Sultan's order to establish the *jizya* overturned previous custom and is said by the historian to have taken place through direct consultation with the ulema. 'Afif notes that the Brahmins protested this new rule, but were unsuccessful in changing the Sultan's view, but influenced the tax rate. The Sultan established three varying rates that tied the tax burden to personal wealth.[68] In the end, it was agreed that the Brahmins would pay the lowest rate.[69]

The event is confirmed importantly in the *Futuhat-i Firuzshahi*, a statement of rule issued by the Sultan and inscribed inside a mosque within the confines of the

---

65 I. H. Siddiqui expresses this view but he does not treat the legal discourses or the changes adopted under Firuz Shah. See Iqtidar Husain Siddiqui, The Sultan and the Hindus: A Re-appraisal of Hindu Muslim Relations in the Sultanate of Delhi during the 13th Century, *Journal of Objective Studies* 6, no. 2 (1994): 39–49.

66 Jackson 1999, 286.

67 'Afif 1888, 382.

68 Ghaznavi stipulates the rates of *jizya* and delineates two categories, a *jizya* payment established by agreement between parties and the annual fixed rate of 12, 24, and 48 dirhams relative to the economic status of the subject. See Ghaznavi 1954, 67. These rates are comparable to those described in the *Chachnama* and in the *Adab al-harb* and referenced in Jackson 1999, 284. Also see Mubarak Shah 1967, 404. Those who fell below a certain economic level were exempted from the tax all together. For a study of this question from Ayyubid Egypt and Syria see Eli Alshech, Islamic Law, Practice, and Legal Doctrine: Exempting the Poor from the Jizya under the Ayyubids (1171–1250), *Islamic Law and Society* 10, no. 3 (2003): 348–375.

69 'Afif 1888, 383–384.

capital. It is a record of the Sultan's attempt to place his rule firmly on the basis of a Sunni-Hanafi interpretation of sharia. In doing so, the Sultan announced his intention to do away with a variety of practices that in his view were previously used, but ran contrary to Islamic law. He frames this in terms of innovations (*bidat*) that had crept into Islam and the need to return to a correct version of Islam that is based on the Quran and the example of the Prophet Muhammad. He referred to the "innovations" as false customs and infidel practices, but the first of these to be removed were certain punishments, described in the text as *siyasa*.[70] Another critical area highlighted for reform was the tax policy of the Sultanate. Firuz Shah claims that all sorts of taxes were collected by previous regimes that were not allowed according to sharia. The "acceptable" taxes listed according to sharia described in the *Futuhat-i Firuzshahi* are: the land tax (*kharaj-i arazi*), one-tenth of produce (*ʿushur*), charity (*zakat*), tax/tribute on Hindus (*jizya-yi hunud*), inheritance (*tarikat*), one-fifth of war booty and mines of precious metals (*khums-i ghanaʾim wa maʿadin*).[71] Specifically referring to the case of the Hindus the text says, "The unclean and idolatrous Hindus (of Marmak?) and idol worshippers (*but parast*) have agreed to pay the *jizya* and their persons and property were accorded protection (*zimma*). But some among them laid the foundations for new temples within the city and in its environs. Under the sharia of the Prophet Muhammad, construction of new temples dedicated to idol worship is forbidden."[72] The text then goes on to describe that these structures were taken down, the leaders were killed, and their followers punished (*taʿzirat*). Therefore, it appears to refer to a renewed or initial strict application of the sharia, framed within a pietistic appeal to the example of the Prophet.

Firuz Shah was known for his public displays of personal piety, and it is a period of particular interest for the development of Islamic legal history, as it was under Firuz Shah that two of the most important legal texts previously discussed were created, the *Fiqh-i Firuzshahi* and the *Fatawa al-tatarkhaniya*. Ali Anooshahr shows in his reading of the introduction of the *Fatawa al-tatarkhaniya*, also printed in this volume, that its authors emphasized the Sunni sectarian nature of the law and the important role to be played by the ulema in relation to defining the boundaries and meanings of being Muslim. He also points out that the

70 For a discussion of *siyasa* in this context see Auer 2009, 247–249.

71 Firuz Shah Tughluq, Futūḥāt-i Fīrūzshāhī, *Journal of the Royal Asiatic Society of Bengal* 7, no. 1 (1941a), 61–89, here 70. Firuz Shah Tughluq, The Victories of Sulṭān Fīrūz Shāh of Tughluq Dynasty: English Translation of *Futūḥāt-i Fīrūz Shāhī* by N.B. Roy, *Islamic Culture* 15, no. 1 (1941b), 449–464, here 453–454.

72 Firuz Shah Tughluq, *The Futuhat-i Firuz Shahi,* edited and translated by Azra Alavi, Delhi: Idarah-i Adabiyat-i Delli, 1996, 26. Tughluq (1941a), 75.

authors made arguments relative to the position of the sultan, who is presented in a fashion that indicates a status lower than that of the religious scholar. Along with religious and theological concerns, there appears to be a political attempt to clarify the boundaries of confessional identity in order to bring rebellious actors in line. Discussions of *jizya* are framed within a larger context that includes the language of rebellion (*fasad*) and Muslim religious identity. For instance, Fakhr-i Mudabbir begins his chapter on *jizya* and *kharaj* with the quote from Quran 8:1 that is followed with a discussion of the meaning of "believer" (*muʿmin*). Thus, the Sultan's reaffirmation of sharia may reflect his increased difficulty to manage the extent of communal diversity represented in the kingdom and his frustrated efforts to establish his authority. The realm of authority had been expanded under Firuz Shah's predecessor Muhammad b. Tughluq, perhaps beyond what was feasible within the existing administrative capacity of the Sultanate. Muhammad b. Tughluq had failed to definitively establish the authority of Delhi from his newly created capital in Dawlatabad. Thus, Firuz Shah was left with an imperial realm stretched beyond its means and facing challenges from a variety of corners.

There is also an element of the politics of the period. Firuz Shah came to power in a disputed transition to power. Muhammad b. Tughluq, who had ruled for 27 years, died unexpectedly on an expedition to Thatta. Firuz Shah, who was accompanying, was his cousin and commander of the army (*amir hajib*). He received the support of the former Sultan's entourage, who nominated him successor to Muhammad b. Tughluq. At the same time, there were two other claimants to the throne. One was a nephew to Muhammad b. Tughluq, Dawar Malik. The other was a child said to be the son of Muhammad b. Tughluq, and enthroned in Delhi by the vizier Khwaja Jahan Ahmad b. Ayaz.[73] It appears in the brief interregnum following Muhammad b. Tughluq's death, Firuz Shah benefited from the support of the increasing influence of the ulema. Firuz Shah was easily able to return to Delhi from his expedition and claim the throne. While the newly enthroned ruler may have had genuine religious leanings, there was also a political dimension to his religious overtures.

73 For an analysis of the conflicting accounts of Firuz Shah's ascension see Jackson 1999, 166–167.

Conclusion

On the whole, the regulation of the category of *zimmi* can be seen as one important element of the discourse of diversity employed by religious scholars to establish order over heterogeneous polities operating under the influence of a Muslim court. The discussion of the *jizya* is framed in the context of getting control of religious communities whose religious and political ideologies could pose a danger to the form of Sunni Islam propagated and patronized under Firuz Shah. In certain cases, this referred to Muslim religious communities that were viewed as deviant from the perspective of the Sunni oriented ruling elite. The process of defining communities within Islamic law through *jizya* and *zimmi* was a reciprocal process of defining the "other" while defining the Muslim community. In a system of governance that was, in significant aspects, defined by religion, the ultimate symbol of submission to that form of governance was to be a Sunni. Similarly, non-Muslim communities also posed the potential threat of rebellion. Their submission to the sultan required a symbol of acquiescence, *zimma*/status and *jizya*. These legal categories were understood as the imperial mechanisms for managing confessional diversity inside and outside the Islamic polity.

References

Encyclopaedia of Islam, second edition, P. Bearman, Th. Bianquis, C.E. Bosworth, E. van Donzel and W.P. Heinrichs (eds.).

Encyclopaedia of the Qur'an, Jane Dammen McAuliffe (ed.).

'Afif, Shams Siraj, *Tarikh-i Firuzshahi*, Calcutta: Asiatic Society, 1888.

Ahmad, Aziz, Trends in the Political Thought of Medieval Muslim India, *Studia Islamica* 17 (1962): 121–130.

Ahmad, Aziz, *Studies in Islamic Culture in the Indian Environment*, Oxford: Clarendon Press, 1964.

Ahmed, Manan, The Long Thirteenth Century of the Chachnama, *Indian Economic & Social History Review* 49, no. 4 (2012): 459–491.

'Ala', 'Alim ibn, *al-Fatawa al-tatarkhaniyah fi al-fiqh al-hanafi*, Beirut: Dar al-Kutub al-'Ilmiyah, 2005.

Alam, Muzaffar, Competition and Co-existence: Indo-Islamic Interaction in Medieval North India, *Itinerario* 13, no. 1 (1989): 37–59.

Alam, Muzaffar, *The Languages of Political Islam: India 1200–1800*, Chicago: University of Chicago Press, 2004.

Alam, Muzaffar, A Muslim State in a Non-Muslim Context, in: *Mirror for the Muslim Prince: Islam and the Theory of Statecraft*, Mehrzad Boroujerdi (ed.), 160–189, Syracuse: Syracuse University Press, 2013.

Alshech, Eli, Islamic Law, Practice, and Legal Doctrine: Exempting the Poor from the Jizya under the Ayyubids (1171–1250), *Islamic Law and Society* 10, no. 3 (2003): 348–375.
Aquil, Raziuddin, On Islam and Kufr in the Delhi Sultanate: Towards a Re-interpretation of Ziya' al-Din Barani's *Fatawa-i Jahandari*, in: *Rethinking a Millennium: Perspectives on Indian History from the Eighth of the Eighteenth Century, Essays for Harbans Mukhia*, Rajat Datta (ed.), 168–197, Delhi: Aakar, 2008.
Auer, Blain, Concepts of Justice and the Catalogue of Punishments under the Sultans of Delhi (7th–8th/13th–14th Centuries), in: *Public Violence in Islamic Societies: Power, Discipline, and the Construction of the Public Sphere, 7th—19th Centuries CE*, Maribel Fierro, Christian Lange (eds.), 238–255, Edinburgh: Edinburgh University Press, 2009.
Baladhuri, Ahmad ibn Yahya, *Kitab futuh al-buldan,* Leiden: E. J. Brill, 1866.
Barani, Ziya' al-din, *Tarikh-i Firuzshahi*. Sayyid Ahmad Khan (ed.), Vol. 33, Bibliotheca Indica, Calcutta: Asiatic Society, 1862.
Barani, Ziya' al-din, *The Political Theory of the Delhi Sultanate (including a translation of Ziauddin Barani's Fatawa-i Jahandari, circa, 1358–9 A.D.)*, translated by Afsar Umar Salim Khan, Allahabad: Kitab Mahal, 1961.
Barani, Ziya' al-din, *Fatava-yi Jahandari*. Afsar Salīm Khān (ed.), 1st ed. Vol. 25, Intishārāt-i Idārah-yi Taḥqīqāt-i Pākistān. Lahore: Research Society of Pakistan, 1972.
Chandra, Satish, Jizyah and the State in India during the 17th Century, *Journal of the Economic and Social History of the Orient/Journal de l'histoire économique et sociale de l'Orient* 12, no. 3 (1969), 322–340.
Elliot, H. M., Dowson, John, *The History of India as Told by its Own Historians: The Muhammadan Period,* London: Trübner and Co., 1867.
Emon, Anver M., *Religious Pluralism and Islamic Law: "Dhimmīs" and Others in the Empire of Law,* Oxford: Oxford University Press, 2012.
Ernst, Carl W., Admiring the Works of the Ancients: The Ellora Temples as Viewed by Indo-Muslim Authors, in: *Beyond Turk and Hindu: Rethinking Religious Identities in Islamicate South Asia*, David Gilmartin, Bruce B. Lawrence (eds.), 98–120, Gainesville, FL: University Press of Florida, 2000.
Ernst, Carl W., Muslim Studies of Hinduism? A Reconsideration of Arabic and Persian Translations from Indian Languages, *Iranian Studies* 36, no. 2 (2003): 173–195.
Ernst, Carl W., Situating Sufism and Yoga, *Journal of Royal Asiatic Society* 15, no. 1 (2005): 15–43.
Ernst, Carl W., Accounts of Yogis in Arabic and Persian Historical and Travel Texts, *Jerusalem studies in Arabic and Islam* 33 (2007): 409–426.
Ernst, Carl W., The Limits of Universalism in Islamic Thought: the Case of Indian Religions, *The Muslim World* 101, no. 1 (2011): 1–19.
Friedmann, Yohanan, Medieval Muslim Views of Indian Religions, *Journal of the American Oriental Society* 95, no. 2 Apr. – Jun. (1975): 214–221.
Friedmann, Yohanan, The Origins and Significance of the Chach Nāma, in: *Islam in Asia*, Yohanan Friedmann (ed.), 23–37, Jerusalem: Magnes Press, 1984.
Friedmann, Yohanan, *Tolerance and Coercion in Islam: Interfaith Relations in the Muslim Tradition*, Cambridge: Cambridge University Press, 2003.
Gabbay, Alyssa, *Islamic Tolerance: Amīr Khusraw and Pluralism,* New York: Routledge, 2010.
Ghaznavi, 'Abd al-Hamid Muharrir, Dastur-ul-albab fi 'ilm-il-Hisab, *Medieval India Quarterly* (1954), 59–99.

Haleem, Muhammad, Abdel, The Jizya Verse (Q. 9:29): Tax Enforcement on Non-Muslims in the First Muslim State, *Journal of Qur'anic Studies* 14, no. 2 (2012): 72–89.
Hardy, Peter, Is the *Chach Nama* intelligible to the historian as political theory?, *Sind Quarterly* (1980): 16–22.
Hasan, Nurul, Sahifa-i Na't-i Muhammadi of Zia-ud-Din Barani, *Medieval India Quarterly* 1, no. 3 & 4 (1954): 100–105.
Islam, Riazul, A Note on the Position of the Non-Muslim Subjects in the Sultanate of Delhi under the Khaljis and the Tughluqs, *Journal of the Pakistan Historical Society* 45, no. 3 (1997), 215–229.
Islam, Zafarul, The *Fatāwā Fīruz Shāhī* as a Source for the Socio-Economic History of the Sultanate Period, *Islamic Culture* 60, no. 2 (1986), 97–117.
Islam, Zafarul, Fīrūz Shāh Tughluq's Attitude towards Non-Muslims – A Reappraisal, *Islamic Culture* 64, no. 4 (1990): 65–79.
Islam, Zafarul, The Contribution of the Tughluq Sultans to Islamic Jurisprudence, *Majallat al-Taʾrīkh al-Islāmī* 2, no. 3–4 (1997): 516–528.
Islam, Zafarul, *Fatāwā Literature of the Sultanate Period,* New Delhi: Kanishka Publishers, 2005.
Jackson, Peter, *The Delhi Sultanate: A Political and Military History,* Cambridge: Cambridge University Press, 1999.
Johansen, Baber, *The Islamic Law on Land Tax and Rent: The Peasants' Loss of Property Rights as Interpreted in the Hanafite Legal Literature of the Mamluk and Ottoman Periods,* London: Croom Helm, 1988.
Kister, M. J., "An Yadin,' An Attempt at Interpretation, *Arabica* (1964): 272–278.
Kuhrami, Sadr al-Din, Yaʿqub Muzaffar, *Fiqh-i Firuzshahi*, BL I.O. Islamic 2987.
Kumar, Sunil, The Value of the *Ādāb al-Mulūk* as a Historical Source: An Insight into the Ideals and Expectations of Islamic Society in the Middle Period (A.D. 945–1500), *Indian Economic and Social History Review* 22, no. 3 (1985): 307–327.
Kumar, Sunil, Politics, the Muslim Community and Hindu-Muslim Relations Reconsidered: North India in the Early Thirteenth Century, in *Rethinking a Millennium: Perspectives on Indian History from the Eighth of the Eighteenth Century, Essays for Harbans Mukhia*, Rajat Datta (ed.), 139–167, Delhi: Aakar, 2008.
Majumdar, Ramesh Chandra (ed.), *The Delhi Sultanate,* Bombay: Bharatiya Vidya Bhavan, 1960; reprint, 1980.
McAuliffe, Jane Dammen, Fakhr al-Dīn Rāzī on *āyat al-jizyah* and *āyat al-sayf*, in: *Conversion and Continuity: Indigenous Christian Communities in Islamic Lands, Eighth to Eighteenth Centuries*, Michael Gervers, Ramzi Jibran Bikhazi (eds.), 103–119, Toronto: Pontifical Institute of Mediaeval Studies, 1990.
Mubarak Shah, Muhammad ibn Mansur (Fakhr-i Mudabbir), *Adab al-harb wa-l-shajaʿa,* Tehran: Intisharat-i Iqbal, 1967.
al-Nawawi, Muhyi al-din, *an-Nawawī's Forty Hadith: An Anthology of the Sayings of the Prophet Muhammad*, translated by Ezzeddin Ibrahim, Denys Johnson-Davies, Cambridge: Islamic Texts Society, 1997.
Nizami, Khaliq Ahmad, *Royalty in Medieval India,* New Delhi: Munshiram Manoharlal Publishers, 1997.
Nizami, Khaliq Ahmad, *Religion and Politics in India during the Thirteenth Century,* New Delhi: Oxford University Press, 2002.
Qureshi, Ishtiaq Husain, *The Administration of the Sultanate of Delhi,* Lahore: Sh. Muhammad Ashraf, 1944.

Rubin, Uri, Quran and *Tafsīr*, The Case of "an yadin', *Der Islam* 70, no. 1 (1993): 133–144.
Siddiqui, Iqtidar Husain, The Sultan and the Hindus: A Re-appraisal of Hindu Muslim Relations in the Sultanate of Delhi during the 13th Century, *Journal of Objective Studies* 6, no. 2 (1994): 39–49.
Siddiqui, Iqtidar Husain, *Authority and Kingship under the Sultans of Delhi (Thirteenth-Fourteenth Centuries)*, Delhi: Manohar, 2006.
Srivastava, Kanhaiya Lall, *The Position of Hindus under the Delhi Sultanate 1206–1526*, New Delhi: Munshiram Manoharlal, 1980.
Stilt, Kristen, *Islamic Law in Action: Authority, Discretion, and Everyday Experiences in Mamluk Egypt*, Oxford: Oxford University Press, 2011.
Tughluq, Firuz Shah, Futūḥāt-i Fīrūzshāhī, *Journal of the Royal Asiatic Society of Bengal* 7, no. 1 (1941a), 61–89.
Tughluq, Firuz Shah, The Victories of Sulṭān Fīrūz Shāh of Tughluq Dynasty: English Translation of *Futūḥāt-i Fīrūz Shāhī* by N.B. Roy, *Islamic Culture* 15, no. 1 (1941b),449–476.
Tughluq, Firuz Shah, *The Futuhat-i Firuz Shahi*, edited and translated by Azra Alavi, Delhi: Idarah-i Adabiyat-i Delli, 1996.
Varisco, Daniel Martin, review of *Tolerance and Coercion in Islam: Interfaith Relations in the Muslim Tradition*, by Yohanan Friedmann, *Islamic Law & Society* 13, no. 2 (2006), 285–288.
Zaman, Muhammad Qasim, review of *Tolerance and Coercion in Islam: Interfaith Relations in the Muslim Tradition*, by Yohanan Friedmann, *The Journal of Religion* 87, no. 3 (2007), 470–473.

Karl Haerter

Cultural diversity, deviance, public law and criminal justice in the Holy Roman Empire of the German Nation

Introduction: Cultural diversity and the society of orders (*Ständegesellschaft*)

Although cultural diversity, defined as "diverse cultures within the borders of particular political communities", challenges the law, the interaction of cultural diversity with public and criminal law has rarely been researched from a historical perspective.[1] The modern concept of cultural diversity is based on the precondition of a mostly uniform state with cohesive laws that is confronted with cultural differences between a dominating monoculture and groups which diverge with regard to crucial cultural/social dimensions such as religion, ethnicity, language, gender and sexual preferences, age, socioeconomic or legal status, migration or 'foreignness'.[2] The resulting cultural differences, however, are not only a phenomenon of modern societies, which are characterized by increasing globalization and legal systems that should guarantee the right to equality before the law and the right to non-discrimination, but they can be traced back to the early modern period. If we conceptualize 'culture' as collective 'ways of life', resulting from and manifesting in shared social practices, customs, habits, attitudes and values,[3] the early modern European society was characterized by both the ideal conception of a uniform, hierarchical Christian society of orders (*Stän-*

1 Marie-Claire Foblets, Jean-François Gaudreault-DesBiens, Alison Dundes Renteln (eds.), *Cultural Diversity and the Law: State Responses from around the World*, Brussels: Bruylant, 2010. On criminal law and diversity from a current perspective, see: Will Kymlicka, Claes Lernestedt, Matt Matravers (eds.), *Criminal Law and Cultural Diversity*. Oxford: Oxford University Press, 2014, 1–9.
2 Foblets 2010. Steven Vertovec (ed.), *Routledge International Handbook of Diversity Studies*. London: Taylor & Francis Ltd, 2015, 1–17.
3 Dagmar Freist, Recht und Rechtspraxis im Zeitalter der Aufklärung am Beispiel der Taufe jüdischer Kinder. In *Juden im Recht. Neue Zugänge zur Rechtsgeschichte der Juden im Alten Reich*, Andreas Gotzmann, Stephan Wendehorst (eds.), 109–137, Berlin: Duncker & Humblot, 2007, here 137–139. Joachim Eibach, Recht – Kultur – Diskurs. Nullum Crimen sine Scientia, *Zeitschrift für neuere Rechtsgeschichte* 23 (2001): 102–120. Martin P. Schennach, Recht – Kultur – Geschichte. Rechtsgeschichte und Kulturgeschichte. Wissenschaftshistorische und methodische Annäherungen, *Zeitschrift für Neuere Rechtsgeschichte* 36 (2014): 2–31.

DOI 10.1515/9783110423327-004

degesellschaft), as well as an increasing variety of different cultures. The Holy Roman Empire of the German Nation (hereinafter the Empire) in particular can be described as a multi-cultural polycentric composite imperial system with in terms of power, law, society and culture extremely diverse and unequal members (imperial estates) and a broad variety of orders (*Stände*) and social groups that formed the diverse *Ständegesellschaft*.[4]

Since the sixteenth century – augmented by the first wave of European colonization and the Protestant Reformation – we can observe the spread of various religions/'confessions' (denomination), increasing migration, and the growth of social and 'ethnic' minorities.[5] Thus, the ideal type of the pre-modern society of orders was neither homogenous nor static, immobile nor secluded, but was instead characterized by an increasing social, spatial and cultural differentiation of the three main strata (clerics, nobility, burgher/peasants) and various groups. The diverse imperial system to a certain extent allowed the promotion (and revocation) of an estate-based status and social mobility.[6] However, as of the sixteenth century, the emerging early modern (territorial) state strived to establish a homogenous, uniform, disciplined society of subjects (*Untertanenverband*) as well as a cohesive state-based legal system through processes termed as confessionalization, social disciplining, state building and monopolization of legislative and judicial powers.[7] Hence, studies dealing with the law and cultural

---

4 Ole Peter Grell, Bob Scribner, (eds.), *Tolerance and intolerance in the European Reformation*. Cambridge: Cambridge University Press, 1996. Sheilagh Ogilvie, Bob Scribner (eds.), *Germany. A new social and economic history, Vol. 1: 1450–1630, Vol. 2: 1630–1800*, London: Arnold, 1996. Robert von Friedeburg, *Lebenswelt und Kultur der unterständischen Schichten in der Frühen Neuzeit*, München: Oldenbourg, 2002. Bernd Roeck, *Civic Culture and Everyday Life in Early Modern Germany*, Leiden: Brill, 2006. Karl Härter, The Early Modern Holy Roman Empire of German Nation (1495–1806): A Multi-layered Legal System. In *Law and Empire. Ideas, Practices, Actors*, Jeroen Duindam, Jill Diana Harries, Caroline Humfress, Nimrod Hurvitz (eds.), 111–131, Leiden/Boston: Brill, 2013a.

5 Winfried Schulze, (ed.), *Ständische Gesellschaft und soziale Mobilität*, München: Oldenbourg, 1988. Leslie Page Moch, *Moving Europeans. Migration in Western Europe since 1650*, 2. Aufl., Bloomington: Indiana University Press, 2003. Joachim Bahlke (ed.), *Glaubensflüchtlinge. Ursachen, Formen und Auswirkungen frühneuzeitlicher Konfessionsmigration in Europa*, Münster: Lit, 2008. Henning P. Jürgens, Thomas Weller (eds.), *Religion und Mobilität. Zum Verhältnis von raumbezogener Mobilität und religiöser Identitätsbildung im frühneuzeitlichen Europ*, Göttingen: Vandenhoeck & Ruprecht, 2010.

6 Schulze 1988. John G. Gagliardo, *Germany under the old regime 1600 – 1790*, London: Routledge, 1991, 152–176. Grell 1996, 233–258. Ogilvie 1996, 134–163. Marian Füssel, Thomas Weller (eds.), Soziale Ungleichheit und ständische Gesellschaft. Theorien und Debatten in der Frühneuzeitforschung, Zeitsprünge. *Forschungen zur Frühen Neuzeit* 15 (2011).

7 Wolfgang Reinhard, *Geschichte der Staatsgewalt. Eine vergleichende Verfassungsgeschichte Europas von den Anfängen bis zur Gegenwart*, München: Beck, 1999. Heinz Schilling, *Ausgewählte*

diversity in the early modern period are faced with the following basic challenges and preconditions:

- Early modern society was based on political and social inequality, prescribed and protected by the legal order. However, the early modern state strived for the formation of a uniform society of subjects;
- The respective legal order prescribed and protected cultural diversity on the basis of an unequal pre-modern society, and, as a consequence, the state and the legal system attempted to control, criminalize, persecute or exclude cultural behaviour and the respective (social, ethnic, religious, minority) groups that deviated from the legal and social order and the dominating culture;
- The legal system of the Empire itself was characterized by multinormativity, hybridity and judicial pluralism; the emerging pre-modern state, on the other hand, strived to redress legal diversity and to establish a uniform legal system that partly aimed for legal equality.

Research has described the different cultural habits and practices of each strata with such concepts as nobility/court culture (*höfische Kultur/Adelskultur*), elite culture, everyday culture (*Alltagskultur*), popular culture (*Volkskultur*) and lower class culture (*Unterschichtenkultur*).[8] Some studies claim that through the processes of civilizing, (social) discipling and acculturation, cultural differences were levelled and diverging cultural practices and habits were excluded in order to form a basically uniform society.[9] Despite widespread criticism of such linear modernization concepts and their actual impact, from the sixteenth century onwards, the authorities increasingly established and ascribed cultural differences through public (administrative and criminal) law by determining cultural

---

Abhandlungen zur europäischen Reformations- und Konfessionsgeschichte, Luise Schorn-Schütte, Olaf Mörke (ed.), Berlin: Duncker und Humblot, 2002. Benjamin J. Kaplan, *Divided by Faith. Religious Conflict and the Practice of Toleration in Early Modern Europe*, Cambridge Massachusetts: Belknap Press of Harvard Univ. Press, 2007. Heinrich Richard Schmidt, *Konfessionalisierung im 16. Jahrhundert*, München: Oldenbourg, 1992.

8 Steven L. Kaplan (ed.), *Understanding Popular Culture. Europe from the Middle Ages to the Nineteenth Century*, Berlin: De Gruyter, 1984. Friedeburg 2002. Achim Landwehr, Stefanie Stockhorst, *Einführung in die europäische Kulturgeschichte*, Paderborn: UTB/BRO, 2004. Roeck 2006.

9 Schmidt 1992. Heinz Schilling (ed.), *Kirchenzucht und Sozialdisziplinierung im frühneuzeitlichen Europa*, Berlin: Duncker und Humblot, 1994. Heinz Schilling (ed.), *Institutionen, Instrumente und Akteure sozialer Kontrolle und Disziplinierung im frühneuzeitlichen Europa/ Institutions, Instruments and Agents of Social Control and Discipline in Early Modern Europe*. Frankfurt am Main: Klostermann, 1999. Reinhard, 1999. Hans-Jürgen Goertz, James M. Stayer (eds.), *Radikalität und Dissent im 16. Jahrhundert*, Berlin: Duncker & Humblot, 2002.

boundaries, protecting the existing cultures and labelling cultural differences and the concerned groups as divergent and deviant.[10]

Within this setting, religion, foreignness, migration, honour and, to some extent, gender constituted the main categories of cultural diversity, whereas age, sexual preferences and ethnicity had little or no relevance for the early modern perception of cultural differences. Only in the age of Enlightenment a discourse devolped which dealt with foreign 'races' – in particular with the Jews and the Gypsies – and discussed 'ethnicity' in terms of cultural differences.[11] Since the *Ständegesellschaft* was hierarchically structured through the degree of honour of each estate, order or group, cultural diversity was also related to the early modern concept (or concepts) of honour. Transgressing cultural boundaries could affect or damage not only the honour of a single person but of the whole estate, order or group, especially if marginal groups were concerned.[12]

In terms of cultural diversity and dissent, social and legal history has dealt with such issues as the regulation and policing of feasts and clothing, the so called sub-culture of the poor and the disciplining of marginal groups.[13] Cultural

---

10 Karl Härter, Entwicklung und Funktion der Policeygesetzgebung des Heiligen Römischen Reiches Deutscher Nation im 16. Jahrhundert. *Ius Commune* 20 (1993): 61–141. Karl Härter, Kriminalisierung, Verfolgung und Überlebenspraxis der Zigeuner im frühneuzeitlichen Mitteleuropa. In *Sinti, Roma, Gypsies. Sprache – Geschichte – Gegenwart*, Yaron Matras, Hans Winterberg, Michael Zimmermann (eds.), 41–81. Berlin: Metropol-Verlag, 2003a. Karl Härter, Zur Stellung der Juden im frühneuzeitlichen Strafrecht: Gesetzgebung, Rechtswissenschaft und Justizpraxis. In *Juden im Recht. Neue Zugänge zur Rechtsgeschichte der Juden im Alten Reich*, Andreas Gotzmann, Stephan Wendehorst (eds.), 347–379. Berlin: Duncker & Humblot, 2007. Karl Härter, Security and "gute Policey" in Early Modern Europe: Concepts, Laws and Instruments. In *Historical Social Research* 35 (2010), *Special Issue: The Production of Human Security in Premodern and Contemporary History*, Cornel Zwierlein, Rüdiger Graf, Magnus Ressel (eds): 41–65. Achim Landwehr, Norm, Normalität, Anomale. Zur Konstitution von Mehrheit und Minderheit in württembergischen Policeyordnungen der Frühen Neuzeit: Juden, Zigeuner, Bettler, Vaganten. In *Minderheiten, Obrigkeit und Gesellschaft in der Frühen Neuzeit. Integrations- und Abgrenzungsprozesse im süddeutschen Raum*, Mark Häberlein, Martin Zürn (eds.), 41–74, St. Katharinen: Scripta-Mercaturae-Verlag, 2001.

11 Vera Kallenberg, *Von "liederlichen Land-Läuffern" zum "asiatischen Volk". Die Repräsentation der ‚Zigeuner' in deutschsprachigen Lexika und Enzyklopädien zwischen 1700 und 1850. Eine wissensgeschichtliche Untersuchung*, Brussels: Lang, 2010.

12 Sylvia Kesper-Biermann, Ulrike Ludwig, Alexandra Ortmann (eds.), *Ehre und Recht. Ehrkonzepte, Ehrverletzungen und Ehrverteidigungen vom späten Mittelalter bis zur Moderne*, Magdeburg: Meine, 2011.

13 Richard J. Evans (ed.), *The German Underworld. Deviants and Outcasts in German History*, London: Routledge, 1988. Wolfgang Seidenspinner, *Mythos Gegengesellschaft. Erkundungen in der Subkultur der Jauner*, Münster: Waxmann, 1998.

differences were also addressed and protected by numerous administrative and public laws (known as 'police ordinances': *Policeyordnungen*) that dealt with all matters of the good order of society and state (*gute Ordnung des Gemeinwesens*) and focused on social control.[14]

For instance, the early modern authorities issued several administrative laws that extensively prescribed dress codes (*Kleiderordnungen*) for each group, in order to distinguish them culturally, especially with regard to minority groups such as the Jews or the poor.[15] The imperial police ordinances of 1530 and 1548 comprised a dress-code which prescribed in 14 detailed articles the different clothing, dresses, drapers, belts, necklaces and headdresses of peasants, burghers, merchants, craftsmen, academics and their wives and children, as well as for the different ranks of the nobility, including their servants, domestics, officials and soldiers. As for 'infamous women' (prostitutes), executioners and the Jews, the code imposed the obligation to dress in appropriate fashion or even wear additional symbols (such as the yellow ring for the Jews) to allow for immediate identification as part of a socio-culturally deviating minority group. The provisions prohibited luxurious clothing that transgressed the allowed attire of each group and ordered all imperial estates to enforce the code, prosecute transgression and punish the perpetrators with sanctions such as confiscation, fines or even banishment.[16] The prescription and criminalization of cultural differences clearly strived to maintain the social order. Nearly all territorial states, imperial cities and other authorities issued many similar ordinances that also regulated and criminalized the infringement or transgression of cultural boundaries in regard to drinking, dancing, carrying arms, hunting and other distinctive cultural practices.[17]

---

14 Karl Härter, Social Control and the Enforcement of Police-Ordinances in Early Modern Criminal Procedure. In *Institutionen, Instrumente und Akteure Sozialer Kontrolle und Disziplinierung im frühneuzeitlichen Europa / Institutions, Instruments and Agents of Social Control and Discipline in Early Modern Europe*, Heinz Schilling, Lars Behrisch (eds.), 39–63, Frankfurt am Main: Klostermann, 1999. Karl Härter, Michael Stolleis (eds.), *Repertorium der Policeyordnungen der Frühen Neuzeit*, vol. 1–11, Frankfurt am Main: Klostermann, 1996–2016.

15 Neithard Bulst, Robert Jütte (eds.), *Zwischen Sein und Schein. Kleidung und Identität in der ständischen Gesellschaft (= Saeculum 44)*, Freiburg: Alber, 1993. Robert Jütte, *Stigma-Symbole. Kleidung als identitätsstiftendes Merkmal bei spätmittelalterlichen und frühneuzeitlichen Randgruppen (Juden, Dirnen, Aussätzige, Bettler)*, Saeculum Bd. 44 (1993): 65–89.

16 Reichspoliceyordnung 1530 §§ 9–22, in: Matthias Weber (ed.), *Die Reichspolizeiordnungen von 1530, 1548 und 1577. Historische Einführung und Edition*, Frankfurt am Main: Klostermann, 2002, 141–151. Härter 1993.

17 Härter, Stolleis, 1996–2016.

Police ordinances also intensified the regulation of groups which were perceived (or constructed) as socially and culturally divergent in terms of religion, social status, ethnicity or way of life such as foreigners, vagrants, beggars, Gypsies, Jews and various religious groups labelled as sects. Thereby, the early modern authorities reacted to developments such as population growth, the increase of marginal groups, poverty, migration and vagrancy, the diversification and gradual disintegration of the society of orders, and the Protestant Reformation, all of which were accompanied by or produced further cultural diversity and were perceived as threatening the good order of society and state.[18]

The diverse legal system of the Empire and cultural diversity

In the following, I will analyse the interdependence between cultural diversity, deviance, public (administrative/criminal) law and criminal justice by focusing on religious diversity and migration and the respective minority groups, such as the Jews and the Gypsies. This analysis will then be compared to the legal diversity as a structural feature of the Holy Roman Empire of the German Nation, which can be described as a multi-layered legal system with various overlapping legal spaces.[19] The legal system comprised Roman law/*ius commune*, imperial law and legislation (*Reichsrecht*), and in particular customary law and legislation of the different territorial rulers. The diversity of law corresponded to various jurisdictions and courts, ranging from the imperial supreme courts (the Imperial Chamber Court and the Imperial Aulic Court) and the manorial courts of the imperial estates to a variety of lower courts and jurisdictions, not to mention the privileged forums of the clergy and the nobles, or the church jurisdiction. This

---

18 Landwehr 2001. Karl Härter, Recht und Migration in der frühneuzeitlichen Ständegesellschaft: Reglementierung – Diskriminierung – Verrechtlichung. In *Zuwanderungsland Deutschland Migrationen 1500–2005*, R. Beier-de Haan (ed), 50–71, Berlin: Edition Minerva, 2005b.

19 Härter 2013a. Karl Härter, Das Heilige Römische Reich deutscher Nation als mehrschichtiges Rechtssystem, 1495–1806. In *Die Anatomie frühneuzeitlicher Imperien. Herrschaftsmanagement jenseits von Staat und Nation: Institutionen, Personal und Techniken*, Stephan Wendehorst (ed.), 327–347, Berlin: De Gruyter Oldenbourg, 2015. Recent historical research on legal pluralism and empires tends to ignore the Holy Roman Empire; for example Lauren Benton, Richard J. Ross, *Legal pluralism and empires, 1500 – 1850*. New York: New York University Press, 2013. Seán Patrick Donlan, Dirk Heirbaut, *The laws' many bodies. Studies in legal hybridity and jurisdictional complexity, c1600–1900*, Berlin: Duncker & Humblot, 2015.

multi-layered and sometimes overlapping patchwork of imperial, territorial, seigniorial, ecclesiastical, aristocratic, corporative, communal and local jurisdictions comprised to some extent limited legal autonomy for different groups and communities, such as the Jews, the guilds and various local corporations.[20]

While the diversity of the imperial legal culture resulted in ambiguity, uncertainty and conflicts, it also facilitated options for the imperial estates, their subjects and minorities to make use of the imperial legal institutions for instance by appealing to the imperial courts. Notably, members of the three main Christian confessions (Catholic, Lutheran, Calvinist) as well as the Jews were able to instigate legal proceedings concerning religious conflicts and if religious rights or privileges were concerned which the imperial constitution had granted or guaranteed. In this regard, the Empire facilitated not only access to justice, 'forum shopping' or the uses of justice (*Justiznutzung*), but also produced a specific culture of litigation and stimulated the process of juridification (*Verrechtlichung*).[21] On the other hand, imperial jurisdiction was highly restricted in all criminal cases and cases of public order and administration (*Policeysachen*), in which concerned subjects or groups could not appeal to the imperial courts and jurisdiction rested with the territorial states and the imperial cities.[22]

---

20 Andreas Gotzmann, Strukturen jüdischer Gerichtsautonomie in den deutschen Staaten des 18. Jahrhunderts. In *Historische Zeitschrift* 267, 2 (1998): 313–356. Andreas Gotzmann, Stephan Wendehorst (eds.), *Juden im Recht. Neue Zugänge zur Rechtsgeschichte der Juden im Alten Reich*, Berlin: Duncker & Humblot, 2007. Andreas Gotzmann, *Jüdische Autonomie in der Frühen Neuzeit: Recht und Gemeinschaft im deutschen Judentum*, Göttingen: Wallstein, 2008.

21 Siegrid Westphal (ed.), *In eigener Sache: Frauen vor den höchsten Gerichten des Alten Reiches*, Köln: Böhlau, 2005. Anja Amend, Anette Baumann, Stephan Wendehorst, Siegrid Westphal (eds.), *Gerichtslandschaft Altes Reich. Höchste Gerichtsbarkeit und territoriale Rechtsprechung*, Köln: Böhlau, 2007. Härter 2013a. Härter 2015. On religious conflicts and *Religionsprozesse* see, for example: Bernhard Ruthmann, *Die Religionsprozesse am Reichskammergericht (1555 – 1648). Eine Analyse anhand ausgewählter Prozesse*, Köln: Böhlau, 1996. Stefan Ehrenpreis, *Kaiserliche Gerichtsbarkeit und Konfessionskonflikt. Der Reichshofrat unter Rudolf II. 1576 – 1612*, Göttingen: Vandenhoeck & Ruprecht, 2006. Verena Kasper-Marienberg, *'vor Euer Kayserlichen Mayestät Justiz-Thron.' Die Frankfurter jüdische Gemeinde am Reichshofrat in josephinischer Zeit (1765–1790)*, Innsbruck: Studienverlag, 2012. André Griemert, *Jüdische Klagen gegen Reichsadelige. Prozesse am Reichshofrat in den Herrschaftsjahren Rudolfs II. und Franz I. Stephan*, Berlin: de Gruyter, Oldenbourg, 2015.

22 Karl Härter, Das Reichskammergericht als "Reichspoliceygericht". Geschichte der Zentraljustiz in *Mitteleuropa, Festschrift für Bernhard Diestelkamp zum 65. Geburtstag*, Friedrich Battenberg, Filippo Ranieri (eds.), 237–252, Weimar: Böhlau, 1994. Christian Szidzek, *Das frühneuzeitliche Verbot der Appellation in Strafsachen. Zum Einfluß von Rezeption und Politik auf die Zuständigkeit insbesondere des Reichskammergerichts*, Köln: Böhlau, 2002.

As a result, the diverse legal system of the Empire provided different norms and instruments for responding to cultural diversity and deviance. They ranged from granting privileges, judicial autonomy, legal protection and tolerance to social control and disciplining, labelling, segregation, exclusion and criminalization. These norms and instruments primarily dealt with religious diversity, migration and foreignness as main fields of cultural differences and deviance. In this respect, the legal system of the Empire obtained different, ambiguous functions:

- It should maintain and protect cultural habits and privileges of each group of the *Ständegesellschaft* and the respective cultural differences (based on social, political and legal inequality), partly by granting protection and privileges (including separate/autonomous jurisdictions) and by prohibiting the transgression of cultural boundaries and the respective laws;
- It should regulate conflicts resulting from cultural and legal diversity, such as conflicts between religious groups and communities (*Religionsprozesse*), conflicts within a cultural/religious community or conflicts of jurisdiction;
- It labelled manifestations of cultural diversity as deviant or even as criminal behaviour, prohibited or persecuted divergent or deviant cultural activities and practices and strived for the control, disciplining or exclusion of the concerned minority groups;
- It served to consolidate the cultural identity of the dominating *Ständegesellschaft* and to produce cultural homogeneity;
- It was part of a cultural (normative) discourse and a contest of cultural interpretation (*kulturelle Deutungshoheit*).

This covers a variety of norms and instruments ranging from discrimination and criminalization to privileges, special rights and judicial autonomy to the protection of rights and also includes access to justice and extrajudicial or infrajudicial opportunities. In this chapter, I will also take into account the actors and dissidents of cultural diversity and their legal agency to use the legal system and the opportunities of judicial diversity to regulate conflicts. These opportunities include culturally grounded norms, practices, knowledge and arguments used by individual perpetrators or communities within judicial practice to explain, excuse, avoid or mitigate a sentence or punishment or to receive pardon. Although this resembles the modern concept of 'cultural evidence' or 'cultural defence' to some extent, the early modern criminal justice system and its inquisitorial procedure did not grant potential exemptions for cultural minorities from criminal law.[23]

---

23 On the modern concept of cultural evidence/defence and criminal law, see Kymlicka, Lernestedt, Matravers 2014, 4–9.

In the following, the ambivalent function of the multi-layered imperial legal system will be outlined by focusing on how public and penal law and the criminal justice system dealt with exemplary manifestations of cultural diversity and deviance that were interconnected through the categories of religion, minority and migration:

- Religious deviance related to diverging groups, in particular 'heretic sects' such as the Anabaptists;
- Deviance related to the Jews as a minority group that differed religiously and culturally;
- Marginal/migrating groups perceived and/or labelled as culturally different (because of their foreignness or ethnicity), such as the Gypsies.

Jews, Gypsies and religious minority groups perceived as sects constituted the three main social groups which significantly deviated from the early modern Christian society of orders in terms of cultural diversity. They were labelled and prosecuted as culturally deviant, whereas other social or minority groups may have also been negatively labelled (such as the poor or vagrants), but still were considered to be a part of the majority culture or society.[24] Since it is nearly impossible to cover the numerous imperial estates and the great variety of courts, the following analysis is restricted to the level of the early modern imperial legal system – in particular the Imperial Chamber Court – and to some exemplary territorial states, such as the Electorate of Mainz and Württemberg. This is based on extensive research[25] and on other exemplary case studies dealing with the

24 Bernd Roeck, *Außenseiter, Randgruppen, Minderheiten. Fremde im Deutschland der frühen Neuzeit*, Göttingen: Vandenhoeck und Ruprecht, 1993. Martin Rheinheimer, In die Erde können sie nicht kriechen. Zigeunerverfolgung im frühneuzeitlichen Schleswig-Holstein, *Historische Anthropologie* 4 (1996): 330–358. Landwehr 2001; Friedeburg 2002; Gerhard Ammerer, *Heimat Straße. Vaganten im Österreich des Ancien Régime*, München: Oldenbourg-Wiss.-Verlag, 2003. Gerhard Ammerer, Gerhard Fritz (eds.), *Die Gesellschaft der Nichtsesshaften. Zur Lebenswelt vagierender Schichten vom 16. bis zum 19. Jahrhundert: Beiträge der Tagung vom 29. und 30. September 2011 im Kriminalmuseum Rothenburg ob der Tauber*, Affalterbach: Didymos-Verlag, 2013.

25 Härter 2003a; Karl Härter, Zum Verhältnis von "Rechtsquellen" und territorialen Rahmenbedingungen in der Strafgerichtsbarkeit des 18. Jahrhunderts: Vagabondage und Diebstahl in der Entscheidungspraxis der Kurmainzer Landesregierung. In *Justiz = Justice = Justicia? Rahmenbedingungen von Strafjustiz im frühneuzeitlichen Europa*, Harriet Rudolph, Helga Schnabel-Schüle (eds.), 433–465, Trier: Kilomedia, 2003b. Karl Härter, *Policey und Strafjustiz in Kurmainz. Gesetzgebung, Normdurchsetzung und Sozialkontrolle im frühneuzeitlichen Territorialstaat*. Frankfurt am Main: Klostermann, 2005a. Härter 2005b. Härter 2007. Härter 2010. Karl Härter, Die Reichskreise als transterritoriale Ordnungs- und Rechtsräume: Ordnungsnormen, Sicherheitspolitik und Strafverfolgung. In *Reichskreise und Regionen im frühmodernen Europa – Horizonte und Grenzen*

practice of territorial criminal justice regarding the named groups[26] as well as on a thorough examination of the inventory of the court records of the Imperial Chamber Court (*Inventar der Reichskammergerichtsakten*) in the archive of

---

im "spatial turn", Wolfgang Wüst, Michael Müller (eds.), 211–249, Frankfurt am Main: Peter Lang, 2011. Karl Härter, Jüdische Migrationen im frühneuzeitlichen Alten Reich: Rechtliche Rahmenbedingungen, Geleit und Rechtsnutzung. In *Kaiser und Reich in der jüdischen Lokalgeschichte*, Stefan Ehrenpreis, Andreas Gotzmann, Stephan Wendehorst (eds.), 67–92, München: Oldenbourg, 2013b. Karl Härter, Prekäre Lebenswelten vagierender Randgruppen im frühneuzeitlichen Alten Reich. Überlebenspraktiken, obrigkeitliche Sicherheitspolitik und strafrechtliche Verfolgung. In *Die Gesellschaft der Nichtsesshaften. Zur Lebenswelt vagierender Schichten vom 16. bis zum 19. Jahrhundert: Beiträge der Tagung vom 29. und 30. September 2011 im Kriminalmuseum Rothenburg ob der Tauber*, Gerhard Ammerer, Gerhard Fritz (eds.), 21–38, Affalterbach: Didymos-Verlag, 2013c.

26 Sects/anabaptists: Ernst Friedrich Peter Güß, *Das Verhalten der kurpfälzischen Regierung gegenüber dem Täufertum bis zum Dreißigjährigen Krieg*, Stuttgart: Diss., 1958. Barbara Kink, *Die Täufer im Landgericht Landsberg 1527/28*. St. Ottilien: EOS-Verlag, 1997. Ralf Klötzer, *Die Täuferherrschaft von Münster. Stadtreformation und Welterneuerung*, Münster: Aschendorff, 1992. David Mayes, Heretics or Nonconformists? State Policies toward Anabaptists in Sixteenth-Century Hesse, *The Sixteenth Century Journal* 32/4 (Winter 2001): 1003–1026. Eric Piltz, Gerd Schwerhoff (eds.), *Gottlosigkeit und Eigensinn. Religiöse Devianz im konfessionellen Zeitalter*, Berlin: Duncker & Humblot, 2015. Päivi Räisänen, *Ketzer im Dorf. Visitationsverfahren, Täuferbekämpfung und lokale Handlungsmuster im frühneuzeitlichen*, Konstanz: UVK-Verlag-Gesellschaft, 2011. Astrid von Schlachta, *Gefahr oder Segen? Die Täufer in der politischen Kommunikation*, Göttingen: V & R Unipress, 2009. Horst W. Schraepler, *Die rechtliche Behandlung der Täufer in der deutschen Schweiz, Südwestdeutschland und Hessen 1525 – 1618*, Tübingen: Ekkehart Fabian-Verlag, 1957. Hans Hermann Theodor Stiasny, *Die strafrechtliche Verfolgung der Täufer in der Freien Reichsstadt Köln 1529 bis 1618*, Münster: Aschendorff, 1962. Jews: Maria Boes, *Crime and punishment in early modern Germany: Courts and adjudicatory practices in Frankfurt am Main, 1562–1696*, Farnham: Ashgate, 2013. Maria Boes, Jews in the Criminal-Justice System of Early Modern Germany. *Journal of Interdisciplinary History* 30, 3 (1999): 407–435. Meike Bursch, *Judentaufe und frühneuzeitliches Strafrecht. Die Verfahren gegen Christian Treu aus Weener/Ostfriesland 1720–1728*, Frankfurt am Main: Lang, 1996. Joachim Eibach, Stigma und Betrug. Delinquenz und Ökonomie im jüdischen Ghetto. In *Kriminalität und abweichendes Verhalten. Deutschland im 18. und 19. Jahrhundert*, Helmut Berding, Diethelm Klippel, Günther Lottes (eds.), 15–38, Göttingen: Vandenhoeck & Ruprecht, 1999. Barbara Gerber, *Jud Süß. Aufstieg und Fall im frühen 18. Jahrhundert. Ein Beitrag zur historischen Antisemitismus- und Rezeptionsforschung* (= Hamburger Beiträge zur Geschichte der deutschen Juden 16), Hamburg: Christians, 1990. Gotzmann, Wendehorst 2007. Yacov Guggenheim, Meeting on the road: Encounters between German Jews and Christians on the margins of society. In *In and out of the Ghetto. Jewish-Gentile Relations in Late Medieval and Early Modern Germany*, Ronnie Po-chia Hsia (ed.), 125–136, New York: Cambridge University Press, 1995. Yacov Guggenheim, Stefi Jersch-Wenzel, Von den Schalantjuden zu den Betteljuden: Jüdische Armut in Mitteleuropa in der Frühen Neuzeit. In *Juden und Armut in Mittel- und Osteuropa*, Stefi Jersch-Wenzel (ed.), 55–69, Köln: Böhlau 2000. Ronnie Po-chia Hsia, *The Myth of Ritual Murder. Jews and Magic in Reformation Germany*, New Haven: Yale University Press, 1988. Ronnie Po-chia Hsia, The Usurious Jew. Economic Structure and Religious Representations in

Stuttgart which provides a detailed description of more than 5,000 court cases of various imperial estates (among them Württemberg) from which I have selected exemplary cases.[27] The approach – to stress this one more time – is not to provide an overview of the social history of the named groups nor to discuss the vast

---

an Anti-Semitic Discourse. In *In and out of the Ghetto. Jewish-Gentile Relations in Late Medieval and Early Modern Germany*, Ronnie Po-chia Hsia, Hartmut Lehmann (eds.), 161–176, Cambridge: Cambridge University Press, 1995. Vera Kallenberg, *Extrem alltäglich – Jüdinnen und Juden in der Frankfurter Strafgerichtsbarkeit (1780–1814)*, Darmstadt: Diss. phil. Technische Universität, 2015. Gustav Partington, Betteljuden in Lippe. In *Kontinuität und Umbruch in Lippe. Sozialpolitische Verhältnisse zwischen Aufklärung und Restauration 1750–1820*, Johannes Arndt, Peter Nitschke (eds.), 253–272, Detmold: Institut für Lippische Landeskunde, 1994. Rotraud Ries, Bilder und Konstruktionen über einen Grenzgänger. Der Prozess gegen den Ansbacher Hofjuden Elkan Fränkel 1712. In *Minderheiten, Obrigkeit und Gesellschaft in der Frühen Neuzeit. Integrations- und Abgrenzungsprozesse im süddeutschen Raum*, Mark Häberlein, Martin Zürn (eds.), 317–338, St. Katharinen: Scripta-Mercaturae-Verlag, 2001. Norbert Schnitzler, Juden vor Gericht: Soziale Ausgrenzung durch Sanktionen. In *Herrschaftliches Strafen seit dem Hochmittelalter. Formen und Entwicklungsstufen*, Hans Schlosser, Rolf Sprandel, Dietmar Willoweit (eds.), 285–308, Köln: Böhlau, 2002. Otto Ulbricht, Criminality and Punishment of the Jews in the Early Modern Period. In *In and out of the Ghetto. Jewish-Gentile Relations in Late Medieval and Early Modern Germany*, Ronnie Po-chia Hsia, Hartmut Lehmann (eds.), 49–70, Cambridge: Cambridge University Press, 1995. Gypsies: Thomas Fricke, *Zigeuner im Zeitalter des Absolutismus. Bilanz einer einseitigen Überlieferung. Eine sozialgeschichtliche Untersuchung anhand süddeutscher Quellen*, Pfaffenweiler 1996. Gerhard Fritz, *Eine Rotte von allerhandt rauberischem Gesindt. Öffentliche Sicherheit in Südwestdeutschland vom Ende des Dreißigjährigen Krieges bis zum Ende des Alten Reiches*, Ostfildern: Thorbecke, 2004. Walter Hartinger, Zigeuner – Ein halbes Jahrtausend Fremde in Ostbayern? *Zeitschrift für Bayerische Landesgeschichte* 60 (1997): 837–860. Leo Lucassen, Zigeuner im frühneuzeitlichen Deutschland. Neue Forschungsergebnisse, -probleme und -vorschläge. In *Policey und frühneuzeitliche Gesellschaft*, Karl Härter (ed.), 235–262, Frankfurt am Main: Klostermann, 2000. Leo Lucassen, *Zigeuner. Die Geschichte eines polizeilichen Ordnungsbegriffes in Deutschland 1700–1945*, Köln: Böhlau, 1996. Rheinheimer 1996. Wilhelm Rütten, "Lustig ist das Zigeunerleben". *Zeitschrift der Savigny-Stiftung für Rechtsgeschichte Germanistische Abteilung* 114 (1997): 233–260.

27 Alexander Brunotte, Raimund J. Weber, *Akten des Reichskammergerichts im Hauptstaatsarchiv Stuttgart*, vol. 1–8, Stuttgart: Kohlhammer, 1993–2008. Anette Baumann, *Gedruckte Relationen und Voten des Reichskammergerichts vom 16. bis 18. Jahrhundert: ein Findbuch*, Köln: Böhlau, 2004. On the approaches and concepts regarding the analyses of the records of the Imperial Chamber Court: Anette Baumann, *Die Gesellschaft der frühen Neuzeit im Spiegel der Reichskammergerichtsprozesse. Eine sozialgeschichtliche Untersuchung zum 17. und 18. Jahrhundert*, Köln: Böhlau 2001. Anette Baumann, Stefan Ehrenpreis, Stephan Wendehorst, Siegrid Westphal, (eds.), *Prozessakten als Quelle. Neue Ansätze zur Erforschung der Höchsten Gerichtsbarkeit im Alten Reich*, Köln: Böhlau, 2001. Anette Baumann, Peter Oestmann, Stephan Wendehorst, Siegrid Westphal (eds.), *Prozesspraxis im Alten Reich. Annäherungen, Fallstudien, Statistiken*, Köln: Böhlau 2005. Amend, Baumann, Wendehorst, Westphal, 2007.

body of the respective literature, but merely to analyse how the legal system of the Empire and early modern criminal justice dealt with sects, Jews and Gypsies as the main protagonists of cultural diversity.[28]

Cultural diversity and religion: Sects and Anabaptists

Research on religious diversity has primarily focused on the process of confessionalization after the Protestant Reformation that generated different religious cultures (*Konfessionskulturen*) and was characterized by a "remarkable religious variety" and "often ambiguously constructed, poorly defined, and highly fluid religious boundaries".[29] This new religious landscape was not restricted to the three main confessions, the Catholics, Lutherans and the Calvinists, as recognized and guaranteed by the imperial constitution since the Religious Peace of 1555 and the Treaty of Westphalia (1648), but instead produced a broad variety of divergent religious groups over time, such as Anabaptists, Mennonites, Quaker, Pietist, *Zwinglianer*, *Hutterer*, *Schwenkfeldianer* and others.[30]

These developments are strongly related to concepts such as confessionalization, intolerance and the emergence of religious tolerance, religious pluralisation and heterodoxy, heresy and heretic groups. Concerning the function of law and judicial systems, a wealth of studies is dealing with ecclesiastical law, church ordinances, the juridification of religious (confessional) conflicts and the legal

---

28 On the basic concepts and approaches of the history of crime and criminal justice, particularly regarding minority groups (which I can not outline in detail in this essay), see Härter 2005a, 1–26. Gerd Schwerhoff, *Historische Kriminalitätsforschung*. Frankfurt am Main: Campus, 2011.

29 Gary B. Cohen, Howard Louthan, Franz A. J. Szabo (eds.), *Diversity and Dissent: Negotiating Religious Difference in Central Europe, 1500–1800*, New York: Berghahn Books, 2011, 3. Dieter R. Bauer, Norbert Haag, Sabine Holtz, Wolfgang Zimmermann (eds.), *Ländliche Frömmigkeit. Konfessionskulturen und Lebenswelten 1500 – 1850*, Stuttgart: Jan Thorbecke Verlag, 2002. Daniel Christensen, Randolph C. Head (eds.), *Orthodoxies and Heterodoxies in Early Modern German Culture. Order and Creativity 1500–1750*, Leiden: Brill, 2007. Kaspar von Greyerz, Thomas Kaufmann, Anselm Schubert (eds.), *Frühneuzeitliche Konfessionskulturen 1. Nachwuchstagung des VRG Wittenberg 30.09.–02.10.2004*, Gütersloh: Gütersloher Verlagshaus, 2008. Robert Kolb (ed.), *Lutheran Ecclesiastical Culture, 1550–1675*, Leiden: Brill, 2008. C. Scott Dixon, Dagmar Freist, Mark Greengrass (eds.), *Living with Religious Diversity in Early-Modern Europe*, Farnham: Ashgate, 2009.

30 Overview: Hans-Jürgen Goertz, *Religiöse Bewegungen in der Frühen Neuzeit*. München: Oldenbourg, 1993. Goertz, Stayer 2002. Cohen, Louthan, Szabo 2011.

foundation of religious tolerance, parity and emancipation.[31] The imperial recess (*Reichsabschied*) of 1555 finally established the legal recognition of the Lutheran confession, the right of religiously dissenting subjects to emigrate and, to some extent, religious tolerance for the imperial cities.[32] The Treaty of Westphalia (1648) extended tolerance and protection for the three main Christian confessions and established formal legal procedures to manage conflicts within the legal system of the Empire. However, the *Reichsabschied* of 1555 and imperial law in general also strived to protect the religious and political order against sects and enabled religious uniformity within the territorial states. This allowed the Protestant and Catholic imperial estates the confessionalization of their territories that intended the formation of homogeneous confessional cultures and therefore produced cultural or religious deviance.[33]

Recently, historical research has discovered religious deviance anew. However, the focus is still on deviant religious behaviour of single dissenters and perpetrators and not on collective cultural diversity and deviance.[34] Undoubtedly, traditional church and criminal law labelled and criminalized dissident religious behaviour and belief as superstition, blasphemy, heresy, etc. Although religious deviance and crime were related to diverging cultural practices, they were most often conceptualized as 'internal' dissenting behaviour of individuals who still somehow belonged to the dominating Christian culture.[35]

The confessionalization and the according public laws (*Policeyordnungen, Kirchenordnungen*) changed the patterns of religious deviance and crime that were increasingly conceptualized as external behaviour of larger, separated groups who differed in terms of religious beliefs as well as cultural attitudes and practices – characterized as "*ungebührliches, unchristliches, ärgerliches Leben*

31 Schmidt 1992. Schilling 1994. Grell, Scribner 1996. Schilling 2002. Andreas Höfele, Stephan Laque, Enno Ruge, Gabriela Schmidt (eds.), *Representing Religious Pluralization in Early Modern Europe*. Berlin: Lit, 2007. Benjamin J. Kaplan 2007. Kaspar von Greyerz, *Religion and Culture in Early Modern Europe, 1500 – 1800*, New York: Oxford University Press, 2008.

32 Reichsabschied 25.09.1555, in: Johann Jakob Schmauss, Heinrich Christian Freiherr von Senkkenberg (eds.), *Neue und vollständigere Sammlung der Reichs-Abschiede [...], Tl. I–IV,* Frankfurt: Knoch, 1747, III, 14–43. Axel Gotthard, *Der Augsburger Religionsfrieden*, Münster: Aschendorff, 2004. Grell, Scribner 1996.

33 Michael Titzmann, Religiöse Abweichung in der Frühen Neuzeit: Relevanz – Formen – Kontexte. In *Heterodoxie in der Frühen Neuzeit*, Hartmut Laufhütte, Michael Titzmann (eds.), 5–118, Tübingen: Niemeyer, 2006. Dixon, Freist, Greengrass 2009.

34 Alexander Kästner, Gerd Schwerhoff (eds.), *Göttlicher Zorn und menschliches Maß. Religiöse Devianz in frühneuzeitlichen Stadtgemeinschaften*, Konstanz: UVK-Verlag-Gesellschaft, 2013. Piltz, Schwerhoff 2015.

35 Piltz, Schwerhoff 2015, 28–32. Titzmann 2006. Freist 2007.

und Wesen" (indecent, unchristian, troublesome life and nature).[36] To some extent, this included existing religious groups such as the Jews who were increasingly regulated through public administrative laws. However, criminalization and prosecution predominantly focused on the sects, notably the Anabaptists. From the authorities' viewpoint, heretical religious sects could also secretly exist within the borders of the imperial estates or the Empire, practice diverging religious as well as cultural customs and endanger the order through the seduction of subjects, disobedience and sedition. Thus, cultural diversity could flourish in obscurity or could lead to revolt, overthrow and the establishment of autonomous communities. The concept (or label) of the sect also played a crucial role for the legal conceptualization of the crime of witchcraft: witches not only entered a pact with the devil but also formed a secret group that practiced religiously and culturally diverging rites (such as the witches' sabbath) that negated (or perverted) the Christian culture as a whole. As a result, religious and cultural deviance was partly criminalized as a social and political crime of sects that threatened public order, security and the Christian culture of the Holy Roman Empire.[37]

Between 1529 and 1566, the Empire issued several imperial laws that criminalized Anabaptist and other sects as seditious groups, breachers of the peace, vagrants, seducer, deceiver and riotous instigators (*Friedbrecher, Landläufer, Verführer, aufrührerische Aufwiegler*) and threatened criminal prosecution and severe capital punishment. Such sects would not only reject Christian sacraments and practice rebaptism, but would also use subversive propaganda, sermons and gatherings to seduce and tempt Christian subjects, instigate apostasy, disobedience against secular authorities, sedition and revolt, as well as establish autonomous communities that would overthrow good order and customs (*alle weltli-*

---

36 Vitus Anton Winter, *Geschichte der baierischen Wiedertäufer im sechszehnten Jahrhundert.* München: Lindauer 1809, 107 (quoting an ordinance by the Bavarian Duke Albrecht from 1559). Karl Härter, Religion, Frieden und Sicherheit als Gegenstand guter Ordnung und Policey: Zu den Aus- und Nachwirkungen des Augsburger Religionsfriedens und des Reichsabschieds von 1555 in der reichsständischen Policeygesetzgebung. In *Der Augsburger Religionsfriede 1555. Ein Epochenereignis und seine regionale Verankerung (= Zeitschrift des historischen Vereins für Schwaben* 98), Wolfgang Wüst, Georg Kreuzer, Nicola Schümann (eds.), 143–164, Augsburg: Wißner, 2005c, here 157–164. Thomas A. Brady, The Entropy of Coercion in the Holy Roman Empire: Jews, Heretics, Witches. In *Diversity and Dissent: Negotiating Religious Difference in Central Europe, 1500–1800*, Gary B. Cohen, Howard Louthan, Franz A. J. Szabo (eds.), 92–113, New York: Berghahn Books, 2011.

37 Von Schlachta 2009. Brady 2011. Piltz, Schwerhoff 2015, 26–33. Gerd Schwerhoff, Böse Hexen und fahrlässige Flucher: Frühneuzeitliche Gottlosigkeiten im Vergleich. In *Gottlosigkeit und Eigensinn. Religiöse Devianz im konfessionellen Zeitalter*, Eric Piltz, Gerd Schwerhoff (eds.), 187–206, Berlin: Duncker & Humblot, 2015, here 191–193.

che Policey Ordnungen und gute Sitten) and destruct the system of property and Christian marriage.[38] Thus, imperial law extended the religious crime of heresy by secular 'political' crimes, such as the 'breach of imperial peace' (*Landfriedensbruch*) and seditious action against the authorities. In this regard, the dissent of sects was not limited to religious belief only, but extended to social, political and cultural deviance as well.

In particular, the overthrow of radical Anabaptists in Münster (1532–1535) in the wake of the 1525 peasants' revolt was considered an attempt to establish an autonomous theocratic community – the Anabaptist kingdom of Münster – that was characterised by a different political, 'socialist' or even 'communist' system and dissenting cultural habits such as polygamy.[39] After the Bishop of Münster had militarily suppressed the Anabaptist community, a trial followed in which the leaders were convicted to harsh capital punishment. Thereafter, the imperial laws commissioned the Imperial Chamber Court, the Imperial Circles (*Reichskreise*) and the imperial estates with the prosecution of sects in order to maintain peace and security and assigning the criminal courts of the imperial estates (*Peinliche und Halsgerichte*) with the task of prosecuting and punishing all sects.[40] In the sixteenth century, between 850 and 1,100 Anabaptists and sectarians were executed within the Empire, most of them in the first half of the century and in the Habsburg territories.[41]

---

38 Reichsabschied 22.04.1529, in: Schmauss, Senckenberg 1747 II, 292–306. Mandat 22.04.1529 (*Constitution oder Mandat wider die Widertäuffer*), in: Schmauss, Senckenberg 1747 II, 302–306. Reichsabschied 19.11.1530, in: Schmauss, Senckenberg 1747 II, 306–332. Reichsabschied 25.04.1535, in: Schmauss, Senckenberg 1747 II, 407–419 (cit.). Reichsabschied 10.06.1544, in: Schmauss, Senckenberg 1747 II, 495–517. Reichsabschied 14.02.1551, in: Schmauss, Senckenberg 1747 II, 609–632. Reichsabschied 30.05.1566, in: Schmauss, Senckenberg 1747 III, 211–244. Härter 2005c, 157–163.

39 James M. Stayer, *The German peasants' war and anabaptist community of goods*. Montreal: McGill-Queen's University Press: 1991. Klötzer 1992. von Schlachta 2009. Astrid von Schlachta, Erzählungen von Devianz. Die wiedertauffer zwischen interner Absonderung und äußerer Exklusion, in *Gottlosigkeit und Eigensinn. Religiöse Devianz im konfessionellen Zeitalter*, Eric Piltz, Gerd Schwerhoff (eds.), 311–332, Berlin: Duncker & Humblot, 2015.

40 Reichsabschied 1551 § 88 & 94, in: Schmauss, Senckenberg 1747 II, 609–632. Reichsabschied 1555, in: Schmauss, Senckenberg 1747 III, 14–136.

41 Brady 2011, 100, based on Claus Peter Clasen, *Anabaptism. A Social History, 1525–1618: Switzerland, Austria, Moravia, South and Central Germany*, London: Cornell University Press, 1972. E. William Monter, Heresy Executions in Reformation Europe, 1520–1565. In *Tolerance and Intolerance in the European Reformation*, Ole Grell, Bob Scribner (eds.), 48–64, Cambridge: Cambridge University Press, 1996.

However, in addition to responding with military suppression and criminal punishment, the Empire and authorities also established different regulations to deal with sects and religious deviance. This included the distinction between different types of criminals such as ring-leaders, preachers, misled followers, single perpetrators or members of a secret society or conspiracy, as well as between different types of wrongdoing such as the proselytizing and seduction of Christian subjects, the distribution of seditious pamphlets and the hosting of sectarians. All of these infractions could be punished with a broad variety of penalties and sanctions. Moreover, the imperial laws included the provision that all sectarians who immediately recanted their "error", accepted penitence and punishment and supplicated could be pardoned based on circumstances such as social status, age or character.

Numerous Catholic and Lutheran territorial states issued laws and ordinances that criminalized sects, enhanced the means of social control through censorship, control of gatherings, local visitations, prohibition of contact or segregation and threatened various punishments that ranged from the death penalty to expulsion and confiscation of property. However, these laws also included penitence, the mitigation of sanctions and pardon in the case that members of sects repented and revoked their false beliefs.[42] The imperial estates and the Swiss federation all prosecuted Anabaptists, sects and even 'crypto-Lutherans' or 'crypto-Calvinists' and punished or expelled such sectarians, most often combined with the confiscation of their property.[43] As late as 1731, the Archbishop of Salzburg expelled Protestant subjects as religiously "deviant rebels, seditious instigators and destroyers of internal peace" ("*Rebellen ... boßhaffte Aufwigler und Zerstörer der innerlichen Landes-Ruhe*").[44] In this regard, criminal justice served as a means of religious and cultural demarcation and was meant to strengthen the religious and cultural identity of the territorial state through exemplary harsh punishment and expulsion.

However, during the early modern period, diverging religious communities and sects continued to exist, most notably in the territorially fragmented southwest of the Empire. These sect members had learned to culturally adapt, especially in local communities and villages. Furthermore, in many territorial states, the actual practices of prosecution and punishment were actually more lenient than the harsh

---

42 Cf. the entry "Sekten" and "Täufer" in: Härter, Stolleis, 1996–2016. It lists more than 200 laws. See also Schraepler 1957. Güß 1958. Härter 2005c, 157–164. Räisänen 2011.

43 See Stiasny 1962. Kink 1997. Räisänen 2011.

44 Emigrationspatent cited: Gabriele Emrich, *Die Emigration der Salzburger Protestanten 1731 – 1732. Reichsrechtliche und konfessionspolitische Aspekte*, Münster: Lit-Verlag, 2002, 32–33. Rudolf Leeb, Martin Scheutz, Dietmar Weikl (eds.), *Geheimprotestantismus und evangelische Kirchen in der Habsburgermonarchie und im Erzstift Salzburg (17./18. Jahrhundert)*. Wien: Böhlau, 2009.

laws threatened, and suspect or prosecuted sectarians could make use of judicial diversity, legal leeway and cultural strategies to escape harsh punishments.[45]

The Duchy of Württemberg, for instance, established a complex procedure that included formal controls and visitations, denunciation, criminal prosecution, interrogation and a final trial. However, local officials and communities were part of these proceedings and could give some support to prosecuted sectarians who could also make use of social and cultural strategies and arguments. They claimed, for instance, that their belief was a 'private matter' of their household and was not practiced in public. Prosecuted secterians also stressed that they would not try to seduce or convert subjects to their beliefs and in any case did not intend to instigate revolt or sedition. Some tried to explain their belief, neglected fundamental differences between their belief and the dominating confession and referred to piety and common religious practices, such as the reading of the Bible. Others stressed simplicity, humility or harmlessness, claimed that they had no specific or clear knowledge of the religious differences and affirmed that they were socially and culturally integrated into the local community and had never intended to form a culturally diverging sect or autonomous society. Although this could not prevent religious dissenters from prosecution, the procedure enabled negotiations on the dimension of religious and cultural deviance, often resulting in lenient sanctions that allowed the convicted delinquent to stay in the local community. Convicted sectarians also successfully supplicated for the mitigation of punishments and pardon by promising remorse, correction, subservience and culturally appropriate behaviour.[46]

Furthermore, some cases are known in which convicted Anabaptists or their families successfully appealed to the Imperial Chamber Court in cases in which territorial courts or governments had unlawfully confiscated their property or withdrawn their legal capacity.[47] After the Thirty Years War and The Peace of Westphalia (1648), more territorial states began to tacitly tolerate religiously diverging groups if they seemed to be integrated into local communities and behaved in an appropriate social and cultural manner, as well as showed no signs of disobedience or sedition.[48] In the eighteenth century, the Imperial Chamber Court ceased

45 Schraepler 1957. Güß 1958. Mayes 2001. Michaela Schmölz-Häberlein, Täufer, Juden und ländliche Gemeinden im badischen Hochberg im 18. Jahrhundert. In *Nachbarn, Gemeindegenossen und die anderen. Minderheiten und Sondergruppen im Südwesten des Reiches während der Frühen Neuzeit*, André Holenstein, Sabine Ullmann (eds.), 275–299, Epfendorf: Bibliotheca-Academica-Verlag, 2004. Räisänen 2011.

46 Räisänen 2011, 289–322.

47 Cf. the repertories of the court records of the Imperial Chamber Courts: Brunotte, Weber 1993–2008.

48 Schmölz-Häberlein 2004.

the prosecution of imperial estates that tolerated groups such as the Mennonites or Pietists, and, in 1763, adopted the principle that sects should no longer be criminally prosecuted if they were not threatening the internal security of the state.[49] Religious diversity was to some extent still considered to be culturally divergent, but was no longer conceptualized as a serious crime or a threat to the political order. Some imperial estates tolerated religious diversity if the concerned groups were under formal or informal social control and behaved as disciplined and culturally appropriate subjects (or were perceived as such). In this regard, religiously diverging groups achieved a more or less similar status to that of the Jews.[50]

Cultural diversity, foreignness and migration: Jews and Gypsies

In the early modern period, the Empire and the imperial estates issued numerous administrative public and penal laws that concerned marginal and migrating groups and minorities, such as the Jews, the Gypsies, and the poor. They constructed religious and cultural differences and labelled or criminalized cultural practices and the transgression of cultural boundaries.[51] This was accompanied by a juridical-political discourse that manifested itself in various publications of jurists, public officials and administrative practitioners who dealt with Jews, Gypsies, vagrants and their way of life (*Lebensart* or *Lebenswandel*). These publications often stressed social and cultural differences, stereotypes and deviant behaviour. Although cultural differences constituted only one factor in the labelling of these groups as deviant, public law, police ordinances and official publications such as 'reports from the files' (*Aktenmässige Berichte*) and 'wanted lists' (*Räuber- und Diebslisten*) criminalized them as socially and culturally divergent, dangerous groups that formed a specific 'criminal culture' or 'underworld' (bands of thieves and robbers in particular) that threatened the *Ständegesellschaft* and public security (*Landessicherheit*).[52]

---

49 Johann Melchior Hoscher, *Sammlung merkwürdiger am Kaiserlichen Reichs-Kammergerichte entschiedener Rechtsfälle mit ausführlicher Erörterung wichtiger Rechtsfragen*, vol. 1–6. Lemgo: Meyer, 1789–1794, Vol. 1, 150.

50 Schmölz-Häberlein 2004.

51 Landwehr 2001. Härter 2010. Härter 2003a. Härter 2007.

52 See, for example: Paul Nicol Einert, *Entdeckter Jüdischer Baldober, Oder Sachsen-Coburgische Acta Criminalia Wider eine Jüdische Diebs- und Rauber-Bande, Worinnen Zu jedermänniglicher Wahrnehmung/ vor die Jüdische Nachstellungen sich hüten zu lernen, Besonders aber Zum nütz-*

Moreover, the criminal law of the Empire (the *Constitutio Criminalis Carolina* and the *ius commune*) discriminated marginal groups such as Jews, Gypsies and vagrants as infamous and treated them unequally, as they did not belong to the regular groups of the *Ständegesellschaft* and their grade of honour was lower (or they received none). The imperial penal code of 1532 and the *ius commune* criminal law of the Empire comprised provisions that diminished the legal status and protection of 'infamous people' with regard to the criminal procedure, apprehension and detention and the application of torture, testimony or the oath, as they were considered dishonourable, infamous and of an inferior status of honour.[53] Jews

---

lichen Gebrauch Derer Criminal-Gerichte, Viele bisher noch nicht bekannt gewesene Bosheiten und Diebs-Streiche, des Jüdischen Volcks, deutlich geoffenbaret und zum Behuff künfftiger Inquisitionsprocesse, mit practischen Anmerckungen erläutert werden, Coburg: Bey J.G. Steinmarck., 1737. Johann Jakob Bierbrauer, *Beschreibung derer berüchtigten Jüdischen Diebes, Mörder- und Rauber-Banden [...] vornemlich [in] hiesigen hochfürstl., sodann auch denen umliegenden Landen und Städten*. Kassel: Estienne, 1758. Johann Jodocus Beck, *Tractatus de iuribus iudaeorum, von Recht der Juden. Worinnen von denen Gesetzen, denen sie unterworffen, deren Heyrathen, Contracten, Wucher, Testamenten, Successionen oder Erbfolgen, Verbrechen und deren Bestraffungen [...] gehandelt wird*. Nürnberg: Lochner, 1731, 318. Johann Benjamin Weissenbruch, *Ausführliche Relation von der Famosen Ziegeuner- Diebs- Mord- u. Rauberbande, welche den 14. u. 15. Nov. Ao. 1726 zu Giessen durch Schwerdt, Strang u. Rad resp. justificirt worden, Worinnen, Nach praemittirter Historie von dem Ursprung und Sitten derer Ziegeuner ac. die vornehmste und schwereste Begangenschafften mit allen Umständen erzehlet, auch was durante Processu sowol ante- als in- et postTorturam vorgenommen worden, enthalten ist*. Frankfurt am Main: Krieger, 1727. Johann Andreas Koll, *Zuverläßige und Acten-mäßige Nachricht von dem famosen Ziegeuner Antoine la Grave vulgo Grossen Galantho, worinnen dessen Diebereyen, Mordthaten, Straßen-Räuberey, Lands-Friedbrüchige Facta und Huren-Händel erzählet, auch Rechts-beständige Ursachen angeführet werden, nach welchen derselbe am 2ten Iunii 1733. hier in Darmstadt mit dem Rad vom Leben zum Tod gebracht worden. Deme noch beygefügt Wahrhaffte Relation, so wohl von Frantz Leimburger, vulgo Netely, als auch Georg Daniel Kleinen, vulgo Speck-Daniel, welche gleichfalß an obgedachtem dato wegen ihrer practicirten vielfältigen qualificirten Diebereyen mit dem Schwerdt ihren wohlverdienten Lohn bekommen haben. Auff Hochfürstl. gnädigsten Special-Befehl, zur Information des Publici zum Druck befördert vom Fürstl. Heßisch-Darmstädt. würckl. Proceß-Rath, Cammer-Consulenten und peinl. Richter daselbsten*. Gießen: Lammers, 1733. Evans 1988. Seidenspinner 1998. Härter 1999. Fritz 2004. Härter 2005a, 930–1122. Härter 2007. Härter 2010. Ammerer, Fritz 2013.

53 Härter 2003. Siegrid Westphal, Der Umgang mit kultureller Differenz am Beispiel von Haftbedingungen von Juden in der Frühen Neuzeit. In *Juden im Recht. Neue Zugänge zur Rechtsgeschichte der Juden im Alten Reich*, Andreas Gotzmann, Stephan Wendehorst (eds.), 139–161, Berlin: Duncker & Humblot, 2007. Joachim Eibach, Rudolf Schlögl (eds.), Ungleichheiten vor Gericht, *Geschichte und Gesellschaft* 35 (2009). Satu Lidman, Unehrlich, kriminell und gottlos? Vorurteile und rechtliche Maßnahmen gegen vagierende Personengruppen im frühneuzeitlichen Bayern. In *Die Gesellschaft der Nichtsesshaften. Zur Lebenswelt vagierender Schichten vom 16. bis zum 19. Jahrhundert: Beiträge der Tagung vom 29. und 30. September 2011 im Kriminalmuseum Rothenburg ob der Tauber*, Gerhard Ammerer, Gerhard Fritz (eds.), 223–243, Affalterbach: Didymos-Verlag, 2013, 229–232.

in particular were not regarded as credible witnesses and not permitted an 'oath of purgation' (*Purgationseid*) that could terminate criminal procedure, but were instead forced to swear an *oath more Judaico* that culturally segregated, discriminated and humiliated them.[54]

However, although perceived as a distinct religious group, the Jews were not generally considered as deviant per se. The Empire provided them with the legal status of Roman or imperial citizens (*Reichsbürger*), and in the sixteenth century, the emperor and the Imperial Diet consolidated legal protection based on imperial laws and the right of the imperial estates to host, tax and regulate Jews (*Judenregal*) and to grant the status of a 'protected Jew' (*Schutzjude*).[55] Hence, several imperial cities and territorial states allowed them to settle and establish Jewish communities (*Landjudenschaften*) that possessed limited administrative and judicial autonomy regarding religious matters and related offences that belonged to the lower jurisdiction.[56]

Moreover, the Jews were able to use the various imperial, territorial and municipal courts to regulate internal conflicts, as well as conflicts with Christians. Many of them were acquainted with the levels and opportunities of the diverse legal system of the Empire.[57] All in all, in the territorial states and imperial cities where Jews were allowed to live, they socially and economically interacted with Christians and were not fully segregated in everyday life. However, several ghettos did exist, such as in Frankfurt/Main and Worms, and the differences

---

54 Beck 1731, 422–519. Christian Gottlieb Gmelin, *Abhandlung von den besonderen Rechten der Juden in peinlichen Sachen*, Tübingen: Cotta, 1785, 95–109. Westphal 2007. Härter 2007.

55 Brady 2011, 95. Friedrich Battenberg, *Judenverordnungen in Hessen-Darmstadt. Das Judenrecht eines Reichsfürstentums bis zum Ende des Alten Reiches. Eine Dokumentation*, Wiesbaden: Kommission für die Geschichte der Juden in Hessen, 1987. Friedrich Battenberg, Rechtliche Rahmenbedingungen jüdischer Existenz in der Frühneuzeit zwischen Reich und Territorium. In *Judengemeinden in Schwaben im Kontext des Alten Reiches*, Rolf Kießling (ed.), 53–79, Berlin: Akademie Verlag, 1995. Friedrich Battenberg, Juden als "Bürger" des Heiligen Römischen Reichs im 16. Jahrhundert: Zu einem Paradigmenwechsel im "Judenrecht" in der Reformationszeit. In *Christen und Juden im Reformationszeitalter*, Rolf Decot (ed.), 175–179, Mainz: von Zabern, 2006.

56 Gotzmann 1998. Gotzmann 2008. Friedrich Battenberg, Die jüdischen Gemeinden und Landjudenschaften im Heiligen Römischen Reich. Zwischen landesherrlicher Kontrolle und Autonomie. In *Selbstverwaltung in der Geschichte Europas in Mittelalter und Neuzeit Tagung der Vereinigung für Verfassungsgeschichte in Hofgeismar vom 10. bis 12. März 2008/ Für die Vereinigung herausgegeben*, Helmut Neuhaus (eds.), 101–142, Berlin: Duncker & Humblot, 2010.

57 Gotzmann, Wendehorst 2007. Kasper-Marienberg 2012. Stefan Ehrenpreis, Andreas Gotzmann, Stephan Wendehorst (eds.), *Kaiser und Reich in der jüdischen Lokalgeschichte*, München: Oldenbourg, 2013, Griemert 2015.

between Jews and Christians were socially, culturally and spatially marked in a clearly visible manner.[58]

The imperial police ordinances of 1530 and the Jewish ordinances of the imperial estates (*Judenordnungen*) imposed the marking of the Jews through specific clothing, symbols or badges, labelling them as a culturally diverging group.[59] Administrative and penal laws also criminalized certain relations between Jews and Christians, most notably sexual intercourse and marriage, and proscribed public activities and feasting of Jews on Christian Sundays and holidays. They also banned the habitation of Jews near Christian churches or spaces (such as processional routes), forbade Christians to work as servants for Jews and criminalized 'Jewish usury' (*Judenwucher*) and 'receiving' (*Hehlerei*). The threatened punishments and sanctions ranged from humiliating death penalties (hanging upside down by the feet or together with an animal) to expulsion, banishment and fines with a considerable range of flexibility and discretion in adjudication.[60]

Although religious crimes such as ritual murder, repeated baptisms and apostasy played a certain role (at least as myths and source of stereotypes),[61] these administrative and penal laws did not solely criminalize Jewish religion, customs or the culture itself. The main purposes of these laws were to protect the Christian religion and culture, to control or prohibit social and cultural relations between the Christians and Jews and to segregate, discipline and control the Jewish communities. Hence, the labelling and criminalization of cultural devi-

---

58 Rolf Kießling (ed.), *Judengemeinden in Schwaben im Kontext des Alten Reiches*. Berlin: Akademie Verlag, 1995. Rolf Kießling, Sabine Ullmann (eds.), *Landjudentum im deutschen Südwesten während der Frühen Neuzeit*. Berlin: Akademie Verlag, 1999. Sabine Ullmann, Der Streit um die Weide. Ein Ressourcenkonflikt zwischen Christen und Juden in den Dorfgemeinden der Markgrafschaft Burgau. In *Devianz, Widerstand und Herrschaftspraxis in der Vormoderne*, Mark Häberlein (ed.), 99–136, Konstanz: Universitätsverlag Konstanz, 1999. Friedrich Battenberg, *Die Juden in Deutschland vom 16. bis zum Ende des 18. Jahrhunderts*. München: Oldenbourg, 2001. Sabine Hödl, Peter Rauscher, Barbara Staudinger (eds.), *Hofjuden und Landjuden. Jüdisches Leben in der Frühen Neuzeit*, Berlin: Philo, 2003.

59 Weber 2002, 151. Jütte 1993.

60 Battenberg 1987. Rochus Scholl, *Juden und Judenrecht im Herzogtum Pfalz-Zweibrücken. Ein Beitrag zur Rechtsgeschichte eines deutschen Kleinstaates am Ende des Alten Reiches*, Frankfurt am Main, 1996. Imke König, *Judenverordnungen im Hochstift Würzburg (15.–18. Jh.)*. Frankfurt am Main: Klostermann, 1999. Werner Marzi, *Judentoleranz im Territorialstaat der Frühen Neuzeit. Judenschutz und Judenordnung in der Grafschaft Nassau-Wiesbaden-Idstein und im Fürstentum Naussau-Usingen*, Wiesbaden: Kommission für die Geschichte der Juden in Hessen, 1999. Eibach 1999. Härter 2007.

61 Hsia 1988. Ronnie Po-chia Hsia, *Trent 1475. Stories of a Ritual Murder Trial*, New Haven: Yale University Press, 1992. Bursch 1996.

ance concerned cultural relations between the majority and the minority of the *Ständegesellschaft*.

A main impact of these laws was to generate and disseminate culturally-based labels and stereotypes of Jewish deviance and criminality, such as the 'thieving, usurious or fraudulent Jew' (*Wucherjude*), which as well as their status as 'infamous people' influenced prosecution, criminal procedure and court practice.[62] If Jews fell victim of crimes, their legal credibility and their capacity to testify as witnesses or to swear an oath was less than that of the Christians. Conversely, Christian perpetrators used anti-Jewish stereotypes and religious, ethnic and cultural arguments to defend their wrongdoing against the 'arch-enemies of Christianity' or 'foreign Polish yids' and *Betteljuden* – and frequently received a more lenient punishment than convicted Jewish delinquents. Moreover, Jews often suffered harsher treatment and worse conditions within the inquisitorial criminal procedure, in particular regarding apprehension, the pre-trial detention, prison conditions and the application of torture. As Jews and members of an infamous group, they were per se suspect, treated like other 'infamous' people (such as Gypsies or vagrants) and separated from Christian delinquents.[63]

In general, Jews were tried for crimes that Christians also frequently committed, although criminal courts mainly prosecuted Jews for property crimes such as thieving, receiving, fraud or usury and rarely for deviant religious behaviour or religious crimes only.[64] However, the transgression of cultural borders could lead to criminal prosecution: if Jews had violated Christian Sundays or holidays by working, feasting or tumultuous activities, if they had employed Christians as servants (*Shabbat goy*) or if sexual relations had occurred between a male Jew and a female Christian, criminal courts imposed penalties that, in addition to fines, prison or capital punishment, were intended to spatially or socially exclude Jewish delinquents through banishment, expulsion, corporal punishment and additional humiliating, shaming practices such as the pillory.[65]

In the Electorate of Mainz, for instance, the criminal court punished three Jews who had made public 'tumult' at Easter with public shaming punishments exe-

---

62 Gerber 1990. Hsia 1995. Ulbricht 1995. Boes 1999. Eibach 1999. Ries 2001. Schnitzler 2002. Härter 2005a, 973–978, 1104–1117. Härter 2007. Maria Boes, Zweifach im Visier: Jüdische Opfer von Straftaten und Rechtsprechung im Römisch-Deutschen Reich der Frühen Neuzeit. In *Juden im Recht. Neue Zugänge zur Rechtsgeschichte der Juden im Alten Reich*, Andreas Gotzmann, Stephan Wendehorst (eds.), 221–241, Berlin: Duncker & Humblot, 2007. Boes 2013. Kallenberg 2015.
63 Ulbricht 1995. Boes 2007. Westphal 2007. Härter 2007.
64 Ulbricht 1995. Boes 1999. Eibach 1999. Härter 2005a, 973–978, 1104–1117. Härter 2007. Boes 2007. Boes 2013. Kallenberg 2015.
65 Ulbricht 1995. Boes 1999. Härter 2005a, 973–978. Härter 2007. Boes 2007. Boes 2013.

cuted on the Sabbath.[66] In the well-known case of the 'court Jew' (*Hofjude*) Joseph Oppenheimer, the criminal court of Württemberg sentenced '*Jud Süß*' in 1737/38 to harsh humiliating capital punishment for the alleged crimes of fraud, treason, sexual intercourse with Christian ladies and the transgressing of social and cultural boundaries. Since Oppenheimer had not only served as political advisor and state official (*Finanzrat*), but had behaved as a member of the prince's court, he was hanged from very high gallows and his corpse was exposed for several years in a narrow cage outside the capital of Stuttgart. The case attracted a great deal of media attention and several illustrated broadsheets appeared depicting the humiliating punishment that clearly mirrored the cultural transgression.[67] Such punishments served to mark the social and cultural boundaries and to exclude members of the minority group from the majority culture.

On the other hand, Jews could use cultural diversity and legal agency as options to act within the diverse criminal justice system with its different actors, logics and extrajudicial proceedings such as petitioning and supplicating. In pretrial detention, *Schutzjuden* could successfully request to live in accordance with their religious norms and exercise essential cultural practices regarding Sabbath, food or the use of religious scripts, as they were culturally separated under different conditions. The authorities were more likely to accept cultural diversity within criminal procedure if Jewish communities or families petitioned and paid for the supply of detainees.[68] More importantly, during the often intense inquisitorial interrogations, Jewish defendants used cultural arguments and stereotypes to argue, deflect from or defend themselves. On the whole, Jewish families and communities as well as individual delinquents possessed a considerable knowledge of how to use judicial and extrajudicial means, such as supplications, complaints, intercessions or appeals, to the imperial high courts or the emperor to negotiate the mitigation of punishments, pardon, safe conduct or protection and to act within the criminal justice system on the basis of their cultural knowledge.[69] Ultimately,

---

66 Bayerisches Staatsarchiv Würzburg, Mainzer Regierungsarchiv, Kriminalakten 2793. cf. Härter 2007, 373.

67 Gerber 1990. Gudrun Emberger, Robert Kretzschmar (eds.), *Die Quellen sprechen lassen. Der Kriminalprozess gegen Joseph Süß Oppenheimer 1737/38*, Stuttgart: Kohlhammer, 2009. For similar punishments (cages), see Ries 2001. Karl Härter, Strafen mit und neben der Zentralgewalt: Pluralität und Verstaatlichung des Strafens in der Frühen Neuzeit. In *Vergeltung. Eine interdisziplinäre Betrachtung der Rechtfertigung und Regulation von Gewalt*, Günther Schlee, Bertram Turner (eds.), 105–126, Frankfurt am Main: Campus Verlag, 2008, 105.

68 Westphal 2007.

69 Kallenberg 2015. Vera Kallenberg, Der Streit um den "Judenpurschen": Interagierende Herrschafts-und Handlungsräume in der deutsch-jüdischen Geschichte Hessen-Kassels und

however, this had to correspond with the fiscal interests of the authorities and their prime intent to protect and maintain the order of the *Ständegesellschaft*.

As mentioned, throughout the early modern period, the Empire, the Imperial Circles (*Reichskreise*) and the imperial estates increasingly issued numerous administrative laws, police ordinances and criminal laws to protect the *Ständegesellschaft* against foreign migrating marginal groups. After the Thirty Years War in particular, a growing number of these laws and the concomitant juridical-political discourse established and disseminated the culturally-based stereotypes and socio-cultural labels of *Betteljuden*, Gypsies and criminal vagrants that would intrude the country and threaten society, public order and the security of the land (*allgemeine Landessicherheit*) through the spreading of infectious diseases, deviant behaviour and various crimes.[70] Hence, the cultural diversity and deviance of *Betteljuden* and Gypsies were not based on religion, but on the categories of migration, foreignness and, to some extent, of ethnicity. The Gypsies were considered to be converted Catholics refugees who originated from Jewish people, Egypt (Egyptians = Gypsies) or India and constituted a divergent cultural group with their own complexion (dark skin), language, clothing, customs and norms, characterised by a mobile way of life, all in all labelled as the 'Gypsy culture' (*zigeunerische Kultur und Lebensweise*).[71] In a similar way the authorities and the respective public laws labelled the culture of the wandering *Betteljuden* as deviant.[72]

---

der Reichsritterschaft der Freiherrn von Thüngen um 1800. Ein Fallbeispiel. In *Kaiser und Reich in der jüdischen Lokalgeschichte*, Stefan Ehrenpreis, Andreas Gotzmann, Stephan Wendehorst (eds.), 93–118, München: Oldenbourg, 2013. Härter 2005a, 495–515. Härter 2007. Härter 2013b. Ulbricht 1995, 70. André Holenstein, Bitten um den Schutz. Staatliche Judenpolitik und Lebensführung von Juden im Lichte von Schutzsupplikationen aus der Markgrafschaft Baden(-Durlach) im 18. Jahrhundert. In *Landjudentum im deutschen Südwesten während der Frühen Neuzeit*, Rolf Kießling, Sabine Ullmann (eds.), 97–153, Berlin: Oldenbourg, 1999.

70 See the entries 'Fahrende Leute', 'Betteljuden' and 'Zigeuner' in: Härter, Stolleis 1996–2016. They list more than 3,000 ordinances. Gerhard Fritz, *Quellen zur Geschichte der öffentlichen Sicherheit in Südwestdeutschland zwischen 1648 und 1806*. Remshalden: 2006 (with an edition of exemplary ordinances). Härter 2011.

71 For a summary of contemporary views, see Weissenbruch 1727, 14–17. Heinrich Moritz Gottlieb Grellmann, *Die Zigeuner. Ein historischer Versuch über die Lebensart und Verfassung Sitten und Schicksahle dieses Volks in Europa, nebst ihrem Ursprunge*, Dessau, Leipzig 1783, second edition Göttingen: Johann Christian Dieterich, 1787. For a modern view: Kallenberg 2010. Yaron Matras, Die Sprache der Roma: Ein historischer Umriss. In *Sinti, Roma, Gypsies. Sprache – Geschichte – Gegenwart*, Yaron Matras, Hans Winterberg, Michael Zimmermann (eds.), 231–261, Berlin: Metropol-Verlag, 2003.

72 Partington, 1994; Guggenheim 1995. Guggenheim, Jersch-Wenzel 2000. Sabine Ullmann, Das Ehepaar Merle und Simon Ulman in Pfersee: Eine jüdische Familie an der Grenze zum Betteljudentum. In *Minderheiten, Obrigkeit und Gesellschaft in der Frühen Neuzeit*, Mark Häberlein (ed.),

Although recent research has questioned if such a distinct culture ever existed, the authorities perceived and labelled Gypsies and *Betteljuden* as culturally deviant due to their way of living (*Lebensart*) as foreign, masterless, permanently migrating people, forming a distinct 'people' or 'nation' ('*Zigeuner-Volck*'), characterised by different surnames, complexion, look and language (*Jiddish*, *Rotwelsch*, or a derivative of the Indian language) and a status as infamous people with habits, such as idleness, laziness, begging, cheating, fortune telling and thieving.[73] According to the 1758 treatise of the Hessian official and judge Bierbrauer, the Jewish people, would make a living by chaffer, usuriousness and outsmarting the Christians, and most of them would wander through the Empire as tricky and thieving *Betteljuden*, protected by the Jewish communities, stealing and robbing from the Christians. He based this on the alleged Jewish custom "that all the goods of the world belong to the seed of Abraham" (*daß die Güther der ganzen Welt dem Saamen Abrahams zugehöreten*).[74] The judicial treatise of the judge and official Weissenbruch in 1727 similarly spoke of the Gypsies as savage godless people of Egyptian or Jewish origin that constituted a 'mixed' 'evil race' (*böse Race*) and 'evil nation' (*böse Nation*) with customs such as a mobile lifestyle, polygamy, painting their skin dark, using a secret language and secret surrogate names and a social hierarchy with a distinct leader.[75]

Public laws and ordinances disseminated the same stereotypes and patterns of socio-cultural deviance: The wandering Gypsies, crooks, *Betteljuden* and masterless vermin would endanger society, disobey divine and secular law and act against the natural order and other persons as troublemakers and enemies of the society ("herum vagirende ruchlose / und dem gemeinen Weesen höchstschädliche Zigeuner / Jauner / Bettel=Juden und anders Herrenlose Diebs=Gesind [...] sich alles Gehorsams gegen Gött= und Weltliche Gesetze entziehen, und wider dieselbe, ja wider die von der Natur eingepflanzte Billigkeit selbsten, ihre gantze

269–291, St. Katharinen: Scripta Mercaturae, 2001. Friedrich Battenberg, Grenzerfahrung und Mobilität von Juden in der Vormoderne: Ein Problemaufriss. In *Räume und Wege. Jüdische Geschichte im Alten Reich 1300–1800*, Rolf Kießling, Peter Rauscher, Barbara Staudinger (eds.), 207–217, Berlin: Akademie Verlag, 2007. Härter 2007. Härter 2013b.

73 Maureen Anne Bell, Walter Otto Weyrauch, Autonomous Lawmaking: The Case of the "Gypsies". *Yale Law Journal* 103 (1993): 323–399. Fricke 1996. Lucassen 1996. Kallenberg, 2010. Matras 2003. For attempts to investigate the lifeworld and social practices of vagrants, Gypsies and *Betteljuden*, see Guggenheim, Jersch-Wenzel 2000. Ullmann 2001. Yaron Matras, Hans Winterberg, Michael Zimmermann (eds.), *Sinti, Roma, Gypsies. Sprache – Geschichte – Gegenwart*, Berlin: Metropol-Verlag, 2003. Ammerer 2003. Ammerer, Fritz 2013. Härter, 2013b. Härter 2013c.

74 Bierbrauer 1758, Vorbericht.

75 Weissenbruch 1727, 1–19.

Lebens=Art durch eine verdammliche Verbündnuß dahin richten, ihren Nächsten Haab und Gut, auch Leib und Leben boßhaffter Weise anzugreißen und zu beleidigen, als offenbahre Feinde und Stöhrer der menschlichen Gesellschafft). Hence, their 'way of life' should be regarded as a crime in itself, as an ordinance of 1748 imposed: "*dem gemeinen Weesen höchst nachtheiligen Lebens-Wandels, so vor ein beständiges Corpus Delicti zu achten*".[76]

These police ordinances and penal laws prohibited entry, transit and stay of *Betteljuden*, Gypsies and vagrants in the respective countries, threatened various punishments that ranged from expulsion or prison workhouses to harsh capital punishment and assigned the criminal justice system to enforce these provision. Although various territorial and municipal criminal courts prosecuted *Betteljuden* and Gypsies (or vagrants labelled as such), they seldom convicted delinquents on the basis of cultural deviance only, nor did they predominantly impose harsh capital punishment. Instead, the actual penal practice showed a great variety of various sentences and was most often based on evidence that a property crime had been committed or could be ascribed to a suspect. However, the culturally-based labels and stereotypes of Jews and Gypsies influenced prosecution, inquisitorial procedure and adjudication. First, police forces, court officials, staff and patrols controlled and apprehended *Betteljuden* and Gypsies because they were suspect per se, searched, interrogated, tortured them (at times) and put them into pre-trial detention. If no evidence could be found that crimes had been committed in the region or that the suspects belonged to a band or could be classified as 'criminal vagrants' (if they carried weapons, loot or were on a wanted list), the judicial and administrative authorities most often expelled *Betteljuden* and Gypsies or imposed arbitrary, extraordinary penalties (*poena extraordinaria*, in contrast to the regular ordinary capital and corporal punishments), based on the legal presumption that their way of life constituted a crime in itself.[77]

If criminal courts could produce sufficient evidence – often through intensive forced interrogations and sometimes by the use of torture – *Betteljuden* and Gypsies were frequently sentenced to harsh punishments, at times even the death penalty. While this penal practice did not differ from the sentences criminal vagrants generally received, it showed considerable differences to delinquents

---

76 Patent des Schwäbischen Kreises 5. Februar 1714, in: Fritz 2006, Nr. 37. Patent des Schwäbischen Kreises 13. August 1718, in: Fritz 2006, Nr. 40. Chur- und Ober-Rheinische Gemeinsame Poenal-Sanction 4.9.1748, Frankfurt 1748. Kurmainzer Verordnung 28.2.1727, in: Härter, Stolleis 1996–2016, Vol. 1, Nr. 592.

77 Fricke 1996. Ammerer 2003. Härter 2003. Fritz 2004. Härter 2003a. Härter 2005a, 973–1117. Härter 2007.

who – as resident subjects – belonged to the society of orders. Most notably, in the case of property crimes, the ordinary subjects usually received milder sentences than delinquents labelled as thieving *Betteljuden*, Gypsies and vagrants. In the early modern territorial state of the Electorate of Mainz, for instance, the criminal court prosecuted 681 'vagrants' and 1,120 'subjects' for property crimes. However, 55 percent of the convicted subjects received milder penalties, such as fines or short imprisonment in special 'burgher jails' (*Bürgertürme*), and only eight per cent received capital punishment. In contrast seventy-nine vagrants – among them 24 Gypsies and six *Betteljuden* – were convicted to death and more than 90 per cent of the 'criminal vagrants' received harsh punishments, such as forced labour, the galleys, prison-workhouse and expulsion, often combined with additional humiliating penalties (flogging, whipping post, pillory) that marked them as infamous people.[78]

Therefore, the adjudicative and penal practice of criminal courts in the Empire showed considerable differences between the punishment of diverging marginal groups such as *Betteljuden*, Gypsies and vagrants on the one hand, and resident subjects on the other. The latter had a much wider range of opportunities to evade harsh pre-trial detention and torture and could negotiate milder punishments or even pardon within the criminal procedure. They could make use of dispensations, supplications and petitions, arguing with their utility (*Nützlichkeit*), industriousness, social reputation and integration into local communities and prospective disciplined behaviour.

In contrast, Gypsies and *Betteljuden* were not often able to use such means or arguments, although they sometimes referred to cultural strategies to deflect from or defend themselves. In some interrogations, Gypsies stressed that they were descendants of refugees from Egypt and good baptised Christians, properly married according to their Gypsy custom and therefore not guilty of fornication, adultery or concubinage. Having relations with a second wife, argued the Gypsy La Grave, could not be considered as adultery because he had not forsaken his first wife and would still feed both wives in his household according to the customs of the Gypsies.[79] Most often, they defended their way of life and the inevitable deviant behaviour by invoking poverty, displacement, the search for subsistence and their custom to wander, sometimes stressing that peasants or local communities had helped or interacted with them. A few *Betteljuden* were also

78 Härter 2003. Härter 2005a, 532, 1080–1122.

79 Interrogation record of five Gypsies, Bayerisches Staatsarchiv Würzburg, Mainzer Regierungsarchiv, Kriminalakten 1737 and 1086. cf. Härter 2005a, 970–972. Statement in the interrogation of La Grave, in: Koll 1733, 75.

able to receive support from local Jewish communities that vouched or supplicated for them and offered fines as a substitute for harsh punishment.[80] Overall, however, the options for cultural defence were considerably limited by the fact that 'foreign' migrating marginal groups such as *Betteljuden* and Gypsies were considered a serious threat to public security and the *Ständegesellschaft* with its dominating culture of industrious resident subjects.

Conclusion

In the early modern period, the legal system of the Empire developed distinctive patterns to deal with cultural diversity that was perceived as deviant. They primarily concerned the diversification of diverging religious groups labelled as sects and the growth of migrating marginal groups labelled as Gypsies, *Betteljuden* or vagrants. Both manifestations of cultural diversity and deviance were strongly related to religion, migration and foreignness. In this regard, the authorities, the juridical-political discourse and the law constructed cultural diversity in the form of marginal groups that existed within or intruded upon the *Ständegesellschaft*, practiced diverging customs and attempted to tempt or endanger the resident subjects. Hence, cultural deviance was conceptualised as a more or less serious threat to the (ideal) uniform society of subjects and its dominating culture, as well as to the order and security of the early modern state. However, throughout the early modern period, the threat of cultural diversity – or the respective narratives – changed from internal religious deviance and religious crimes of sects to external migrating marginal groups and property crimes. Although this could have been primarily caused by general socio-economic and political developments, the diverse responses of the legal system of the Empire had an impact on the manifestations of cultural diversity and deviance.

First, the Empire and the imperial estates responded with public administrative and penal law – most notably police ordinances – that criminalized the various manifestations of cultural deviance and the respective groups and practices. The laws, however, did not only require the criminal justice system to prosecute and punish the perpetrators, but also differentiated the means of disciplining and social control and, therefore, also intended adaption or even assimilation. This was paralleled by the legal toleration of diverging religious groups – among

80 For further examples, see Ammerer 2003. Härter 2005a, 969–978. Härter 2013c. Kallenberg 2015.

them the Jews – through privileges and a specific legal status by the Empire or the imperial estates, which, to some extent, allowed a diverging religious culture if the concerned groups did not transgress socio-cultural boundaries, 'seduce' or tempt ordinary subjects or threaten public order and security and, on the local level, behaved accordingly and assimilated (or were perceived to do so). At the end of the eighteenth century, some imperial estates (among them Prussia and Austria) even attempted to apply this method to the Gypsies and forced them to settle in segregated Gypsy colonies (*Zigeunerkolonien*). However, these colonies largely failed.[81] The legal adaption and disciplining of cultural diversity also meant that the autonomy of the concerned groups was strictly reduced to religious issues and all forms of legal autonomy regarding norms and conflict regulation were abolished.

However, the diverse multi-layered legal system of the Empire with its various overlapping legal spaces allowed the actors to use judicial and extrajudicial means such us petitioning or supplicating to deal with the regulation and repression of cultural diversity. Concerned groups or actors could utilise their legal and cultural agency to defend their respective practices, regulate cultural conflicts and therefore negotiate the boundaries and the scope of cultural diversity and deviance. While this may seem to have invoked modern functions of the law, the options for cultural defence were considerably limited to strategies of adaption, good order and social control, and by no means based on constitutional rights (such as the right to non-discrimination or equality before the law). Instead, they were based on the diversity of the imperial legal system. Moreover, concerning the external threat of cultural diversity, the criminalization, prosecution and punishment of deviant, foreign, migrating groups such as *Betteljuden*, Gypsies and vagrants remained as a main pattern of the legal system that ultimately intended segregation, exclusion and – in its most radical form – extermination. Although the latter was considerably limited to the exemplary capital punishment of serious criminals, procedure, adjudication and penal practice of the criminal justice system within the early modern Empire was strongly influenced by stereotypes and patterns of cultural deviance that resulted in discrimination and exclusion, at the very least.

81 Ulrich Friedrich Opfermann, "*Daß sie den Zigeuner-Habit ablegen*". *Die Geschichte der "Zigeuner-Kolonien" zwischen Wittgenstein und Westerwald*, 2d ed. Frankfurt am Main: Lang, 1997.

References

Amend, Anja, Baumann, Anette, Wendehorst, Stephan, Westphal, Siegrid (eds.), *Gerichtslandschaft Altes Reich. Höchste Gerichtsbarkeit und territoriale Rechtsprechung*, Köln: Böhlau, 2007.

Ammerer, Gerhard, *Heimat Straße. Vaganten im Österreich des Ancien Régime*, München: Oldenbourg-Wiss.-Verlag, 2003.

Ammerer, Gerhard, Fritz, Gerhard (eds.), *Die Gesellschaft der Nichtsesshaften. Zur Lebenswelt vagierender Schichten vom 16. bis zum 19. Jahrhundert: Beiträge der Tagung vom 29. und 30. September 2011 im Kriminalmuseum Rothenburg ob der Tauber*, Affalterbach: Didymos-Verlag, 2013.

Bahlke, Joachim (ed.), *Glaubensflüchtlinge. Ursachen, Formen und Auswirkungen frühneuzeitlicher Konfessionsmigration in Europa*, Münster: Lit, 2008.

Battenberg, Friedrich, *Judenverordnungen in Hessen-Darmstadt. Das Judenrecht eines Reichsfürstentums bis zum Ende des Alten Reiches. Eine Dokumentation*, Wiesbaden: Kommission für die Geschichte der Juden in Hessen, 1987.

Battenberg, Friedrich, Rechtliche Rahmenbedingungen jüdischer Existenz in der Frühneuzeit zwischen Reich und Territorium. In *Judengemeinden in Schwaben im Kontext des Alten Reiches*, Rolf Kießling (ed.), 53–79, Berlin: Akademie Verlag, 1995.

Battenberg, Friedrich, *Die Juden in Deutschland vom 16. bis zum Ende des 18. Jahrhunderts*. München: Oldenbourg, 2001.

Battenberg, Friedrich, Juden als "Bürger" des Heiligen Römischen Reichs im 16. Jahrhundert: Zu einem Paradigmenwechsel im "Judenrecht" in der Reformationszeit. In *Christen und Juden im Reformationszeitalter*, Rolf Decot (ed.), 175–179, Mainz: von Zabern, 2006.

Battenberg, Friedrich, Grenzerfahrung und Mobilität von Juden in der Vormoderne: Ein Problemaufriss. In *Räume und Wege. Jüdische Geschichte im Alten Reich 1300–1800*, Rolf Kießling, Peter Rauscher, Barbara Staudinger (eds.), 207–217, Berlin: Akademie Verlag, 2007.

Battenberg, Friedrich, Die jüdischen Gemeinden und Landjudenschaften im Heiligen Römischen Reich. Zwischen landesherrlicher Kontrolle und Autonomie. In *Selbstverwaltung in der Geschichte Europas in Mittelalter und Neuzeit Tagung der Vereinigung für Verfassungsgeschichte in Hofgeismar vom 10. bis 12. März 2008/ Für die Vereinigung herausgegeben*, Helmut Neuhaus (eds.), 101–142, Berlin: Duncker & Humblot, 2010.

Bauer, Dieter R., Haag, Norbert, Holtz, Sabine, Zimmermann, Wolfgang (eds.), *Ländliche Frömmigkeit. Konfessionskulturen und Lebenswelten 1500 – 1850*, Stuttgart: Jan Thorbecke Verlag, 2002.

Baumann, Anette, *Die Gesellschaft der frühen Neuzeit im Spiegel der Reichskammergerichtsprozesse. Eine sozialgeschichtliche Untersuchung zum 17. und 18. Jahrhundert*, Köln: Böhlau, 2001.

Baumann, Anette, *Gedruckte Relationen und Voten des Reichskammergerichts vom 16. bis 18. Jahrhundert: ein Findbuch*, Köln: Böhlau, 2004.

Baumann, Anette, Ehrenpreis, Stefan, Wendehorst, Stephan, Westphal, Siegrid (eds.), *Prozessakten als Quelle. Neue Ansätze zur Erforschung der Höchsten Gerichtsbarkeit im Alten Reich*, Köln: Böhlau, 2001.

Baumann, Anette, Oestmann, Peter, Wendehorst, Stephan, Westphal, Siegrid (eds.), *Prozesspraxis im Alten Reich. Annäherungen, Fallstudien, Statistiken*, Köln: Böhlau, 2005.

Beck, Johann Jodocus, *Tractatus de iuribus iudaeorum, von Recht der Juden. Worinnen von denen Gesetzen, denen sie unterworffen, deren Heyrathen, Contracten, Wucher, Testamenten, Successionen oder Erbfolgen, Verbrechen und deren Bestraffungen [...] gehandelt wird*. Nürnberg: Lochner, 1731.
Bell, Maureen Anne, Weyrauch, Walter Otto, Autonomous Lawmaking: The Case of the "Gypsies". *Yale Law Journal* 103 (1993): 323–399.
Benton, Lauren, Ross, Richard J., *Legal pluralism and empires, 1500 – 1850*. New York: New York University Press, 2013.
Bierbrauer, Johann Jakob, *Beschreibung derer berüchtigten Jüdischen Diebes, Mörder- und Rauber-Banden [...] vornemlich [in] hiesigen hochfürstl., sodann auch denen umliegenden Landen und Städten*. Kassel: Estienne, 1758.
Boes, Maria, Jews in the Criminal-Justice System of Early Modern Germany. *Journal of Interdisciplinary History* 30, 3 (1999): 407–435.
Boes, Maria, Zweifach im Visier: Jüdische Opfer von Straftaten und Rechtsprechung im Römisch-Deutschen Reich der Frühen Neuzeit. In *Juden im Recht. Neue Zugänge zur Rechtsgeschichte der Juden im Alten Reich*, Andreas Gotzmann, Stephan Wendehorst (eds.), 221–241, Berlin: Duncker & Humblot, 2007.
Boes, Maria, *Crime and punishment in early modern Germany: Courts and adjudicatory practices in Frankfurt am Main, 1562–1696*, Farnham: Ashgate, 2013.
Brady, Thomas A., The Entropy of Coercion in the Holy Roman Empire: Jews, Heretics, Witches. In *Diversity and Dissent: Negotiating Religious Difference in Central Europe, 1500–1800*, Gary B. Cohen, Howard Louthan, Franz A. J. Szabo (eds.), 92–113, New York: Berghahn Books, 2011.
Brunotte, Alexander, Weber, Raimund J., *Akten des Reichskammergerichts im Hauptstaatsarchiv Stuttgart*, vol. 1–8, Stuttgart: Kohlhammer, 1993–2008.
Bulst, Neithard, Jütte, Robert (eds.), *Zwischen Sein und Schein. Kleidung und Identität in der ständischen Gesellschaft (= Saeculum 44)*, Freiburg: Alber, 1993.
Bursch, Meike, *Judentaufe und frühneuzeitliches Strafrecht. Die Verfahren gegen Christian Treu aus Weener/Ostfriesland 1720–1728*, Frankfurt am Main: Lang, 1996.
Christensen, Daniel, Head, Randolph C. (eds.), *Orthodoxies and Heterodoxies in Early Modern German Culture. Order and Creativity 1500–1750*, Leiden: Brill, 2007.
Clasen, Claus Peter, *Anabaptism. A Social History, 1525–1618: Switzerland, Austria, Moravia, South and Central Germany*, London: Cornell University Press, 1972.
Cohen, Gary B., Louthan, Howard, Szabo, Franz A. J. (eds.), *Diversity and Dissent: Negotiating Religious Difference in Central Europe, 1500–1800*, New York: Berghahn Books, 2011.
Dixon, C. Scott, Freist, Dagmar, Greengrass, Mark (eds.), *Living with Religious Diversity in Early-Modern Europe*, Farnham: Ashgate, 2009.
Donlan, Seán Patrick, Heirbaut, Dirk, *The laws' many bodies. Studies in legal hybridity and jurisdictional complexity, c1600–1900*, Berlin: Duncker & Humblot, 2015.
Ehrenpreis, Stefan, *Kaiserliche Gerichtsbarkeit und Konfessionskonflikt. Der Reichshofrat unter Rudolf II. 1576 – 1612*, Göttingen: Vandenhoeck & Ruprecht, 2006.
Ehrenpreis, Stefan, Gotzmann, Andreas, Wendehorst, Stephan (eds.), *Kaiser und Reich in der jüdischen Lokalgeschichte*, München: Oldenbourg, 2013.
Eibach, Joachim, Stigma und Betrug. Delinquenz und Ökonomie im jüdischen Ghetto. In *Kriminalität und abweichendes Verhalten. Deutschland im 18. und 19. Jahrhundert*, Helmut Berding, Diethelm Klippel, Günther Lottes (eds.), 15–38, Göttingen: Vandenhoeck & Ruprecht, 1999.

Eibach, Joachim, Recht – Kultur – Diskurs. Nullum Crimen sine Scientia, *Zeitschrift für neuere Rechtsgeschichte* 23 (2001): 102–120.

Eibach, Joachim, Schlögl, Rudolf (eds.), Ungleichheiten vor Gericht, *Geschichte und Gesellschaft* 35 (2009).

Einert, Paul Nicol, *Entdeckter Jüdischer Baldober, Oder Sachsen-Coburgische Acta Criminalia Wider eine Jüdische Diebs- und Rauber-Bande, Worinnen Zu jedermänniglicher Wahrnehmung/ vor die Jüdische Nachstellungen sich hüten zu lernen, Besonders aber Zum nützlichen Gebrauch Derer Criminal-Gerichte, Viele bisher noch nicht bekannt gewesene Bosheiten und Diebs-Streiche, des Jüdischen Volcks, deutlich geoffenbaret und zum Behuff künfftiger Inquisitionsprocesse, mit practischen Anmerckungen erläutert werden*, Coburg: Bey J.G. Steinmarck., 1737.

Emberger, Gudrun, Kretzschmar, Robert (eds.), *Die Quellen sprechen lassen. Der Kriminalprozess gegen Joseph Süß Oppenheimer 1737/38*, Stuttgart: Kohlhammer, 2009.

Emrich, Gabriele, *Die Emigration der Salzburger Protestanten 1731 – 1732. Reichsrechtliche und konfessionspolitische Aspekte*, Münster: Lit-Verlag, 2002.

Evans, Richard J. (ed.), *The German Underworld. Deviants and Outcasts in German History*, London: Routledge, 1988.

Foblets, Marie-Claire, Gaudreault-DesBiens, Jean-François, Renteln, Alison Dundes (eds.), *Cultural Diversity and the Law: State Responses from around the World*, Brussels: Bruylant, 2010.

Freist, Dagmar, Recht und Rechtspraxis im Zeitalter der Aufklärung am Beispiel der Taufe jüdischer Kinder. In *Juden im Recht. Neue Zugänge zur Rechtsgeschichte der Juden im Alten Reich*, Andreas Gotzmann, Stephan Wendehorst (eds.), 109–137, Berlin: Duncker & Humblot, 2007.

Fricke, Thomas, *Zigeuner im Zeitalter des Absolutismus. Bilanz einer einseitigen Überlieferung. Eine sozialgeschichtliche Untersuchung anhand süddeutscher Quellen*, Pfaffenweiler 1996.

Friedeburg, Robert von, *Lebenswelt und Kultur der unterständischen Schichten in der Frühen Neuzeit*, München: Oldenbourg, 2002.

Fritz, Gerhard, *Eine Rotte von allerhandt rauberischem Gesindt. Öffentliche Sicherheit in Südwestdeutschland vom Ende des Dreißigjährigen Krieges bis zum Ende des Alten Reiches*, Ostfildern: Thorbecke, 2004.

Fritz, Gerhard, *Quellen zur Geschichte der öffentlichen Sicherheit in Südwestdeutschland zwischen 1648 und 1806*. Remshalden: 2006.

Füssel, Marian, Weller, Thomas (eds.), Soziale Ungleichheit und ständische Gesellschaft. Theorien und Debatten in der Frühneuzeitforschung, Zeitsprünge. *Forschungen zur Frühen Neuzeit* 15 (2011).

Gagliardo, John G., *Germany under the old regime 1600 – 1790*, London: Routledge,1991.

Gerber, Barbara, *Jud Süß. Aufstieg und Fall im frühen 18. Jahrhundert. Ein Beitrag zur historischen Antisemitismus- und Rezeptionsforschung* (= Hamburger Beiträge zur Geschichte der deutschen Juden 16), Hamburg: Christians, 1990.

Gmelin, Christian Gottlieb, *Abhandlung von den besonderen Rechten der Juden in peinlichen Sachen*, Tübingen: Cotta, 1785.

Goertz, Hans-Jürgen, *Religiöse Bewegungen in der Frühen Neuzeit*. München: Oldenbourg, 1993.

Goertz, Hans-Jürgen, Stayer, James M. (eds.), *Radikalität und Dissent im 16. Jahrhundert*, Berlin: Duncker & Humblot, 2002.

Gotthard, Axel, *Der Augsburger Religionsfrieden*, Münster: Aschendorff, 2004.
Gotzmann, Andreas, Strukturen jüdischer Gerichtsautonomie in den deutschen Staaten des 18. Jahrhunderts. In *Historische Zeitschrift* 267, 2 (1998): 313–356.
Gotzmann, Andreas, *Jüdische Autonomie in der Frühen Neuzeit: Recht und Gemeinschaft im deutschen Judentum*, Göttingen: Wallstein, 2008.
Gotzmann, Andreas, Wendehorst, Stephan (eds.), *Juden im Recht. Neue Zugänge zur Rechtsgeschichte der Juden im Alten Reich*, Berlin: Duncker & Humblot, 2007.
Grell, Ole Peter, Scribner, (eds.), *Tolerance and intolerance in the European Reformation*. Cambridge: Cambridge University Press, 1996.
Grellmann, Heinrich Moritz Gottlieb, *Die Zigeuner. Ein historischer Versuch über die Lebensart und Verfassung Sitten und Schicksahle dieses Volks in Europa, nebst ihrem Ursprunge*, Dessau, Leipzig 1783, second edition Göttingen: Johann Christian Dieterich, 1787.
Greyerz, Kaspar von, *Religion and Culture in Early Modern Europe, 1500 – 1800*, New York: Oxford University Press, 2008.
Greyerz, Kaspar von, Kaufmann, Thomas, Schubert, Anselm (eds.), *Frühneuzeitliche Konfessionskulturen 1. Nachwuchstagung des VRG Wittenberg 30.09.–02.10.2004*, Gütersloh: Gütersloher Verlagshaus, 2008.
Griemert, André, *Jüdische Klagen gegen Reichsadelige. Prozesse am Reichshofrat in den Herrschaftsjahren Rudolfs II. und Franz I. Stephan*, Berlin: de Gruyter, Oldenbourg, 2015.
Guggenheim, Yacov, Meeting on the road: Encounters between German Jews and Christians on the margins of society. In *In and out of the Ghetto. Jewish-Gentile Relations in Late Medieval and Early Modern Germany*, Ronnie Po-chia Hsia (ed.), 125–136, New York: Cambridge University Press, 1995.
Guggenheim, Yacov, Wenzel, Stefi, Von den Schalantjuden zu den Betteljuden: Jüdische Armut in Mitteleuropa in der Frühen Neuzeit. In *Juden und Armut in Mittel- und Osteuropa*, Stefi Jersch-Wenzel (ed.), 55–69, Köln: Böhlau, 2000.
Güß, Ernst Friedrich Peter, *Das Verhalten der kurpfälzischen Regierung gegenüber dem Täufertum bis zum Dreißigjährigen Krieg*, Stuttgart: Diss., 1958.
Härter, Karl Entwicklung und Funktion der Policeygesetzgebung des Heiligen Römischen Reiches Deutscher Nation im 16. Jahrhundert. *Ius Commune* 20 (1993): 61–141.
Härter, Karl, Das Reichskammergericht als "Reichspoliceygericht". Geschichte der Zentraljustiz in *Mitteleuropa, Festschrift für Bernhard Diestelkamp zum 65. Geburtstag*, Friedrich Battenberg, Filippo Ranieri (eds.), 237–252, Weimar: Böhlau, 1994.
Härter, Karl, Social Control and the Enforcement of Police-Ordinances in Early Modern Criminal Procedure. In *Institutionen, Instrumente und Akteure Sozialer Kontrolle und Disziplinierung im frühneuzeitlichen Europa / Institutions, Instruments and Agents of Social Control and Discipline in Early Modern Europe*, Heinz Schilling, Lars Behrisch (eds.), 39–63, Frankfurt am Main: Klostermann, 1999.
Härter, Karl, Kriminalisierung, Verfolgung und Überlebenspraxis der Zigeuner im frühneuzeitlichen Mitteleuropa. In *Sinti, Roma, Gypsies. Sprache – Geschichte – Gegenwart*, Yaron Matras, Hans Winterberg, Michael Zimmermann (eds.), 41–81. Berlin: Metropol-Verlag, 2003a.
Härter, Karl, Zum Verhältnis von "Rechtsquellen" und territorialen Rahmenbedingungen in der Strafgerichtsbarkeit des 18. Jahrhunderts: Vagabondage und Diebstahl in der Entscheidungspraxis der Kurmainzer Landesregierung. In *Justiz = Justice = Justicia? Rahmenbedingungen von Strafjustiz im frühneuzeitlichen Europa*, Harriet Rudolph, Helga Schnabel-Schüle (eds.), 433–465, Trier: Kilomedia, 2003b.

Härter, Karl, *Policey und Strafjustiz in Kurmainz. Gesetzgebung, Normdurchsetzung und Sozialkontrolle im frühneuzeitlichen Territorialstaat*. Frankfurt am Main: Klostermann, 2005a.

Härter, Karl, Recht und Migration in der frühneuzeitlichen Ständegesellschaft: Reglementierung – Diskriminierung – Verrechtlichung. In *Zuwanderungsland Deutschland Migrationen 1500–2005*, R. Beier-de Haan (ed), 50–71, Berlin: Edition Minerva, 2005b.

Härter, Karl, Religion, Frieden und Sicherheit als Gegenstand guter Ordnung und Policey: Zu den Aus- und Nachwirkungen des Augsburger Religionsfriedens und des Reichsabschieds von 1555 in der reichsständischen Policeygesetzgebung. In *Der Augsburger Religionsfriede 1555. Ein Epochenereignis und seine regionale Verankerung (= Zeitschrift des historischen Vereins für Schwaben* 98), Wolfgang Wüst, Georg Kreuzer, Nicola Schümann (eds.), 143–164, Augsburg: Wißner, 2005c.

Härter, Karl, Zur Stellung der Juden im frühneuzeitlichen Strafrecht: Gesetzgebung, Rechtswissenschaft und Justizpraxis. In *Juden im Recht. Neue Zugänge zur Rechtsgeschichte der Juden im Alten Reich*, Andreas Gotzmann, Stephan Wendehorst (eds.), 347–379. Berlin: Duncker & Humblot, 2007.

Härter, Karl, Strafen mit und neben der Zentralgewalt: Pluralität und Verstaatlichung des Strafens in der Frühen Neuzeit. In *Vergeltung. Eine interdisziplinäre Betrachtung der Rechtfertigung und Regulation von Gewalt*, Günther Schlee, Bertram Turner (eds.), 105–126, Frankfurt am Main: Campus Verlag, 2008.

Härter, Karl, Security and "gute Policey" in Early Modern Europe: Concepts, Laws and Instruments. In *Historical Social Research* 35 (2010), *Special Issue: The Production of Human Security in Premodern and Contemporary History*, Cornel Zwierlein, Rüdiger Graf, Magnus Ressel (eds): 41–65.

Härter, Karl, Die Reichskreise als transterritoriale Ordnungs- und Rechtsräume: Ordnungsnormen, Sicherheitspolitik und Strafverfolgung. In *Reichskreise und Regionen im frühmodernen Europa – Horizonte und Grenzen im "spatial turn"*, Wolfgang Wüst, Michael Müller (eds.), 211–249, Frankfurt am Main: Peter Lang, 2011.

Härter, Karl, The Early Modern Holy Roman Empire of German Nation (1495–1806): A Multi-layered Legal System. In *Law and Empire. Ideas, Practices, Actors*, Jeroen Duindam, Jill Diana Harries, Caroline Humfress, Nimrod Hurvitz (eds.), 111–131, Leiden/Boston: Brill, 2013a.

Härter, Karl, Jüdische Migrationen im frühneuzeitlichen Alten Reich: Rechtliche Rahmenbedingungen, Geleit und Rechtsnutzung. In *Kaiser und Reich in der jüdischen Lokalgeschichte*, Stefan Ehrenpreis, Andreas Gotzmann, Stephan Wendehorst (eds.), 67–92, München: Oldenbourg, 2013b.

Härter, Karl, Prekäre Lebenswelten vagierender Randgruppen im frühneuzeitlichen Alten Reich. Überlebenspraktiken, obrigkeitliche Sicherheitspolitik und strafrechtliche Verfolgung. In *Die Gesellschaft der Nichtsesshaften. Zur Lebenswelt vagierender Schichten vom 16. bis zum 19. Jahrhundert: Beiträge der Tagung vom 29. und 30. September 2011 im Kriminalmuseum Rothenburg ob der Tauber*, Gerhard Ammerer, Gerhard Fritz (eds.), 21–38, Affalterbach: Didymos-Verlag, 2013c.

Härter, Karl, Das Heilige Römische Reich deutscher Nation als mehrschichtiges Rechtssystem, 1495–1806. In *Die Anatomie frühneuzeitlicher Imperien. Herrschaftsmanagement jenseits von Staat und Nation: Institutionen, Personal und Techniken*, Stephan Wendehorst (ed.), 327–347, Berlin: De Gruyter Oldenbourg, 2015.

Härter, Karl, Stolleis, Michael (eds.), *Repertorium der Policeyordnungen der Frühen Neuzeit*, vol. 1–11, Frankfurt am Main: Klostermann, 1996–2016.

Hartinger, Walter, Zigeuner – Ein halbes Jahrtausend Fremde in Ostbayern? *Zeitschrift für Bayerische Landesgeschichte* 60 (1997): 837–860.
Hödl, Sabine, Rauscher, Peter, Staudinger, Barbara (eds.), *Hofjuden und Landjuden. Jüdisches Leben in der Frühen Neuzeit*, Berlin: Philo, 2003.
Höfele, Andreas, Laque, Stephan, Ruge, Enno, Schmidt, Gabriela (eds.), *Representing Religious Pluralization in Early Modern Europe*. Berlin: Lit, 2007.
Holenstein, André, Bitten um den Schutz. Staatliche Judenpolitik und Lebensführung von Juden im Lichte von Schutzsupplikationen aus der Markgrafschaft Baden(-Durlach) im 18. Jahrhundert. In *Landjudentum im deutschen Südwesten während der Frühen Neuzeit*, Rolf Kießling, Sabine Ullmann (eds.), 97–153, Berlin: Oldenbourg, 1999.
Hoscher, Johann Melchior, *Sammlung merkwürdiger am Kaiserlichen Reichs-Kammergerichte entschiedener Rechtsfälle mit ausführlicher Erörterung wichtiger Rechtsfragen*, vol. 1–6. Lemgo: Meyer, 1789–1794.
Hsia, Ronnie Po-chia, *The Myth of Ritual Murder. Jews and Magic in Reformation Germany*, New Haven: Yale University Press, 1988.
Hsia, Ronnie Po-chia, *Trent 1475. Stories of a Ritual Murder Trial*, New Haven: Yale University Press, 1992.
Hsia, Ronnie Po-chia, The Usurious Jew. Economic Structure and Religious Representations in an Anti-Semitic Discourse. In *In and out of the Ghetto. Jewish-Gentile Relations in Late Medieval and Early Modern Germany*, Ronnie Po-chia Hsia, Hartmut Lehmann (eds.), 161–176, Cambridge: Cambridge University Press, 1995.
Jürgens, Henning P., Weller, Thomas (eds.), *Religion und Mobilität. Zum Verhältnis von raumbezogener Mobilität und religiöser Identitätsbildung im frühneuzeitlichen Europ*, Göttingen: Vandenhoeck & Ruprecht, 2010.
Jütte, Robert, *Stigma-Symbole. Kleidung als identitätsstiftendes Merkmal bei spätmittelalterlichen und frühneuzeitlichen Randgruppen (Juden, Dirnen, Aussätzige, Bettler)*, Saeculum Bd. 44 (1993): 65–89.
Kallenberg, Vera, *Von "liederlichen Land-Läuffern" zum "asiatischen Volk". Die Repräsentation der 'Zigeuner' in deutschsprachigen Lexika und Enzyklopädien zwischen 1700 und 1850. Eine wissensgeschichtliche Untersuchung*, Brussels: Lang, 2010.
Kallenberg, Vera, Der Streit um den "Judenpurschen": Interagierende Herrschafts-und Handlungsräume in der deutsch-jüdischen Geschichte Hessen-Kassels und der Reichsritterschaft der Freiherrn von Thüngen um 1800. Ein Fallbeispiel. In *Kaiser und Reich in der jüdischen Lokalgeschichte*, Stefan Ehrenpreis, Andreas Gotzmann, Stephan Wendehorst (eds.), 93–118, München: Oldenbourg, 2013.
Kallenberg, Vera, *Extrem alltäglich – Jüdinnen und Juden in der Frankfurter Strafgerichtsbarkeit (1780–1814)*, Darmstadt: Diss. phil. Technische Universität, 2015.
Kaplan, Benjamin J., *Divided by Faith. Religious Conflict and the Practice of Toleration in Early Modern Europe*, Cambridge Massachusetts: Belknap Press of Harvard Univ. Press, 2007.
Kaplan, Steven L. (ed.), *Understanding Popular Culture. Europe from the Middle Ages to the Nineteenth Century*, Berlin: De Gruyter, 1984.
Kasper-Marienberg, Verena, *'vor Euer Kayserlichen Mayestät Justiz-Thron.' Die Frankfurter jüdische Gemeinde am Reichshofrat in josephinischer Zeit (1765–1790)*, Innsbruck: Studienverlag, 2012.
Kästner, Alexander, Schwerhoff, Gerd (eds.), *Göttlicher Zorn und menschliches Maß. Religiöse Devianz in frühneuzeitlichen Stadtgemeinschaften*, Konstanz: UVK-Verlag-Gesellschaft, 2013.

Kesper-Biermann, Sylvia, Ludwig, Ulrike, Ortmann, Alexandra (eds.), *Ehre und Recht. Ehrkonzepte, Ehrverletzungen und Ehrverteidigungen vom späten Mittelalter bis zur Moderne*, Magdeburg: Meine, 2011.

Kießling, Rolf (ed.), *Judengemeinden in Schwaben im Kontext des Alten Reiches*. Berlin: Akademie Verlag, 1995.

Kießling, Rolf, Ullmann, Sabine (eds.), *Landjudentum im deutschen Südwesten während der Frühen Neuzeit*. Berlin: Akademie Verlag, 1999.

Kink, Barbara, *Die Täufer im Landgericht Landsberg 1527/28*. St. Ottilien: EOS-Verlag, 1997.

Klötzer, Ralf, *Die Täuferherrschaft von Münster. Stadtreformation und Welterneuerung*, Münster: Aschendorff, 1992.

Kolb, Robert (ed.), *Lutheran Ecclesiastical Culture, 1550–1675*, Leiden: Brill, 2008.

Koll, Johann Andreas, *Zuverläßige und Acten-mäßige Nachricht von dem famosen Ziegeuner Antoine la Grave vulgo Grossen Galantho, worinnen dessen Diebereyen, Mordthaten, Straßen-Räuberey, Lands-Friedbrüchige Facta und Huren-Händel erzählet, auch Rechts-beständige Ursachen angeführet werden, nach welchen derselbe am 2ten Iunii 1733. hier in Darmstadt mit dem Rad vom Leben zum Tod gebracht worden. Deme noch beygefügt Wahrhaffte Relation, so wohl von Frantz Leimburger, vulgo Netely, als auch Georg Daniel Kleinen, vulgo Speck-Daniel, welche gleichfalß an obgedachtem dato wegen ihrer practicirten vielfältigen qualificirten Diebereyen mit dem Schwerdt ihren wohlverdienten Lohn bekommen haben. Auff Hochfürstl. gnädigsten Special-Befehl, zur Information des Publici zum Druck befördert vom Fürstl. Heßisch-Darmstädt. würckl. Proceß-Rath, Cammer-Consulenten und peinl. Richter daselbsten*. Gießen: Lammers, 1733.

König, Imke, *Judenverordnungen im Hochstift Würzburg (15.–18. Jh.)*. Frankfurt am Main: Klostermann, 1999.

Kymlicka, Will, Lernestedt, Claes, Matravers, Matt (eds.), *Criminal Law and Cultural Diversity*. Oxford: Oxford University Press, 2014.

Landwehr, Achim, Norm, Normalität, Anomale. Zur Konstitution von Mehrheit und Minderheit in württembergischen Policeyordnungen der Frühen Neuzeit: Juden, Zigeuner, Bettler, Vaganten. In *Minderheiten, Obrigkeit und Gesellschaft in der Frühen Neuzeit. Integrations- und Abgrenzungsprozesse im süddeutschen Raum*, Mark Häberlein, Martin Zürn (eds.), 41–74, St. Katharinen: Scripta-Mercaturae-Verlag, 2001.

Landwehr, Achim, Stockhorst, Stefanie, *Einführung in die europäische Kulturgeschichte*, Paderborn: UTB/BRO, 2004.

Leeb, Rudolf, Scheutz, Martin, Weikl, Dietmar (eds.), *Geheimprotestantismus und evangelische Kirchen in der Habsburgermonarchie und im Erzstift Salzburg (17./18. Jahrhundert)*. Wien: Böhlau, 2009.

Lidman, Satu, Unehrlich, kriminell und gottlos? Vorurteile und rechtliche Maßnahmen gegen vagierende Personengruppen im frühneuzeitlichen Bayern. In *Die Gesellschaft der Nichtsesshaften. Zur Lebenswelt vagierender Schichten vom 16. bis zum 19. Jahrhundert: Beiträge der Tagung vom 29. und 30. September 2011 im Kriminalmuseum Rothenburg ob der Tauber*, Gerhard Ammerer, Gerhard Fritz (eds.), 223–243, Affalterbach: Didymos-Verlag, 2013.

Lucassen, Leo, *Zigeuner. Die Geschichte eines polizeilichen Ordnungsbegriffes in Deutschland 1700–1945*, Köln: Böhlau, 1996.

Lucassen, Leo, Zigeuner im frühneuzeitlichen Deutschland. Neue Forschungsergebnisse, -probleme und -vorschläge. In *Policey und frühneuzeitliche Gesellschaft*, Karl Härter (ed.), 235–262, Frankfurt am Main: Klostermann, 2000.

Marzi, Werner, *Judentoleranz im Territorialstaat der Frühen Neuzeit. Judenschutz und Judenordnung in der Grafschaft Nassau-Wiesbaden-Idstein und im Fürstentum Naussau-Usingen*, Wiesbaden: Kommission für die Geschichte der Juden in Hessen, 1999.
Matras, Yaron, Die Sprache der Roma: Ein historischer Umriss. In *Sinti, Roma, Gypsies. Sprache – Geschichte – Gegenwart*, Yaron Matras, Hans Winterberg, Michael Zimmermann (eds.), 231–261, Berlin: Metropol-Verlag, 2003.
Matras, Yaron, Winterberg, Hans, Zimmermann, Michael (eds.), *Sinti, Roma, Gypsies. Sprache – Geschichte – Gegenwart*, Berlin: Metropol-Verlag, 2003.
Mayes, David, Heretics or Nonconformists? State Policies toward Anabaptists in Sixteenth-Century Hesse, *The Sixteenth Century Journal* 32/4 (Winter 2001): 1003–1026.
Moch, Leslie Page, *Moving Europeans. Migration in Western Europe since 1650*, 2. Aufl., Bloomington: Indiana University Press, 2003.
Monter, E. William, Heresy Executions in Reformation Europe, 1520–1565. In *Tolerance and Intolerance in the European Reformation*, Ole Grell, Bob Scribner (eds.), 48–64, Cambridge: Cambridge University Press, 1996.
Ogilvie, Sheilagh, Scribner, Bob (eds.), *Germany. A new social and economic history, Vol. 1: 1450–1630, Vol. 2: 1630–1800*, London: Arnold, 1996.
Opfermann, Ulrich Friedrich, "*Daß sie den Zigeuner-Habit ablegen". Die Geschichte der "Zigeuner-Kolonien" zwischen Wittgenstein und Westerwald*, 2d ed. Frankfurt am Main: Lang, 1997.
Partington, Gustav, Betteljuden in Lippe. In *Kontinuität und Umbruch in Lippe. Sozialpolitische Verhältnisse zwischen Aufklärung und Restauration 1750–1820*, Johannes Arndt, Peter Nitschke (eds.), 253–272, Detmold: Institut für Lippische Landeskunde, 1994.
Piltz, Eric, Schwerhoff, Gerd (eds.), *Gottlosigkeit und Eigensinn. Religiöse Devianz im konfessionellen Zeitalter*, Berlin: Duncker & Humblot, 2015.
Räisänen, Päivi, *Ketzer im Dorf. Visitationsverfahren, Täuferbekämpfung und lokale Handlungsmuster im frühneuzeitlichen*, Konstanz: UVK-Verlag-Gesellschaft, 2011.
Reinhard, Wolfgang, *Geschichte der Staatsgewalt. Eine vergleichende Verfassungsgeschichte Europas von den Anfängen bis zur Gegenwart*, München: Beck, 1999.
Rheinheimer, Martin, In die Erde können sie nicht kriechen. Zigeunerverfolgung im frühneuzeitlichen Schleswig-Holstein, *Historische Anthropologie* 4 (1996): 330–358.
Ries, Rotraud, Bilder und Konstruktionen über einen Grenzgänger. Der Prozess gegen den Ansbacher Hofjuden Elkan Fränkel 1712. In *Minderheiten, Obrigkeit und Gesellschaft in der Frühen Neuzeit. Integrations- und Abgrenzungsprozesse im süddeutschen Raum*, Mark Häberlein, Martin Zürn (eds.), 317–338, St. Katharinen: Scripta-Mercaturae-Verlag, 2001.
Roeck, Bernd, *Außenseiter, Randgruppen, Minderheiten. Fremde im Deutschland der frühen Neuzeit*, Göttingen: Vandenhoeck und Ruprecht, 1993.
Roeck, Bernd, *Civic Culture and Everyday Life in Early Modern Germany*, Leiden: Brill 2006.
Ruthmann, Bernhard, *Die Religionsprozesse am Reichskammergericht (1555 – 1648). Eine Analyse anhand ausgewählter Prozesse*, Köln: Böhlau, 1996.
Rütten, Wilhelm, "Lustig ist das Zigeunerleben". *Zeitschrift der Savigny-Stiftung für Rechtsgeschichte Germanistische Abteilung* 114 (1997): 233–260.
Stayer, James M., *The German peasants' war and anabaptist community of goods*. Montreal: McGill-Queen's University Press, 1991.
Schennach, Martin P., Recht – Kultur – Geschichte. Rechtsgeschichte und Kulturgeschichte. Wissenschaftshistorische und methodische Annäherungen, *Zeitschrift für Neuere Rechtsgeschichte* 36 (2014): 2–31.

Schilling, Heinz (ed.), *Kirchenzucht und Sozialdisziplinierung im frühneuzeitlichen Europa*, Berlin: Duncker und Humblot, 1994.
Schilling, Heinz (ed.), *Institutionen, Instrumente und Akteure sozialer Kontrolle und Disziplinierung im frühneuzeitlichen Europa/ Institutions, Instruments and Agents of Social Control and Discipline in Early Modern Europe*. Frankfurt am Main: Klostermann, 1999.
Schilling, Heinz, *Ausgewählte Abhandlungen zur europäischen Reformations- und Konfessionsgeschichte*, Luise Schorn-Schütte, Olaf Mörke (ed.), Berlin: Duncker und Humblot, 2002.
Schlachta, Astrid von, *Gefahr oder Segen? Die Täufer in der politischen Kommunikation*, Göttingen: V & R Unipress, 2009.
Schlachta, Astrid von, Erzählungen von Devianz. Die wiedertauffer zwischen interner Absonderung und äußerer Exklusion, in *Gottlosigkeit und Eigensinn. Religiöse Devianz im konfessionellen Zeitalter*, Eric Piltz, Gerd Schwerhoff (eds.), 311–332, Berlin: Duncker & Humblot, 2015.
Schmauss, Johann Jakob, Senckenberg, Heinrich Christian Freiherr von (eds.), *Neue und vollständigere Sammlung der Reichs-Abschiede [...], Tl. I–IV*, Frankfurt: Knoch, 1747.
Schmidt, Heinrich Richard, *Konfessionalisierung im 16. Jahrhundert*, München: Oldenbourg, 1992.
Schmölz-Häberlein, Michaela, Täufer, Juden und ländliche Gemeinden im badischen Hochberg im 18. Jahrhundert. In *Nachbarn, Gemeindegenossen und die anderen. Minderheiten und Sondergruppen im Südwesten des Reiches während der Frühen Neuzeit*, André Holenstein, Sabine Ullmann (eds.), 275–299, Epfendorf: Bibliotheca-Academica-Verlag, 2004.
Schnitzler, Norbert, Juden vor Gericht: Soziale Ausgrenzung durch Sanktionen. In *Herrschaftliches Strafen seit dem Hochmittelalter. Formen und Entwicklungsstufen*, Hans Schlosser, Rolf Sprandel, Dietmar Willoweit (eds.), 285–308, Köln: Böhlau, 2002.
Scholl, Rochus, *Juden und Judenrecht im Herzogtum Pfalz-Zweibrücken. Ein Beitrag zur Rechtsgeschichte eines deutschen Kleinstaates am Ende des Alten Reiches*, Frankfurt am Main, 1996.
Schraepler, Horst W., *Die rechtliche Behandlung der Täufer in der deutschen Schweiz, Südwestdeutschland und Hessen 1525 – 1618*, Tübingen: Ekkehart Fabian-Verlag, 1957.
Schulze, Winfried (ed.), *Ständische Gesellschaft und soziale Mobilität*, München: Oldenbourg, 1988.
Schwerhoff, Gerd, Böse Hexen und fahrlässige Flucher: Frühneuzeitliche Gottlosigkeiten im Vergleich. In *Gottlosigkeit und Eigensinn. Religiöse Devianz im konfessionellen Zeitalter*, Eric Piltz, Gerd Schwerhoff (eds.), 187–206, Berlin: Duncker & Humblot, 2015.
Schwerhoff, Gerd, *Historische Kriminalitätsforschung*. Frankfurt am Main: Campus, 2011.
Seidenspinner, Wolfgang, *Mythos Gegengesellschaft. Erkundungen in der Subkultur der Jauner*, Münster: Waxmann, 1998.
Stiasny, Hans Hermann Theodor, *Die strafrechtliche Verfolgung der Täufer in der Freien Reichsstadt Köln 1529 bis 1618*, Münster: Aschendorff, 1962.
Szidzek, Christian, *Das frühneuzeitliche Verbot der Appellation in Strafsachen. Zum Einfluß von Rezeption und Politik auf die Zuständigkeit insbesondere des Reichskammergerichts*, Köln: Böhlau, 2002.
Titzmann, Michael, Religiöse Abweichung in der Frühen Neuzeit: Relevanz – Formen – Kontexte. In *Heterodoxie in der Frühen Neuzeit*, Hartmut Laufhütte, Michael Titzmann (eds.), 5–118, Tübingen: Niemeyer, 2006.
Ulbricht, Otto, Criminality and Punishment of the Jews in the Early Modern Period. In *In and out of the Ghetto. Jewish-Gentile Relations in Late Medieval and Early Modern Germany*,

Ronnie Po-chia Hsia, Hartmut Lehmann (eds.), 49–70, Cambridge: Cambridge University Press, 1995.

Ullmann, Sabine, Der Streit um die Weide. Ein Ressourcenkonflikt zwischen Christen und Juden in den Dorfgemeinden der Markgrafschaft Burgau. In *Devianz, Widerstand und Herrschaftspraxis in der Vormoderne*, Mark Häberlein (ed.), 99–136, Konstanz: Universitätsverlag Konstanz, 1999.

Ullmann, Sabine, Das Ehepaar Merle und Simon Ulman in Pfersee: Eine jüdische Familie an der Grenze zum Betteljudentum. In *Minderheiten, Obrigkeit und Gesellschaft in der Frühen Neuzeit*, Mark Häberlein (ed.), 269–291, St. Katharinen: Scripta Mercaturae, 2001.

Vertovec, Steven (ed.), *Routledge International Handbook of Diversity Studies*. London: Taylor & Francis Ltd, 2015.

Weber, Matthias (ed.), *Die Reichspolizeiordnungen von 1530, 1548 und 1577. Historische Einführung und Edition*, Frankfurt am Main: Klostermann, 2002.

Weissenbruch, Johann Benjamin, *Ausführliche Relation von der Famosen Ziegeuner- Diebs- Mord- u. Rauberbande, welche den 14. u. 15. Nov. Ao. 1726 zu Giessen durch Schwerdt, Strang u. Rad resp. justificirt worden, Worinnen, Nach praemittirter Historie von dem Ursprung und Sitten derer Ziegeuner ac. die vornehmste und schwereste Begangenschafften mit allen Umständen erzehlet, auch was durante Processu sowol ante- als in- et postTorturam vorgenommen worden, enthalten ist*. Frankfurt am Main: Krieger, 1727.

Westphal, Siegrid (ed.), *In eigener Sache: Frauen vor den höchsten Gerichten des Alten Reiches*, Köln: Böhlau, 2005.

Westphal, Siegrid, Der Umgang mit kultureller Differenz am Beispiel von Haftbedingungen von Juden in der Frühen Neuzeit. In *Juden im Recht. Neue Zugänge zur Rechtsgeschichte der Juden im Alten Reich*, Andreas Gotzmann, Stephan Wendehorst (eds.), 139–161, Berlin: Duncker & Humblot, 2007.

Winter, Vitus Anton, *Geschichte der baierischen Wiedertäufer im sechszehnten Jahrhundert*. München: Lindauer, 1809.

Part II: **Legal Pluralism**

Sumit Guha

The *qazi*, the *dharmadhikari* and the judge

Political authority and legal diversity in pre-modern India

Introduction

Max Weber initiated the global study of comparative law in all its diversity. His writing explored many interesting ideas, but I will focus on a few of them. He believed that achieving the "highest degree of formal juridical precision" would maximize the chance of correctly predicting the legal consequences of any action. This was the ideal type of a rationalized law that allowed the judicial process to work with mechanical regularity. In such a system, the consequences of actions were exactly calculable. But neither patrimonial sovereigns nor ecclesiastical authorities cared to rigorously implement such a system. Rather, they wanted a system to work toward fulfilling "the expediential and ethical goals of the authorities in question."[1] That forced a choice between maintaining an "abstract formalism" and realizing "substantive goals," which Weber saw as governed by desired outcomes that would conform to concrete ethical and political needs.[2] Logic and coherence were less important here. The ideal type of this alternative kind of adjudication he termed "khadi [*qazi*] justice". It included the justice administered by worthies, such as English Justices of the Peace, and some versions of trial by jury.[3] We may think of Weber's description of justice oriented to substantive goals as judge-centered rather than law-centered.

That then brings us to the Indian sub-continent, where by the early modern period a variety of judges operated in different fora. This paper will look at three sources of justice in Western India who overlapped and coexisted and yet worked out of very distinct religio-political traditions: Islamic judges who were usually appointed by rulers but soon became hereditary, state-recognized Hindu custodians of *dharma* and, lastly, English Protestant merchants turned judges. Nor was this the only area where legal diversity existed. The unification and rationalization of legal systems under the aegis of the state was not even an ambition in earlier times in most parts of the world. That was especially true of the Indian

1 Max Weber, *Economy and Society: An Outline of Interpretive Sociology*, Guenther Roth, Claus Wittich (eds.), 2 vols., Berkeley: University of California Press, 1978,II: 810.

2 Weber 1978, II: 811

3 Weber 1978, II: 813, 814

DOI 10.1515/9783110423327-005

subcontinent. Even in long-lived centralized monarchies it was very gradually that states molded all law-givers into at least a notional hierarchy who applied a uniform set of rules and procedures.[4] Political centers in Indian life before the mature British imperial regime never achieved this.[5] Even the British colonial government in practice supported and protected diverse legal arrangements by its tacit non-interference with the internal self-regulation inherent in the caste and occupational structures of Indian society.[6] That is important because prior to the 20th century, community autonomy was a key foundation for legal diversity. It limited both the information and the powers available to central authority. As long as the state remained quiescent, community leaders could decide outcomes even in defiance of formal civil or criminal law. Viewed through the lens of functionalist sociology, we would see community autonomy as reinforcing the existing social order and limiting conflict. At the same time, much pre-modern legal process was centrally connected to the earning perquisites or fees. The desire to increase revenues was a centripetal force that drew royal appointees towards interference in disputes even as it attracted those who were 'forum-shopping'. On the other hand, the early modern state usually lacked the understanding or capacity to manage complex disputes. It therefore often profited from them by exacting fees for installing worthies into positions of community authority and power. The centre of political gravity was shifting downward to the more rooted levels of the system. The system of rule remained essentially horizontal and relied on local intermediate groups.[7]

My paper will explore legal processes and law-finding in this political context. It has three parts: in the first I briefly look at the functioning of *qazis* as law officers under the Sultanates and Mughal empire, then I review the legal practices of the Maratha regime that replaced the former and finally I examine how the early English regime in western India sought to establish a legal system in the colonial enclave in Bombay that it received from the English Crown.

4 In England this was still being completed at the end of the nineteenth century. F. W. Maitland, F. C. Montague, *A Sketch of English Legal History*, New York: G.P. Putnam's Sons, 1915, 146–187.

5 Vithal Trimbak Gune, *The Judicial System of the Marathas, 1400–1800*, Poona: Deccan College, 1953. Sumit Guha, Rules, Laws and Powers: A Perspective from the Past, in *Rules, Laws, Constitutions: A Perspective for Our Times*, S. Saberwal (ed.), 83–96, New Delhi: Sage Publications, 1998.

6 L. T. Kikani, *Caste in the Courts*. Rajkot: Ganatra, 1912.

7 Farhat Hasan *State and Locality in Mughal India: Power Relations in Western India, c.1572–1730*. Cambridge: Cambridge University Press, 2006, 50.

Qazi

Islamic judges had a long history in West Asia before they began to be installed in the urban centers under the Sultanate of Delhi (c.1200–1400), first in North and then South India. This effort was pushed forward by the Mughal empire in the sixteenth century. C.A. Elliott states that in North India the emperor Akbar appointed one in every pargana, whether there was a Muslim population or not. Their deeds of appointment tasked them, *inter alia* with enforcing Islamic law, solemnizing marriages and attesting documents.[8] One would then expect them to enlarge their roles locally since a part of their income came from fees and fines. We have documents from western India showing that Aurangzeb (1658–1707) charged them also with assessing and collecting the *jizya* tax from non-Muslims.[9]

Farhat Hasan summarizes the nature of the office in India. The post required the holder to be a *sayyid*, and appointments were usually confined to a few distinguished families. By the end of the seventeenth century they had become hereditary. Muzaffar Alam observes that letters of appointment often came after the heir had assumed the office. In Mughal manuals he was required to settle disputes and inflict punishments in accordance with the sharia.[10] His duties as stipulated in a letter of appointment issued under Aurangzeb were "to decide disputes, to settle claims, to appease enmities, to perform the marriage ceremony gratis for orphans, to decide inheritance disputes, to write decrees, to incite people to religion ..." All inhabitants (the document continued) should be aware that letters and documents attested with his seal or written in his hand were valid.[11] Hasan has studied the working of this office in Gujarat under Mughal rule and J.S. Grewal has published the records of the property transactions in the city of Batala from the seventeenth and eighteenth century. [12] Both of them point out how all sorts of transactions, regardless of community membership, came before the *qazi* but equally how many matters were settled without recourse to him. Grewal's

8 C. A. Elliott, *The Chronicles of Oonao, A District in Oudh*, Printed for private circulation only. Allahabad: 1862, 114.

9 A. R. Kulkarni, Jiziya in the Maratha Country, in *Medieval Deccan History. Commemoration Volume in Honour of P.M. Joshi*, A. R. Kulkarni, M. A. Nayeem, T. R. De Souza (eds.), 156–184, Bombay: Popular Prakashan, 1996.

10 Muzaffar Alam, *The Crisis of Empire in Mughal North India: Awadh and the Punjab, 1707–48*, Delhi, New York: Oxford University Press, 1986, 112. Hasan 2006, 99–100.

11 Elliott 1862, 114.

12 J. S. Grewal (ed.), *In the by-Lanes of History: Some Persian Documents from a Punjab Town*, Simla: Indian Institute of Advanced Study, 1975. And Hasan 2006, passim.

summary of the situation down to the colonial period (in Batala, 1848) is likely to have held across much of India:

> Much of discretion appears to have been left with the individual to go or not to go the *qazi's* court; and unless a person decided to go to the court he remained outside its jurisdiction. Thus there was no necessary incompatibility between 'the custom' and the Law. In the countryside probably the custom remained the king; but in the towns it was gradually overshadowed by the *sharia't*; familiarity with its provisions would add to its popularity. In Batala, the *brahman*, the *khatri*, the goldsmith and the Hindu carpenter frequented the *qazi's* court as much as the *sayyid* and the Muslim mason. This may explain, among other things, the continuation of the *qazi's* office at Batala during the Sikh period.[13]

Parallel to this, the sharia as applied by the *qazis* increasingly assimilated local norms and customs. Local non-Muslim communities invoked it to legitimate their transactions and also had their agreements registered with the Islamic judge.[14] This was likely the result of the authoritative nature of his attestation of documents which would support either party in any future dispute. But the documents studied by Hasan often bear the attestation of community heads or leaders as well, and, as he points out, state authority (of the *qazi*) was "integrated with and served to bolster the local arrangements of power and control."[15] This was also the pattern strongly manifested in the countryside of western India.

For the countryside – where the overwhelming majority of the people dwelt, we must begin with V.T. Gune's path-breaking study of judicial processes 1400–1800. He concluded that the "medieval period gave more importance to tradition and custom than to the written law."[16] This is borne out by innumerable documents. The *qazi* was present in many adjudications. Gune collected a sample of deeds and found the *qazi* present in 27 of them but (he noted) that the *qazi* was usually only present in the administrative headquarters. Another clue to his position may be found in where his name and seal appeared in the document. Most award-deeds (*mahzar*) listed state officials (collectively termed the *diwan*) first, followed by a list of local community leaders (*gota*). Initially under the Sultans and later under Aurangzeb, the *qazi* was grouped with state officials and listed at the head of the document. With the rise of Maratha power in the 18th century, he gradually moved to the level of an ordinary hereditary officer and part of the regional community. In many places, they came to depend on local potentates to retain their land-grants – so, for example, we find one Sharfuddin Mahmad

13 Grewal 1975, 32.
14 Hasan 2006, 72–74.
15 Hasan 2006, 95.
16 Gune 1953, 69.

(sic) Qazi of the important town of Wai, which was still notionally Mughal territory, petitioning the Maratha commander Ramachandra Pant around 1700. After fulsome compliments, he claims that every ruler of the Bhosle line from Shahaji Raje (in this area c. 1624–38?) to Rajaram (d.1700) had patronized and assisted him. He also reminds Ramachandra Pant that he too did so. He then asks Ramachandra not to allow an outsider named Gangaji Shankar to interfere with the hereditary *deshpande* (or registrar) Chintamani Keshav Thite, who was the rightful claimant and had a deed or *mahzar* from the present *qazi*'s father to that effect. He also took the opportunity to plead for an additional land grant for himself as he had a large family. The *qazi* clearly belonged to a family well rooted in local society and on good terms with the deshpande even though their functions might seem to rival each other.[17]

Following the expulsion of Mughal power, the status of the *qazi* underwent a decline. Whereas earlier he had been part of the official class, he was (Gune states) first listed as a member of the *gota* or local community in an award issued in 1731.[18] While it may appear a degradation, such a change in affiliation had obvious advantages to the holders of the office. The post would now become hereditary as all local offices were under Maratha rule. It would no longer be buffeted by the winds of political change or the tiresome requirements of scholarship. But the cost would be that *qazis* now needed to be even more mindful of local opinion and feeling. This led a contemptuous observer to write of them in the eighteenth century that "the registers of the *deshpandya* [hereditary registrar, usually a Brahmin] and words of *zamindars* are their law and holy books."[19] Nor indeed was this adaptation something limited to India – Wael Hallaq has argued that the *qazis* like other officials had always to consider the effects of their decisions on their own social, economic and moral networks.[20] Sometimes indeed, *qazi* offices originated in grants from the Brahmin Peshwas – as for example we see with Shaikh Dawud, son of Shaikh Hasan, who served as intelligence officer (*harkar*) in the Portuguese lands of Sashti conquered by the Marathas in 1738–39. The document claimed that the hereditary office of *qazi* apparently already existed in the region –something implausible if it had been under Portuguese rule. The Maratha administration probably appointed a temporary judge to the

---

17 Shivacharitrasahitya Volume 5, in *Bharata Itihasa Samshodhan Mandal Quarterly*, vol. 16, 1935–1936, Pune: 1936, 25–26.

18 Gune 1953, 23–24.

19 Cited in Sumit Guha, An Indian Penal Regime: Maharashtra in the Eighteenth Century, *Past and Present* 147 (1995): 101–126, here 104.

20 Wael B. Hallaq, *Sharīa: Theory, Practice, Transformations*, Cambridge: Cambridge University Press, 2009, 213.

post. Shaikh Dawud now successfully petitioned for it to be given him as a new hereditary property (*watan*) in reward for his efforts during the campaign. This was done and the new *qazi* was told to collect the customary fees on marriages and conduct other business according to custom.[21]

This flexibility on the other hand is what probably preserved *qazi* posts into the nineteenth century. It could also be turned to advantage when practices not permissible in classical Islamic law, but current among the majority Hindu community, were introduced. This was even done by the *qazi* of Chalisgaon's widow who petitioned and was allowed to adopt an heir who would succeed to the hereditary post.[22] Elsewhere, many custodians of the local mosque or shrine came to depend on fees for slaughtering animals, with religious roles as a secondary occupation. A dispute in Pune illustrates the change that had occurred. The *qazi* with the British army cantoned near Pune, used to both kill animals and issue *fatwas*. His right to do the former was challenged by the city *qazi* who produced documents from the king of Bijapur and Peshwa to attest to his hereditary monopoly of these twin pursuits in the Pune subdivision. The British cantonment commander in 1818 pathetically described how "Shaikh Issoof"

> a very respectable and well-behaved man, to enable him to maintain himself, and be present for the duties of his situation has always been considered as having the privilege of what little profit might be derived from performing the Jabah Halal to all cattle slain in the Poona Brigade, by himself or assistant, to the exclusion of all other Molnas, who neither live in the Bazar, attend to the duties of a Cauzee at Courts Martial, or follow the force in times of danger, as without the priviledge Shaikh Issoof must be compelled to starve or leave the Bazar without a Molna.[23]

In some Gujarat towns, petitions against the new British demand that legal documents, including second marriage certificates (*natra-chithi*), be drawn up on stamped paper claimed that this imposed an unsupportable burden on poor Muslims who could not even pay the *qazi*'s fee for such papers, much less the government tax.[24] Maratha customary law governed the posts of even specialists in Islamic law. Wasdeo Mahadeo, long-time administrator of the coastal territories of Kalyan and Bhiwandi, testified before the Civil court in 1818 that under the Peshwa's government in disputes between Muslims over hereditary property,

---

21 G.C. Vad (ed.), *Selections from the Satara Raja's and Peshwa Diaries*, 8 vols., Poona: Deccan Vernacular Education Society, 1902, vol. VIII, 18–19.

22 D. B. Parasnis, *Itihasa Sangraha* (periodical) 1907–1916, no.1–3, 271–272.

23 *Bombay Judicial Proceedings*, British Library, 399/35 dt. 23 June 1824, henceforth *BJP*.

24 *BJP*, P/400/9, no.32, dt. 24 August 1824.

such as the office of *chaudhuri*, the custom of the country was always followed rather than Islamic law. However, he added they were always allowed to settle family or private disputes among themselves as they chose.[25] Presumably those that could not be so resolved came before state-appointed authorities. We may recollect that Grewal points out that people could choose to take their cases to the *qazi*: clearly fewer people did so as his position weakened with changing regimes. Even where he functioned, he provided but a patina of Islamic law to the shifting dynamics of customary usage. The *qazi* thus survived into the regime of the Peshwas or Chief Ministers who gradually assumed control of the Maratha confederacy in the eighteenth century.

The Peshwa regime

Donald Davis has emphasized the centrality of jurisdiction to medieval Hindu law, meaning thereby the authority to pronounce the law even in the absence of the power to enforce it.[26] I will therefore look at the Maratha system in that context. The Peshwas were Chitpavan Brahmins who took several measures to revive the study of Sanskrit, including its jurisprudence. But it is striking that they did not seek to establish classical Hindu law. An undated memorandum compiled in the early 19th century described the administration of justice under the Peshwas in western Maharashtra between 1774 and 1795 CE. It began by saying that there were two successive Chief Justices (*mukhya nyayadhisha*) in this period: Ramshastri and Ayyashastri. The former became a famous figure in folklore, long revered as a wise and impartial judge. He is the subject of a well-researched biography by Sadashiv Athavale.[27] But the memorandum went on to explain that it was not the custom to call everyone who administered justice (*nyaya-insaf*) a judge. Those given administrative charge had that role ex officio. The governor of the coastal Konkan province had plenipotentiary powers wider than those of other governors. Within cities, such as Pune, minor disputes, thefts, and cases of misconduct were decided at the office of the *kotwal* (Town Commissioner). Justices (*nyayadhisha*) did not hear every complaint; if there was a major

25 *Reports of Civil Causes adjudged by the Court of Sudder Adawlut for the Presidency of Bombay, 1800–1824,* Bombay: Education Society's Press, 1862, vol.2, 39.

26 Donald R. Davis Jr., Centres of Law: Duties, Rights and Jurisdictional Pluralism in Medieval India," in *Legalism: Anthropology and History,* Paul Dresch, Hannah Skoda (eds.), 86–113, Oxford: Oxford University Press, 2013, here 87.

27 Sadashiv Athavale, *Ramshastri Prabhune: Caritra va Patre,* Pune: Srividya Prakasan, 1988.

money dispute or a quarrel over hereditary estates then the plaint would come to the regent Nana Phadnis through his secretaries. It would then be allotted to the appropriate officer to be settled. No one would take up a major case without a government order to do so; in lesser cases some court official might summon the parties, hear their plaints and make an award that satisfied them. But the respondent could not be punished without a government order.

If a dispute concerned estates (*watan*) or debts, evidence was taken in writing from the parties concerned and witnesses. Records and evidence of possession were scrutinized. "There was no practice of settling these on oral testimony alone." Measures were taken to ensure the respondent's attendance; if it was a major offense then a process-fee (*masala*) was collected with the summons. If someone was recalcitrant, his house or property could be seized to secure his attendance. It was rare for a respondent to evade a summons. But if he was sheltered by a powerful commander, then it might be necessary to issue a decree on the basis of other evidence with the annotation that the defendant had not appeared.

More usually, both were present whereupon the justice would usually gather a jury (*pancha*) acceptable to both, hear their assessment and give a decision with a summary of evidence and his own conclusions. If the written evidence in a debt dispute proved insufficient then a partial verdict might be given. Disputes over landed property often came before the justices. Here the jury would be drawn from the hereditary gentry of the county and adjoining ones. In money-cases involving books of account, the jury would consist of merchants who kept books themselves. Where mortgages of a house or estate were disputed, the jurors would be owners of similar estates and impartial men.

If a claim to a long-held estate was energetically made then the holder was asked to submit a written response and then the jury sat to decide if the case should proceed. The estate might sometimes be temporarily confiscated or it might not. Once written evidence had been taken, then estate-owning (*watandar*) witnesses might be gathered in a temple or made to bathe in a sacred river before recording their evidence. In business disputes various oaths might be administered. Where the case concerned a village boundary dispute, the claims would be recorded, village accounts and sketch-maps scrutinized, and the jury would be the headmen of five nearby villages with the hereditary chief and registrar of the county (*pargana*). They would gather at the spot. If no decision could be reached then the disputants would be asked to undergo an ordeal with the village headman or hereditary watchman asked to walk along the claimed boundary. (The assumption was that false evidence would bring down some calamity on the person or his household.) In all disputes, the winner and loser both paid fees – but the latter's was termed 'penalty'. The fees depended on the size of the estate and their individual capacity. The written award from the government was formally issued only after all fees and dues had been paid.[28]

So under this new Maratha regime, the Islamic judge was no longer the titular head of the judiciary. Should we seek a Hindu equivalent under the Maratha regime that succeeded the Mughals in western India? That does not seem to have been the case. As we noted, the Peshwas did create the office of chief judge (*nyayadhisha*), but the latter largely dealt only with cases that were referred to him by the executive. In his biography of Ramshastri, Athavale points out that no document can be found in which the justice both delivered a verdict and decreed a punishment. That power lay with the executive.[29] Even rituals of caste purification needed official sanction. Sadashiva Ganesha Kelkar was found guilty of murdering the (unnamed) wife of Gunaji Ganesha Tivrekar. He was imprisoned for ten years and then released, but had not yet been religiously purified for the crime. This would mean that he would still be excluded from the company of Brahmins and even of members of his own family. So he petitioned that the government impose a royal fine appropriate to his resources and order that he be purified of the sin. So it was ordered 1792–3, that both the royal fine and the Brahmin fine (*rajdanda va brahmadanda*) be collected from him and he be purified according with the appropriate rituals. The order was addressed to the government officer and the Brahmin assembly of the subdivision of Vijayadurg.[30] This case well illustrates the division of functions and incomes. The rites of purification could be only be administered if the government permitted it – caste membership was no longer just caste business. This sort of authority could also be farmed out to government appointees. So when Anandrao Kashi was appointed police commissioner or *kotwal* of the city of Pune in 1776, his letter of appointment included instructions to settle quarrels and disputes within the city after considering them in an impartial manner. Such fines and fees as could be secured thereby should duly be entered in the income ledgers of his office.[31] Sometimes the government would recognize a headman and assign judicial powers to him. So for instance, Ghasi, son of Dhanraj Naik of the palanquin (*palkhi*) bearer caste (*Kahar*), successfully petitioned for the right to settle all disputes within his caste and that

---

28 G. S. Sardesai, *Selections from the Peshwa Daftar*, 45 vols., Bombay: Government Central Press, 1931, 45: 134–142.
29 Athavale 1988, 9.
30 Vad 1902, VIII, 3, 88–89.
31 Vad 1902, VIII, 3, 126.

whenever a new *palkhi* was established, the leader of the crew should pay Ghasi a fee of five rupees.[32]

Centrally appointed officials could override caste heads too. It was reported that the Brahmins of the sacred city of Nasik drank alcohol and so Sarvottam Samkar was ordered to inquire. The Brahmins led by the hereditary moral censor (*dharmadhikari*) obstructed the inquiry. Therefore the hereditary post of moral censor was seized and the income arising from it was to be collected by a government clerk and credited to the provincial governor's account.[33]

In general, previous practice was deemed legitimate – thus Ramaji Mahadev headman of the village of Pimplas complained that he had hitherto decided all property disputes in that village, but now the district officer had usurped that jurisdiction. He had secured prohibitory orders on this earlier, but the fees and fines were still not being given to him. A new order was issued telling the officer concerned to let Ramaji's jurisdiction continue as heretofore.[34] In general, the norm seems to have developed that previous practice should continue. So, the Adilshahi officer of Wai district reproved a potter who had started digging his clay from a new site that he should not innovate or he would face punishment. A century later, there was a dispute between the village communities of Malegaon and Peth over the boundary between their lands. The Peth men seized the ploughs working on the disputed land and the Malegaon villagers said reprovingly: "Why do you seize the ploughs of Malegaon? And why do you break the old and do the new?"[35] Clearly then, the protocols of determining custom were the key to judicial process. Very often it depended on the testimony of the local community headed by its worthies. That process is exactly what Hasan has also found operative in urban Gujarat.[36]

The use of community heads' testimony was a common practice in Eurasia. As the introduction to this volume has pointed out, laws and rights were variously understood even in the European arena. That was despite the common heritage of ecclesiastical law and the medieval version of Roman law shared across the region. In India, the classical *dharmashastra* usually allowed for expedient variation and judicial discretion in matters of property, marriage, etc. Local customs, many texts argued, needed to be enforced even if they were shocking to those

32 Vad 1902, I, 199, year 1740–41.
33 Vad 1902, VIII, 3, 120.
34 Vad 1902, VIII, 3, 127.
35 Cited in: Guha 1998, 87–88.
36 Hasan 2006, 100–102.

from other regions.[37] We may recollect that Max Weber has pointed to the parallel strains in English common law where a hierarchy of royal courts existed parallel with the rough and ready administration of 'khadi justice' by the local worthies serving as magistrates. Furthermore, as he points out, the jury system acted as an obstacle to complete rationalization of the system.[38]

The line between crime and political subversion was also a blurry one, and at least in the *Arthashastra* both might fall under the head of the 'removal of thorns' – something done by judicial process or expedient violence. That pattern persisted even after a layer of Islamic law was added following the establishment of the Delhi and other sultanates in India. This in fact was exactly analogous to what Radhika Singha has noted as a feature of the Islamic law encountered by the East India Company in north India, where the Muslim law officers would advise the magistrate that offenses where the legal standard of proof was not attained could yet be punished *siyasat*, as an act of government.[39]

How are we to understand the salient features of this as a legal system in a diverse society? At one level, there was no conception of a hierarchy of fora – instead there was a rough idea of the ranking of disputes in order of magnitude. That magnitude seems to have depended not just on money value but on the nature of the property in dispute. So long-lasting property – hereditary claims, village boundaries – was especially important and adjudicated with the most care. On the other hand, the resolution of disputes was evidently a royal process, one in which governmental interests took precedence over abstract concerns. Ruling authority could not afford to give away justice nor could it appear to defy its underlying principles. Yet what were those principles given the diversity of persons, faiths and statuses in this cosmopolitan world? By the 18th century, a broad consensus seems to have settled around custom, ancient usage. As Gune said in 1953, "medieval society gave more importance to tradition and custom than to the written law."[40]

37 P. V. Kane, *History of dharmaśāstra : (ancient and mediæval religious and civil law)* 5 volumes, Poona : Bhandarkar Oriental Research Institute, 1930–1962, III:856–864.

38 Weber 1978, Vol II, 813.

39 Radhika Singha, *A Despotism of Law: Crime and Justice in Early Colonial India*, Delhi, New York: Oxford University Press, 1998, 63.

40 Gune 1953, 69.

The coming of 'English' law

The English East India Company took control of the island of Bombay in 1664, just as the Maratha regime began to rise in western India. It, of course, originated in a legal milieu where the King-in-Parliament was increasingly taking charge of statute law but a judge-made 'Common law' was yet vigorous. We may look at their judicial administration in the 17th and 18th centuries as an example of how this western legal regime was gradually acclimatized to the Indian setting. Bombay, unlike either Calcutta or Madras which were held in subordinate tenures from Indian rulers, was an island held in exclusive English sovereignty. This was a consequence of its cession by another European power – the Portuguese Crown. We also have good legal records from this site, comparable to those from the Maratha regime on the adjoining mainland. It therefore offers us a good example of legal acculturation in a land of diversity. The settlement was for many decades subordinate to the President and Council at Surat, a short voyage north, lodged in a prosperous city with a regular *qazi* supported by the Mughal governor. The politically and economically challenged Company was anxious to make its royal grant into a political and economic asset and sought to do so in the time-honored way by attracting settlers. But there were well established trading ports along the west coast, not merely Surat but also Goa and Diu among others.

The Company also had a notion that the administration of justice was an aspect of the sovereignty delegated to them by the King of England. It figured prominently in the memorandum describing his take-over written by Humfrey Cooke, the first governor.

> In this Island was neither Government nor Justice, but all cases of Law was carried to Tannay [Thane] and Bassin [Vasai], but now it is in his Majesties Jurisdiction there must be a setlement of Justice, according to such Lawes as his Majestie shall think fit.[41]

In practice, it would seem Portuguese estate-holders termed *foreiro mayor*, some lay and some clerical, had functioned as de facto judges. A petition of 225 lesser landholders "Catholiques and Mahometans and Gentiles Incorporated together" claimed that the *foreiros* or "Chief Farmers [of taxes]" used to bribe the Portuguese magistrates into supporting them. The petition asked the English not to permit any such *foreiros* on the island because "every one [of them] was a justiciary in

41 Shafa'at Ahmad Khan, *Anglo-Portuguese Negotiations Relating to Bombay, 1660–1677*, Allahabad University Studies in History, vol. III, London : Oxford University Press, 1922, 467. Spelling as in original.

his own house..."[42] This was supported in another letter, this from Gervase Lucas, a later governor in 1667:

> His Majestie and the Queen will have loud Outcries against me from the Jesuites, Barnardine de Tavora and Igius [Ignatius] de Miranda, which 3 have almost the whole island of Bombaim in their possession, with the Fishing in Salt Water, and power of Tribute over the People, power of punishment, imprisonment, whipping, starving, banishment; all which since my arrival I have secured the Inhabitants from, allowing no power to any to punish but by order of his Majesties Governour upon the place, or by such Justice of peace as are appointed by Governour ...[43]

The actual inauguration of a new legal system had to wait till 1672. At that time, Gervase Lucas, a new governor having come from Surat was presented by various communities with a petition from the "the severall Cast", i.e. assembled communities, for the establishment of English law. Lucas thereupon ordered George Wilcox to set up things as near as possible "according to the Custome and constitution of England". A proclamation was issued abolishing all Portuguese laws from the first of August 1673. Wilcox, a merchant who claimed legal background from three years in the Crown Prerogative office, was the first Judge. He agreed to draw his pay and maintain the establishment, including translators and runners, within a budget of 2000 rupees annually. A scale of fees and charges was laid down and the judicial establishment was designed to be self-supporting.[44] This reflected the chronic penury of the Bombay settlement. Early correspondence is full of plaintive requests for supplies and support for the chronically deficit establishment. This was fundamentally administration of justice by local worthies in the King's name even while it mimicked the forms of the royal courts. In practice (as we shall see), it was close to Max Weber's description of English justices of the peace, who dealt with the daily troubles and misdemeanors of the masses, as applying what he terms "khadi justice" with a focus on substantive outcomes rather than pre-set rules.[45] Not all Company officials believed that English judicial institutions could be transplanted. A prominent Director, Josiah Childe declared in 1688:

> The Company hope all Gentlemen know that the Governments of those Eastern parts of the world are merely despotical, and that the admired and beloved common laws of this Kingdom are plants too precious to be understood, or grow, so far Eastward, or on any other soil then that of our blessed Nation".[46]

---

42 Khan 1922, 451–453.
43 Khan 1922, 487. Orthography original.
44 Khan 1922, 491–494.
45 Weber 1978, Vol II, 814.
46 Cited in Khan 1922, 567.

But Childe's skepticism was disregarded by the early Company. Attracting merchants and settlers was a pressing concern and the Company was hopeful of drawing them to Bombay with the lure of religious freedom and an attractive judicial system. Supporting a degree of legal pluralism was one option that might bring settlers. A Company letter of 1669 observed, the Company did not "think it convenient to erect a judicature that should clash with our government ..." yet giving the Indian merchants they were courting the power to choose their own leaders "as a kind of moderators or superintendants (*sic*) over them" would do much to draw them to Bombay.[47] This extended much beyond the Gujarati merchants that the Company was eager to conciliate. In practice any major community was consulted on its own affairs.

Indeed, the Company was soon recognizing corporate bodies for the various "casts" to be found on the island and appointing heads of each of them. The administration of Bombay island itself found it necessary to adjudicate such appointments. So in 1723, the Chief Justice of the Crown court declared that:

> various and sundry disputes have arisen concerning ye right of administering the rites and ceremonies of the Gentoos of the Island and have continued a long time undetermined not only to the great prejudice of the person in whom the said right is vested, but also to the great detriment of the Island by the unlimited license of ye Brahmans resorting hither ... as several other ill-practices tending to disturb the peace and good government thereof.

So the claims of different parties having been examined and "twelve men, four from each caste having been examined and the opinion required under their hands whereby it is become their proper act and no objection can ever arise and they having unanimously given it as their opinion that the sole right of administering the said rites and ceremonies is vested in Shama Gharia [sic] Brahman (exclusive of all others....)"[48]

So the Mayor's court in the British colony on Bombay island heard a range of plaints and followed very much the same procedure as the Maratha judge. Muslims ('Moors') were reckoned as one of the 'castes' allowed autonomy. So for example:

> The Codjee [*qazi*] and the Chugulars [*chaugulas* – community leaders] having examined the Woman who accuses her husband of Sodomy give in a Present report that the Woman is a bad woman and they believe it is a Scandalous story raised by the Woman to get a Divorce ... Ordered for troubling the Court fifteen lashes in the publick Buzar & to return to her husband.[49]

---

47 William Foster (ed.), *English Factories in India 1668–9*, London: Clarendon, 1927, 239.
48 J. M. Campbell (ed.), *Materials towards a Statistical Account of the Town and Island of Bombay in Three Volumes*, Vol I., Bombay: Government and Central Press, 1893, 167–168 n.1.
49 *BJP*, P/416/99 Sitting of December 11, 1723.

Cases involving Muslims, such as that above, seem usually to have been settled by the *qazi* and *caugulas* or leaders of the community. But occasionally the *qazi* was the target himself, as for instance when "Esupjee Moorman" complained that he was unfairly treated over the dowry of his first wife when he married a second one. This plaint came before the Mayor's Court.[50]

Other caste leaders were similarly consulted in cases pertaining to their community: for example, Ram Matra was to marry a woman but "two persons to whom her former husband was indebted" impeded the marriage. The "heads of the Casts having Examined the affair, declare this to be no Lawfull Impediment & that the partys may marry. Ordered accordingly."[51] Even what might seem to be normal cases under commercial law were referred to community heads, such as this one involving the Roman Catholic *cast*:

> Louisia D'Silva petitioning the Court concerning a Slave Wench sold her & which proved Sickly & Incapable of service, this having been referred to three principall persons of the Cast they give it as their opinion that their (*sic*) being a great while Elapsed since the bargain was made and no application or complaint in two years; the agreement ought to stand good which the Court confirms.[52]

The practice was described and defended by the Mayor and Council in 1730 when they were charged by the Surat Council of infringing their charter by dabbling in religious disputes. They replied that many cases of "meum and Tuum (sic)" have an "Immediate Relation to the laws and Customs of the Respective Casts" and that the earlier English court in Bombay would "appoint the Heads of the Cast to examine into such disputes and to make report to them for their Information they then confirm'd or reversed as they thought proper ..."[53]

Diverse communities were thus recognized as "castes"; so for example when an affray resulted because the Prabhus insisted on carrying a separate umbrella in a religious procession, the Mayor gathered the "Principall persons of the Sev[eral] Casts of the Island in number Fiveteen (sic), Including the Portugueze Christians Moors and Persees" to ask if they knew of any such customary right.[54]

The first decades of the 19th century saw efforts by the new colonial administration to compile usage and custom and incorporate these into new printed codes that were to guide judges in the Company courts. This resulted in large compila-

50 *BJP*, P/416/99, April 29th 1724.
51 *BJP*, P/416/99, March 4, 1723/4.
52 *BJP*, P/416/99, April 29th, 1724.
53 India office records, V/416/103 fos. 129 ff.
54 *BJP*, 416/99, March 25th, 1724.

tions by Harry Borradaile and Henry Steele for coastal Gujarat and Maharashtra respectively. Amrita Shodhan recently published a careful analysis of the process. She has emphasized the extent that the Company's government was prepared to recognize castes (of all faiths) as political communities, capable of managing their own affairs. In both regions, the role of community consensus dwarfed that of textual law.[55] This is a process that was also reported from Khandesh in the north and Satara to the south.

For the western peninsula, Steele was told that among Brahmins, apart from the general jurisdiction of the Shankaracharyas of the four great monastic establishments, there were officers of the *dharma* who held their offices as hereditary and partible property. They exercised jurisdiction over Brahmins of particular sects or places. They could investigate offenses and levy fines. We saw, however, that in cases of major delinquency the government might set their power aside. The right to officiate at religious ceremonies or to pronounce the auspicious moment was a separate function. It covered all Hindu castes that did not have separate priests of their own.[56]

Max Weber has argued that both autocratic potentates and democratic polities were historically averse to 'rational' abstract and formal justice and preferred justice either according to precedent, revelation or concrete ethical valuation on a case-by-case basis.[57] This propensity was certainly strongly evident in the adjudicatory practices of all the regimes we have considered in western India. But in the 1820s the impulse to a 'rationalization' of the law began to appear, with general propositions being put to community leaders. It was this that produced compilations such as Steele and Borradaile authored. But Borradaile also offers us a glimpse into the resistance of communities to submit to even this degree of formalization of their legal practice. A key element of 'traditional' structures was that headship was adjudicated and enforced by political authorities. We have many instances of this in the Maratha-ruled territories. In the eighteenth century the government of Bombay seems to have favored and consulted one Shamachari Brahmin as an authority on Hindu law and ritual. He may have profited to get himself named into a post analogous to that of hereditary *dharmadhikari*.

Such stable authority seems to have begun to decline in the early nineteenth century in the mobile and competitive world of coastal Gujarat. As a result, Bor-

---

55 Amrita Shodhan, Caste in the Judicial Courts in Gujarat, in *The Idea of Gujarat: History, Ethnography and Text*, Edward Simpson, Aparna Kapadia (eds.), 33–49, New Delhi: Orient Blackswan, 2010.

56 A. T. Steele, *The Law and Custom of Hindoo Castes of the Dekkun*, London: W. H. Allen, 1827, 83.

57 Weber 1978, Vol II, 976–77.

radaile had great difficulty in finding authorities who he could consult as heads of particular castes. By 1820, the succession of rival powers, fragmentation of sovereignty and active market society in Gujarat seems to have moved authority into the hands of caste members several degrees further than Farhat Hasan found a century earlier. Borradaile, tasked with assembling the customary law of Gujarati castes parallel to Steele's inquiry, reported that

> in Gujarat, every member of a Cast upholds his Prerogative of voting in Cast matters with the utmost vigilance, no Bundobust is considered fully valid without the signatures of all members ...
>
> In the Dekhun, it appears one man is allowed to state the Rules in the name of the whole, here it is impossible, every one would cry out, and in the smallest Cast such an attempt would excite suspicion and be opposed...[58]

So each adult male householder was here effectively a sharer in judicial authority – conflicts would then inevitably result in resort to those who had the capacity to enforce verdicts. One obvious agency would be colonial courts and these took over a larger and larger part of caste authority. The other would be economically important 'shets' or financial magnates. He wrote that he did not even try to get a statement of customs from the "Bunyan" castes of Surat because he knew that Atmaram Bhookun, the head of the group was "known to be hostile to the plans of Government ..." He therefore hoped to influence Atmaram through an East India Company officer, Romer. Once his compliance was secured then all other opposition would vanish.[59] The authority of such powerful men can be discerned in Borradaile's narrative of his travails. But if there were such intense internal factions within each community, authority would de facto be thrown into the hands of colonial authorities and their appointed agents.

Conclusion

So where then did the law reside? So many persons and institutions clearly shared in the processes of its making! The law did not just cope with diversity: legal processes actively created it via disagreements and decisions that revised or ignored previous ones. As Borrodaile discovered, the process of recording the

58 *BJP*, P/400/7.
59 *BJP*, Pros. P/400/7 18 July 1827, no.46

verdict of a caste council could itself create a new council. Borradaile tells us that not only did a settlement need the signature of all the members, but they had to sign in order of precedence. "So if one through accident or enmity signs out of his place, all those injured thereby call off and refuse their sanction to the Public Deed and thenceforward make a separate Party."[60] How then, one may ask, was anything such as custom ever recognizable? I would revert to an answer that I have already given in an early exploration of these processes. Apart from a "local community's sense of fairness, the contestants' relations with their neighbors, their local standing and reputation, connections and powers, would all come into the picture. The judicial process, the process of conflict resolution, was designed to allow full play to local political processes."[61] The judicial process was transparently a political process.

References

Alam, Muzzafar, *The Crisis of Empire in Mughal North India: Awadh and the Punjab, 1707–48,* Delhi, New York: Oxford University Press, 1986.

Athavale, Sadashiv, *Ramshastri Prabhune: Caritra va Patre,* Pune: Srividya Prakasan, 1988.

Bombay Judicial Proceedings, British Library.

Campbell, J. M. (ed.), *Materials towards a Statistical Account of the Town and Island of Bombay in Three Volumes*, Vol I., Bombay: Government and Central Press, 1893.

Davis Jr., Donald R., Centres of Law: Duties, Rights and Jurisdictional Pluralism in Medieval India," in *Legalism: Anthropology and History,* Paul Dresch, Hannah Skoda (eds.), 86–113, Oxford: Oxford University Press, 2013.

Elliott, C. A., *The Chronicles of Oonao, A District in Oudh*, Printed for private circulation only. Allahabad: 1862.

Foster, William (ed.), *English Factories in India 1668–9,* London: Clarendon, 1927.

Grewal, J. S. (ed.), *In the by-Lanes of History: Some Persian Documents from a Punjab Town*, Simla: Indian Institute of Advanced Study, 1975.

Guha, Sumit, An Indian Penal Regime: Maharashtra in the Eighteenth Century, *Past and Present* 147 (1995): 101–126.

Guha, Sumit, Rules, Laws and Powers: A Perspective from the Past, in *Rules, Laws, Constitutions: A Perspective for Our Times*, S. Saberwal (ed.), 83–96, New Delhi: Sage Publications, 1998.

Gune, Vithal Trimbak, *The Judicial System of the Marathas, 1400–1800,* Poona: Deccan College, 1953.

Hallaq, Wael B., *Sharīa: Theory, Practice, Transformations,* Cambridge: Cambridge University Press, 2009.

60 Ibidem.

61 Guha 1998, 93.

Hasan, Farhat, *State and Locality in Mughal India: Power Relations in Western India, c.1572–1730*. Cambridge: Cambridge University Press, 2006.
Kane, P. V., *History of dharmaśāstra : (ancient and mediæval religious and civil law)* 5 volumes, Poona : Bhandarkar Oriental Research Institute, 1930–1962.
Khan, Shafa'at Ahmad, *Anglo-Portuguese Negotiations Relating to Bombay, 1660–1677*, Allahabad University Studies in History, vol. III, London: Oxford University Press, 1922.
Kikani, L. T., *Caste in the Courts*. Rajkot: Ganatra, 1912.
Kulkarni, A. R., Jiziya in the Maratha Country, in *Medieval Deccan History. Commemoration Volume in Honour of P.M. Joshi*, A. R. Kulkarni, M. A. Nayeem, T. R. De Souza (eds.), 156–184, Bombay: Popular Prakashan, 1996.
Maitland, F. W., Montague, F. C., *A Sketch of English Legal History*, New York: G.P. Putnam's Sons, 1915.
Parasnis, D. B., *Itihasa Sangraha* (periodical) 1907–1916, no.1–3.
Reports of Civil Causes adjudged by the Court of Sudder Adawlut for the Presidency of Bombay, 1800–1824, Bombay: Education Society's Press, 1862, vol.2.
Sardesai, G. S., *Selections from the Peshwa Daftar*, 45 vols., Bombay: Government Central Press, 1931.
Shivacharitrasahitya Volume 5, in *Bharata Itihasa Samshodhan Mandal Quarterly*, vol. 16, 1935–1936, Pune: 1936.
Shodhan, Amrita, Caste in the Judicial Courts in Gujarat, in *The Idea of Gujarat: History, Ethnography and Text*, Edward Simpson, Aparna Kapadia (eds.), 33–49, New Delhi: Orient Blackswan, 2010.
Singha, Radhika, *A Despotism of Law: Crime and Justice in Early Colonial India*, Delhi, New York: Oxford University Press, 1998.
Steele, A. T., *The Law and Custom of Hindoo Castes of the Dekkun*, London: W. H. Allen, 1827.
Vad, G. C. (ed.), *Selections from the Satara Raja's and Peshwa Diaries*, 8 vols., Poona: Deccan Vernacular Education Society, 1902.
Weber, Max, *Economy and Society: An Outline of Interpretive Sociology*, Guenther Roth, Claus Wittich (eds.), 2 vols., Berkeley: University of California Press, 1978.

Corinne Lefèvre

Beyond diversity

Mughal legal ideology and politics

Introduction

In his *Muntakhab al-tawarikh*, the historian ʿAbd al-Qadir Badaʾuni (d. c. 1615) recorded the following dispute between the Mughal emperor Akbar (r. 1556–1605) and the scholars (ulema, sing. *ʿalim*) of his court:

> The first of the questions (*musa'il*) which the emperor asked in these days[1] was this: 'How many freeborn women may a man legally marry by *nikah*[2]?' The ulema answered that four was the limit fixed by the Prophet. The emperor thereupon remarked that in his early youth he had not regarded the question and had married what number of women he pleased [...], [but] he now wanted to know what the remedy (*ʿilaj*) [for his situation] was. Each [of the present] said something [different]. Then, the emperor remarked that Shaikh ʿAbd al-Nabi[3] had once told him that one of the *mujtahids*[4] had allowed as many as nine wives. Some of the ulema replied that [...] some had even allowed eighteen from a too literal translation of [...] the Qurʾan [...]; but this tradition (*riwayat*) is rejected. [...] After much discussion (*radd-u-badal*), the ulema, having collected all the different traditions (*jamʿ-i riwayat-i mutanauwiʿ*) on the subject, opined (*fatwa dadand*) that, by *muʿta* [temporary marriage], a man was allowed (*mubah*) to marry any number of wives he pleased and that such marriages were considered licit (*ja'iz*) by Imam Malik Rahmatallah[5] [...]. [At this point] Naqib Khan fetched a copy of the *Muwatta* by Imam Malik, and pointed to a Hadith according to which *muʿta* was forbidden (*manʿa*).
>
> [Another] night [...], the emperor sent for me [...] and asked me what my opinion was on this subject. I said: 'The conclusion to be drawn from so many conflicting traditions and different schools of law (*riwayat-i mukhtalaf wa mazahib-i gun-a-gun*) in a word is this: the followers of Imam Malik Rahmatallah and the Shiites are unanimous in looking upon *muʿta* as permissible (*mubah*); Imam Shafiʿi and the great Imam [Hanifa][6] [...] look upon *muʿta* as

1 That is to say, in the period following 1575, when Akbar began to stage religious debates in the *ʿibadat khana* (house of praise) of his new capital Fatehpur Sikri.

2 *Nikah* is the "regular" form of marriage in Islam.

3 Between 1566 and 1579, Shaikh ʿAbd al-Nabi (d. 1583) served as *sadr al-sudur*, the head officer in charge of *madad-i maʿash* grants (revenue of tax-free lands given in charity to religious or worthy individuals) and of the appointment of judges throughout the empire.

4 A *mujtahid* is an individual who is qualified to exercise *ijtihad* (lit. "exerting effort", independent reasoning) on questions concerning the sharia.

5 Malik b. Anas (d. 796) was the eponymous founder of the Maliki school of law (*mazhab*).

6 Al-Shafiʿi (d. 820) and Abu Hanifa (d. 767) were the eponymous founders of the Shafiʿi and

DOI 10.1515/9783110423327-006

> illegal (*haram*). But should a *qazi* [judge] of the Maliki school sign an order (*hukm*) [making *mu'ta*] lawful, *mu'ta* also becomes lawful according to the great Imam [Hanifa] [...].' This pleased His Majesty very much [...].
>
> The emperor then said: 'I appoint Qazi Husain 'Arab Maliki as *qazi* for this case (*mas'ala*) [concerning my wives] [...].' Qazi Husain immediately [...] issued a decree according to his own school of law making *mu'ta* licit (*ja'iz*). [...] From this day onward, the road of opposition and discord (*rah-i khilaf wa ikhtilaf*) lay open until the advent of the time of *ijtihad*.[7]

This passage is interesting for several reasons. First, and in view of the comparative perspective underlying the present volume, the story narrated by Bada'uni interestingly echoes another legal conflict which had opposed political and religious authorities a few decades earlier in Europe, a dispute whose roots also lay in matrimony and which had eventually similarly resulted in the emancipation of royal power from ecclesiastical control: the reference is here, of course, to Henri VIII of England's (r. 1509–1547) clash with the Pope regarding the annulment of his marriage with Catherine of Aragon and to the ensuing creation of an independent Church of England with the king as its supreme head. Second, and more importantly for the purpose of this essay, the episode recorded by Bada'uni encapsulates a number of important points concerning the legal dimensions of the Mughal empire.

The first and most salient issue is the absence of a unanimously agreed version of sharia (Islamic law) throughout the Muslim world in general and in Mughal India in particular: even though the Hanafi *mazhab* is often said to have prevailed within the empire, the events described by Bada'uni indicate, along with other pieces of evidence, that this hegemony was far from being absolute and that "pragmatic eclecticism"[8] across the boundaries of other Sunni (Maliki, Shafi'i) as well as Shiite legal schools also existed. Besides the inner diversity of Islamic law, Mughal rulers also had to deal with the existence of an altogether different set of socio-religious norms that have long been deemed binding for the vast majority of their subjects, that is to say the Hindu *dharma*. Just as sharia, "Hindu Law" was, in practice, equally plural and made up of multiple layers

---

Hanafi schools of law respectively.

7 I have slightly modified the English translation given in 'Abd al-Qadir Bada'uni, *Muntakhab al-tawarikh*, translated by G. S. A. Ranking, W. H. Lowe, T. W. Haig, 3 vols. Delhi: Renaissance Publishing House, 1986 (reprint), II: 211–213. For the Persian original, see 'Abd al-Qadir Bada'uni, *Muntakhab al-tawarikh*, Kabir al-Din Ahmad, M. A. Ahmad 'Ali, W. N. Lees (eds.), 3 vols. Calcutta: Asiatic Society of Bengal, 1864–1869, II: 207–210.

8 The phrase is borrowed from Ahmed Fekry Ibrahim, The Codification Episteme in Islamic Juristic Discourse between Inertia and Change. *Islamic Law and Society* 22 (2015): 157–220, here 159, where the reader will find an in-depth reflection on this form of pragmatism in Islamic law.

of codes such as special rules for castes (*jatidharma*), regions (*deshadharma*) or kingdoms (*rajadharma*).[9] As pointed out by Donald R. Davis, "one partially unifying feature of these social locations of the law was their relationship to the jurisprudential tradition of *dharmashastra*, a huge scholastic corpus of Sanskrit texts and commentaries devoted to religious and legal duty."[10] The existence of these two different sets of religiously inspired laws did not mean, however, that they exclusively applied to Muslims and Hindus respectively. As several scholars have demonstrated in recent years, Hindus did not hesitate to turn to sharia and the *qazis*' courts for purposes of notarial registration, to sustain their claims in litigation or to obtain rulings more to their own advantage – all such cases signaling the reality of forum shopping for the non-Muslim subjects of the Mughal empire.[11] In addition to the norms deriving from the Muslim and Hindu traditions, a third set of rules – *zawabit* (sing. *zabitat*) or state legislation – that may be roughly equated with administrative *cum* penal law also impacted a number of aspects of Mughal society. Originating in the monarchs' *siyasa* (political) power and their ensuing legislative capacity – a capacity which was, however, far from unanimously accepted by the ulema, this set developed cumulatively through the *farmans* or edicts of succeeding emperors.[12] To sum up, then, there

9 Ingo Strauch, Dharma. In *Brill's Encyclopedia of Hinduism*, Knut A. Jacobsen, Helene Basu, Angelika Malinar and Vasudha Narayanan (eds.), vol. 2, 736–743, Leiden: Brill, 2010.

10 Donald R. Davis Jr., Centres of Law: Duties, Rights and Jurisdictional Pluralism in Medieval India. In *Legalism. Anthropology and History*, Paul Dresch, Hannah Skoda (eds.), 86–113, Oxford: Oxford University Press, 2012, here 88.

11 Farhat Hasan, *State and Locality in Mughal India. Power Relations in Western India, c. 1572–1730*, Cambridge: Cambridge University Press, 2004, ch. 6. M. L. Bhatia, *The Ulama Islamic Ethics and Courts Under the Mughals. Aurangzeb Revisited*, New Delhi: Manak, 2006, ch. 6. Nandini Chatterjee, Reflections on Religious Difference and Permissive Inclusion in Mughal Law. *Journal of Law and Religion* 29:3 (2014): 396–415. See also Sanjay Subrahmanyam, Peasants before the Law: Recent Historiography on Colonial India. *Études rurales* 149–150 (1999): 199–209, here 200, for an example of Christian appeal to the *qazi*'s court.

12 Even though some scholars have argued that the Mughals continued to stick to the *tura-i chingizi* – a body of rules supposedly instituted during Chingiz Khan's reign and also referred to as *yasa* – long after they settled in India, a close scrutiny of contemporary Indo-Persian sources shows that the impact of the *tura* on Mughal law-making was actually very limited and its use mostly confined to situations of acute political crises (especially succession struggles). See Corinne Lefèvre, Recovering a Missing Voice from Mughal India: The Imperial Discourse of Jahāngīr (r. 1605–1627) in his Memoirs. *Journal of the Economic and Social History of the Orient* 50:4 (2007): 452–489, here 466, for a demonstration of this point during Jahangir's reign, and Mansura Haidar, The Yasai Chingizi (Tura) in the Medieval Indian Sources. In *Mongolia. Culture, Economy and Politics (Indian-Mongolian Assessment)*, S. Bira, M. Haidar, R. C. Sharma, K. Warikoo (eds.), 53–66, Delhi: Khama Publishers, 1992, for an analytical survey of Indo-Persian materials bearing on *tura*.

were at least three (complementary and in some cases concurrent) normative frameworks coexisting within the Mughal empire (sharia, *dharma* and *zawabit*), none of which had achieved a significant degree of standardization by the heyday of the dynasty in the 1650s. Besides, all of them had to accommodate the local customs and usages (*ʿurf-u-ʿada*) ingrained in the countless villages, towns and cities whose aggregation constituted the imperial dominions.

How the Mughals addressed the legal diversity that characterized their territories is the second major issue raised by the account of Badaʾuni. It is also the main focus of the present article, which is primarily concerned with the legal ideology and politics of the Mughal empire and not, or only very secondarily, with jurisdictional pluralism and the ways in which subordinate groups and individuals interacted with, and manipulated to their own ends, the legal diversity and pluralism the dynasty allowed for.[13] If the imperial perspective adopted in this essay may appear outdated to specialists of the European and Ottoman early modern powers (fields in which state law and the royal discourse on law have long received considerable attention[14]), it is worth emphasizing here that the Muslim polities which came to dominate large swathes of South Asia between the thirteenth and the eighteenth centuries have so far rarely been examined from this point of view.[15] Far from ambitioning to fill such a vast historiographical gap, the present contribution simply aims at pointing out some of the avenues explored by the Mughals to think about and to manage the legal diversity of their territories.

---

13 For examples of the recent historiographical emphasis on legal pluralism in early modern empires, see: Lauren Benton, *Law and Colonial Cultures. Legal Regimes in World History 1400–1900*, Cambridge: Cambridge University Press, 2002, for a global perspective; Karen Barkey, Aspects of Legal Pluralism in the Ottoman Empire. In *Legal Pluralism and Empires, 1500–1850*, Lauren Benton, Richard J. Ross (eds.), 83–108, New York: New York University Press, 2013, on the Ottoman case; Hasan 2004, and Chatterjee 2014 on the Mughals.

14 See e. g. Lauren Benton, Richard J. Ross, Empires and Legal Pluralism: Jurisdiction, Sovereignty, and Political Imagination in the Early Modern World. In *Legal Pluralism and Empires, 1500–1850*, Lauren Benton, Richard J. Ross (eds.), 1–17, New York: New York University Press, 2013. And Jeroen Duindam, Jill Harries, Caroline Humfress, Nimrod Hurvitz, Introduction. In *Law and Empire. Idea, Practices, Actors*, Jeroen Duindam, Jill Harries, Caroline Humfress, Nimrod Hurvitz (eds.), 1–22, Leiden: Brill, 2013, for two contrasted assessments of this historiographical legacy.

15 For a similar assessment of the historiography of the Mughal empire, see M. Reza Pirbhai, A Historiography of Islamic Law in the Mughal Empire. In *The Oxford Handbook of Islamic Law*, ed. Anver M. Emon and Rumee Ahmed (eds.). Oxford online, 2016, online available under: http://www.oxfordhandbooks.com/view/10.1093/oxfordhb/9780199679010.001.0001/oxfordhb-9780199679010-e-65 (10/04/2016).

Except at its very margins, the rulers did not, by and large, attempt to interfere with "Hindu law": albeit the practice of *sati* (ritual burning of widows) was, for instance, strongly discouraged, it was never officially prohibited by the state.[16] The situation was altogether different concerning the sharia and its traditional exponents, the ulema. True, the inner diversity of Islamic law was at times used by the monarchs to their own benefit, as has been illustrated above with the case of Akbar's appointment of a Maliki (rather than a Hanafi) *qazi* to make his multiple marriages lawful. Another well-known example of "pragmatic eclecticism" as practiced by Mughal rulers dates from the time of Akbar's great-grandson Aurangzeb (r. 1658–1707): while the monarch actively participated in the imperial project of legal centralization and homogenization through his commissioning of the *Fatawa-i ʿAlamgiri* (1664–1672) – the largest compendium of Hanafi jurisprudence (*fiqh*) ever produced in Mughal India on which more will be said below, he did not hesitate to contravene the legal opinions (*fatawa*, sing. *fatwa*) recorded in the text when the latter did not suit his political needs. If we are to believe the *Ahkam-i ʿAlamgiri* attributed to Hamid al-Din Khan, the emperor refused to act according to a decision by the chief *qazi* concerning the fate of war prisoners because he deemed it too lenient. Instead, he gave the judge the following instructions: "This decision [is] according to the Hanafi school; decide the case to some other school, so that control over the kingdom may not be lost. Ours is not the rigid Shia creed, that there should be only one tree in an entire village. Praised be God! There are four schools [of Sunni law] based on truth, [each] according to a particular age and time."[17] The *qazi* complied and proposed a new decision supposedly based on the *Fatawa-i ʿAlamgiri* – and therefore in accordance with the Hanafi *mazhab* – but sentencing the prisoners to death, to which Aurangzeb readily agreed.[18]

If, then, the Mughal monarchs occasionally manipulated the inner diversity of Islamic law (and its accompanying contradictions and ambiguities) for the sake of political expediency,[19] they more generally tended to consider it an impediment to the central authority they strove to establish in their dominions, and they therefore developed a number of strategies to absorb it. One of them was

---

16 See e. g. Badaʾuni 1986, II: 388.

17 Hamid al-din Khan, *Ahkam-i ʿAlamgiri*, translated by J. Sarkar, Anecdotes of Aurangzib, Calcutta: M. C. Sarkar & Sons, 1925, 141–142.

18 The episode is also analyzed by Alan M. Guenther, Hanafi *Fiqh* in Mughal India: The *Fatāwá-i ʿĀlamgīrī*. In *India's Islamic Traditions, 711–1750*, Richard M. Eaton (ed.), 209–230, Delhi: Oxford University Press, 2003, 224.

19 Far from being an exclusive imperial prerogative, manipulation of sharia was a widespread practice among ulema as well as subordinate groups, both Muslims and Hindus (Hasan 2004, ch. 5 and 6).

the elevation of the ruler to the status of law-giver and supreme legal authority in the empire – an option that was inaugurated by Akbar in the second part of his reign, as suggested by Bada'uni in the last sentence of the passage quoted above. In fact, his mention of "the advent of the time of *ijtihad*" is a direct reference to the promulgation, in 1579, of the famous *mahzar* – a document signed by the principal ulema of the empire and declaring the monarch's status to be higher than that of the *mujtahids*, thereby emancipating his domination from the control of Muslim jurists.[20] Such a claim was not, however, limited to Mughal territories but extended to the wider Islamic world and endowed Akbar with a juridical-religious authority theoretically surpassing that of his Safavid and Ottoman competitors.[21] As has been argued by Azfar Moin,[22] Akbar's bold step in legal matters may be linked to the well-known messianic pretensions the ruler nurtured in the context of the upcoming Islamic millennium (1591–1592), one of the Mahdi (Messiah)'s hallmarks being his ability to restore justice to the world through the reformation of religious law. Fortified by Akbar' success in establishing the emperor's superiority over the ulema in matters of legal authority and by the capacity of his successors Jahangir (r. 1605–1627) and Shah Jahan (r. 1628–1658) to uphold such a balance of power, Aurangzeb was able to adopt a more flexible and accommodating attitude towards the jurists and to entrust them with the unfinished imperial project of standardizing Islamic law. The aforementioned *Fatawa-i ʿAlamgiri* is the best-known result of this process of religious-legal homogenization which, as rightly pointed out by Muzaffar Alam and Sanjay Subrahmanyam, ran parallel to increased imperial legislative activity and visibility in the non-religious domains.[23]

The third point raised – albeit more indirectly – by the account of Bada'uni is the question of the evidence available to the historian willing to reconstruct the legal life and proceedings of the Mughal empire. Unlike the Ottoman case which is documented by a rich corpus of *sijills* (registers of cases from the courts of the *qazis*), the Mughal judicial records are much less abundant, especially for the period preceding the middle of the seventeenth century, a scarcity that should

---

20 Having stated the superior status of the Mughal as *sultan-i ʿadil* ("just ruler"), the *mahzar* further acknowledges his ability to opine on religious questions (*musa'il-i din*) on which the *mujtahids* do not agree but also to issue new rulings (*hukm*), provided they do not contradict the Qur'an and are advantageous to mankind (Bada'uni 1864–1869, II: 271–272, and 1986, II: 279–280).

21 Francis W. Buckler, A New Interpretation of Akbar's 'Infallibility' Decree of 1579. *Journal of the Royal Asiatic Society, New Series* 56: 4 (1924): 591–608.

22 A. Azfar Moin, *The Millennial Sovereign. Sacred Kingship and Sainthood in Islam*, New York: Columbia University Press, 2012, ch. 5.

23 Muzaffar Alam, Sanjay Subrahmanyam, Introduction. In *The Mughal State (1526–1750)*, Muzaffar Alam, Sanjay Subrahmanyam (eds.), 1–71, Delhi: Oxford University Press, 2000 (reprint), here 31.

be understood in connection with the absence of centralized imperial archives, with each judge probably keeping his own records.[24] A number of disseminated archival collections do, however, shed occasional light on local urban and rural transactions and disputes. This is for instance the case with two sets of seventeenth-eighteenth-century documents produced in Surat and Cambay that have been thoroughly examined by Farhat Hasan in his *State and Locality*; one should also mention the "proceedings" of the Benares *dharmasabha*s or *parishad*s (councils) of Brahmins – whose function was to settle disputes or prescribe penances in matters of Hindu law through oral or written *responsa* (*nirnayapatra*) – on which Rosalind O'Hanlon has recently worked extensively.[25] The relative dearth of Mughal judicial records notwithstanding, a systematic and in-depth study of the documents and collections so far identified still remains a desideratum today.

This is all the more true of the vast corpus of doctrinal and jurisprudential literature which, in spite of its particular value for understanding the complex intellectual trajectory of law(s) and legal traditions(s) in Mughal India, has generally been left out by historians of the empire. Jurisprudential compilations and compendia especially, whether they belonged to the scholarly tradition of *fiqh* or of *dharmashastra*, have long been discarded on account of their supposed aloofness *vis-à-vis* the world of judicial practice and the Mughal political context more generally. Following in the steps of Wael B. Hallaq who, back in the mid-1990s, had already argued for a much more composite nature of legal manuals, Mouez Khalfaoui has recently made a similar case for the *Fatawa-i 'Alamgiri* by pointing out the fact that the authors of the digest systematically rejected the opinions of the Central Asian branch of the Hanafi *mazhab* when it came to the treatment of non-Muslims and instead favored earlier Iraqi Hanafi jurists and their more accommodating *fatwa*s regarding *kafir*s (or unbelievers).[26] As shown by Ali

24 Pirbhai 2016, who also provides a useful survey of Mughal legal documents.

25 Hasan 2004, ch. 5 and 6; Rosalind O'Hanlon, Speaking from Siva's temple: Banaras scholar households and the Brahman 'ecumene' of Mughal India. *South Asian History and Culture* 2:2 (2011): 253–277 and Rosalind O'Hanlon, Letters Home: Banaras pandits and the Maratha regions in early modern India. *Modern Asian Studies* 44:2 (2010): 201–240. For other recent analyzes of legal documents produced in the Mughal empire, see Bhatia 2006, ch. 6; Chatterjee 2014, and Nandini Chatterjee, *Mahzar-namas* in the Mughal and British Empires: The Uses of an Indo-Islamic Legal Form. *Comparative Studies in Society and History* 58:2 (2016): 379–406.

26 Wael B. Hallaq, Model *Shurūṭ* works and the dialectic of doctrine and practice. *Islamic Law and Society* 2:2 (1995): 109–134; Mouez Khalfaoui, *L'islam indien: pluralité ou pluralisme*. Frankfurt am Main: Peter Lang, 2008 and Mouez Khalfaoui, Together but separate: How Muslim scholars conceived of religious plurality in South Asia in the seventeenth century. *Bulletin of the School of African and Asian Studies* 74:1 (2011): 87–96.

Anooshahr's essay in this volume, the *Fatawa-i ʿAlamgiri* are also reflective of the changed balance of power between the monarch and the ulema since the time of the Delhi Sultanate. Both contributions therefore rightly emphasize that the *Fatawa-i ʿAlamgiri* should be seen as the result of a dynamic dialogue between the Hanafi juridical tradition and the socio-religious and political conditions prevailing in contemporary Mughal India. In addition, these fruitful insights into the *Fatawa-i ʿAlamgiri* are important because they open a promising path for a larger and much needed (re)consideration of the *fiqh* literature produced in the empire.[27] The same possibly holds true for the numerous *dharmashastra*s written under Mughal domination, especially of those which were sponsored by subordinate Raja rulers – like Mitramishra's twenty-two-volumes *Viramitrodaya* patronized by Bir Singh Deo of Orchha in the 1630s[28] – or those which were composed by Brahmin intellectuals connected to the Mughal court, such as the descendants of the famous Narayana Bhatta.[29] As a matter of fact, an interesting way to look at the question of law and diversity in pre-colonial India would be to investigate more closely and more comparatively the parallel genres of legal opinions and manuals in the *fiqh* and *dharmashastra* traditions in the perspective of an intellectual and socio-political history of law: such an investigation would usefully complement the emphasis that has been laid on the "hard evidence" of judicial records in the past decades and also provide a methodological tool for comparison with European *responsa*.

To conclude this brief survey of the sources at hand for the study of law(s) in the Mughal empire, mention should be made of the official documents and texts emanating from central power, be it in the guise of *farmans*, *dastur al-ʿamals* (rules of governance), letters or chronicles. True, the latter do shed light on the activities of emperors as law-makers and judges, as well as on the judicial functions of a number of officials (*subadar*, *faujdar*, *kotwal*, etc.) besides the *qazi*. It is worth emphasizing, however, that the royal ordinances contained in such documents seem to have been seldom collected into more comprehensive codes of law and to have circulated in this form throughout the empire: despite the very

---

27 No systematic description of this corpus has been attempted to this day. Nor is there any equivalent for the Mughal period of Zafarul Islam's work on *fatawa* literature under the Delhi Sultanate, see Zafarul Islam, *Fatāwā Literature of the Sultanate Period*. Delhi: Kanishka, 2005.

28 For a brief description of this monumental text, see Pandurang Vaman Kane, *The History of Dharmaśāstra (Ancient and Mediaeval Religious and Civil Law)*, 5 vols. Poona: Bhandarkar Oriental Research Institute, 1930–1962, here I: 440–446.

29 For further details on their works, see: Kane 1930–1962, I: 432–440. Dara N. Marshall, *Mughals in India. A bibliographical survey of manuscripts*. London, New York: Mansell Publishing, 1967, n°1679 and 1401.

heteroclite materials it included, the *A'in-i Akbari* – the second part of the well-known *Akbar Nama* by Abu'l Fazl (d. 1602) – is probably the one text that most closely approximates this, admittedly Western, idea of a general code of law, as is indeed shown by the text's swift translation into English in the 1770s under the evocative title of *The Institutes of emperor Akbar.*[30] As to the materials explicitly delineating the emperors' vision of the legal diversity inherent to their dominions or recording the particulars of their discussions on this topic with contemporary jurists, they are (at least to my knowledge) remarkably few. One such source is Bada'uni's *Muntakhab al-tawarikh*, but it should be pointed out that, in the end, the information the text provides on the precise content of the religious-legal debates held at Akbar's court are quite scarce, the passage quoted as an opening to this essay being actually the only one detailing the proceedings of such exchanges. By contrast, the recently discovered *Majalis-i Jahangiri* by ʿAbd al-Sattar ibn Qasim Lahauri (d. after 1619) bears ample evidence of Jahangir's profound interest in matters of law and of the various reactions his ambitions in the legal domains elicited from within the ranks of the empire's law experts. It is therefore a good case study for thinking about the dynasty's legal ideology and politics.

Imperial perception and management of legal diversity in the *Majalis-i Jahangiri*

Building on the literary traditions of *munazara* (disputation) and *malfuzat* (teachings of a Sufi master), the *Majalis* are at once a record of the night sessions held at Jahangir's court between 1608 and 1611 and a spiritual handbook (*dastur al-ʿamal*) for the newly enrolled disciples of the monarch.[31] As a *malfuzat*, the *Majalis*' main function was to unveil the messianic nature of the monarch who called himself a "universal manifestation" (*mazhar-i kull*) of God – something Sattar skillfully manages to do through the narration of Jahangir's oneiric encounters with the

---

30 Even though imperial *dastur al-ʿamals* multiplied in the course of the seventeenth century, their content and reach were generally more circumscribed. For further details on the context and purpose of the *A'in-i Akbari*'s English translation by Francis Gladwin, see Robert Travers, *Ideology and Empire in Eighteenth-Century India. The British in Bengal*, Cambridge: Cambridge University Press, 2007, especially ch. 3.

31 For a short intellectual biography of the author of the *Majalis-i Jahangiri*, see Corinne Lefèvre, ʿAbd al-Sattār b. Qāsim Lāhawrī. In *Encyclopedia of Islam, THREE*, Kate Fleet, Gudrun Krämer, Denis Matringe, John Nawas Everett Rowson (eds.), fasc. 1, 6–8, Leiden: Brill, 2015.

divine,[32] the miracles he performed thanks to his capacities as a seer[33] and, most importantly for the present purpose, the discussions he conducted with a wide range of religious specialists, from Brahmins and Muslim ulema and Sufis to Jesuit and Jewish scholars.[34] These discussions are highly instructive on several accounts. First, the religious diversity of their participants testifies to the breadth of the monarch's pretensions. Second, most of these debates concentrate on the legal dimensions of the religious traditions represented at court with, however, the exception of the exchanges with the Jesuits which focused on doctrinal and scriptural questions.[35] Third, Jahangir's interventions in the discussions consistently illustrate his determination to act upon the 1579 *mahzar* and to follow in the steps of his predecessor Akbar as supreme legal authority of the empire and of the various communities it included, be they Muslim or not. By positioning himself along such lines, the monarch also meant to demonstrate his capacity to renew (*tajdid*) the "world of religion" through the exercise of his intellectual faculties (*ʿaql*), which he considered an independent source of knowledge.

Before proceeding to the analysis of the religious-legal discussions recorded in the *Majalis-i Jahangiri*, it is worth stressing the fact that the text also contains a

---

32 ʿAbd al-Sattar ibn Qasim Lahauri, *Majalis-i Jahangiri*, A. Naushahi M. Nizami (eds.), Tehran: Miras-i Maktub, 2006, 26–27, 58 and 110–111.

33 See e. g. ʿAbd al-Sattar 2006, 93–94.

34 For brief descriptions of some of these exchanges, see: Reyaz Ahmad Khan, Jahangir on *Shias* and *Sunnis* in *Majalis-i Jahangiri*. In *Proceedings of the Indian History Congress, 72nd Session*, 302–307. Aligarh: Aligarh Historian Society, 2012 and Reyaz Ahmad Khan, Jahangir and Muslim Theology-Discussions Reported in the *Majalis-i Jahangiri*. In *Proceedings of the Indian History Congress, 71st Session*, 236–242. Calcutta: Indian History Congress, 2011; Shireen Moosvi, The Conversations of Jahangir 1608–11: Table Talk on Religion. In *Proceedings of the Indian History Congress, 68th Session*, 328–332, Delhi: Indian History Congress, 2008. For more in-depth analyses, see Muzaffar Alam, Sanjay Subrahmanyam, Frank disputations: Catholics and Muslims in the court of Jahangir (1608–11). *Indian Economic and Social History Review* 46:4 (2009): 457–511 and Anna Kollatz, *Inspiration und Tradition. Strategien zur Beherrschung von Diversität am Mogulhof und ihre Darstellung in Maǧālis-i Ǧahāngīrī (ca. 1608–11) von ʿAbd al-Sattār b. Qāsim Lāhōrī*, Berlin: EB-Verlag, 2016, especially 117–130 and 216–278.

35 For Jahangir's discussion of Judaism's prescriptions for marital life, see ʿAbd al-Sattar 2006, 265–266, 268. Interestingly enough, the discussion was based on the *Suhuf-i Ibrahim* (Scrolls or Book of Abraham) which the emperor had had translated into Persian by "Yusuf the Jew." Albeit mentioned in the Qurʾan, the *Suhuf-i Ibrahim* are generally considered a lost body of scripture. One is therefore left to wonder what text was actually translated at the Mughal court, even though the nature of the subjects discussed would point in the direction of the Torah (mentioned as such in the text p. 118 as *taurit*). For further details on the Jewish presence at the Mughal court, see Walter J. Fischel, Jews and Judaism at the Court of the Moghul Emperors in Medieval India. *Proceedings of the American Academy for Jewish Research* 18 (1948–1949): 137–177.

number of references to the function of the *diwan-i khass* (the hall of private audience where the debates were conducted) and the assemblies held there as a royal court of justice for all the empire's subjects. A survey of the cases brought before the monarch shows that the *diwan-i khass*, just as the *mazalim* courts of the ʿAbbasid and early Mamluk periods,[36] was mostly concerned with administrative and penal law: in the course of its sessions, Jahangir thus released a convicted heretic out of consideration for his father as well as a number of other prisoners,[37] ruled against a Brahmin who claimed that his stipend had not been paid for twelve years,[38] unmasked the author of a theft thanks to his skilled practice of physiognomy (*tafarrus* or *firasa*),[39] compensated a man for the usurpation of his *madad-i maʿash* grant by a local *jagirdar* (holder of temporary fiscal rights over a specified territory),[40] reprimanded an amir whose abuses of power had been reported by the people of Panjab, [41] and cleared another imperial official of charges of corruption.[42] Interestingly, two other cases recorded by ʿAbd al-Sattar seem further to indicate that the jurisdiction of the *diwan-i khass* also included, like that of the *siyasa* courts of the late Mamluk empire, areas such as property and contract laws that were normally within the purview of the sharia courts of the *qazis*.[43] The first one involved inheritance: upon the parricide of his gamekeeper Ismaʿil, Jahangir adjudicated – in contravention of escheat regulations applying to all Muslims of the empire – that Ismaʿil's money and goods (*naqd-u-jins*) should be transferred to his brother Kamal.[44] The second civil dispute is especially signif-

---

36 Literary meaning "abuses of power", the term *mazalim* (sing. *mazlima*) "came to denote the structure through which the temporal authorities took direct responsibility for dispensing justice" (Jørgen S. Nielsen, Maẓālim. In *Encyclopaedia of Islam, Second Edition*, Charles E. Bosworth, Emeri van Donzel, Wolfhart P. Heinrichs, Charles Pellat (eds.), vol. 6, 933–935, Leiden: Brill, 1986, here 933).

37 ʿAbd al-Sattar 2006, 22–24, 265 and 268.

38 ʿAbd al-Sattar 2006, 95, and *infra* in this essay.

39 ʿAbd al-Sattar 2006, 104–105. On the admissibility of evidence based on *firasa* in the sharia courts of the *qazis*, see Baber Johansen, Signs as Evidence: The Doctrine of Ibn Taymiyya (1263–1328) and Ibn Qayyim al-Jawziyya (d. 1351) on Proof. *Islamic Law and Society* 9:2 (2002): 168–193, here 188–189.

40 ʿAbd al-Sattar 2006, 207–208.

41 ʿAbd al-Sattar 2006, 219–220.

42 ʿAbd al-Sattar 2006, 271–272.

43 For stimulating reflections on these *siyasa* courts and on the Mamluk sultans' increasing intervention in the legal system during the fourteenth-sixteenth centuries, see Yossef Rapoport, Royal Justice and Religious Law: *Siyāsah* and Shariʿa under the Mamluks. *Mamlūk Studies Review* 16 (2012): 71–102.

44 ʿAbd al-Sattar 2006, 246–247.

icant because it relates to exchanges (*mu'amala*): the plaintiff complained that after he had concluded a transaction worth 40 000 rupees with an individual, that same person had torn to pieces the written document (*khatt*) recording the deal and, even though several people had witnessed the scene, none of them was willing to testify. Another remarkable point in this *majlis* is the method used by the monarch to judge the affair: following the plaintiff's suggestion, he ordered the accuser and the accused to be tried by fire ordeal. Seeing the stupefaction that his order had aroused among the participants in the session who equated ordeal with oppression, he hastened to explain his decision: having intuited that the plaintiff was a liar and knowing that he would be the first of the two men to be tried by ordeal, he had meant the burning of his hand to be his punishment rather than a test of his innocence.[45] In most of the instances mentioned above and whatever field of law they pertained to, Jahangir is unequivocally seen performing his judicial duties, pronouncing sentences over cases brought before him as a last resort by people dissatisfied with earlier judgements and using the *diwan-i khass* as a supreme court of appeal. In addition to acting as *qazi al-quzat* (judge of the judges) – a not altogether unconventional role for a Muslim monarch – and as the following pages will show, the ruler also appears in the course of his exchanges with Brahmins and ulema as a full-fledged legist possessing the highest degree of competence in jurisprudence.

Even though debates with Hindu interlocutors are only two in the *Majalis-i Jahangiri*, they interestingly all depict the monarch as a rightful interpreter of *dharma* who was perfectly entitled to act as an arbiter in the legal disputes brought before him. During the twenty-sixth night session, Jahangir thus stepped into a discussion between Rajputs who were trying to decide whether the antelope (*nil-gaw*) belonged to the species (*nau'*) of deer (*ahu*) or of bovid (*gaw*), in order to know whether the consumption of its meat was lawful (*halal*) or unlawful (*haram*). After having listened to the arguments of both parties whose attempt to recast a debate about *dharma* in Islamic terms is noteworthy, the monarch concluded this dispute as follows: "If the antelope belonged to the species of bovid, its female would, like the cow, wear horns on its head; but it does not have any [horns], just as the doe. It is therefore clear that the antelope belongs to the species of deer and not of bovid;" in other words, the deer was *halal* because the cow was not. On hearing such words of wisdom, 'Abd al-Sattar concluded, all the present showered praise on the emperor.[46]

---

45 'Abd al-Sattar 2006, 254–255.

46 'Abd al-Sattar 2006, 64–65. According to the *Nemivijaya nirvana rasa* (1617) by Krpasagara (Marshall 1967, n°938), the Jain monk Nemisagara Upadhyaya also brought before Jahangir a

Taking place a few months later, the second discussion is all the more interesting because it illustrates the combined functions of the imperial *majlis* as a judicial assembly and as a forum for juridical disputes, but also because it is the only debate recorded by ʿAbd al-Sattar involving Hindu scholars. This particular disputation was actually triggered by the arrival in the *diwan-i khass* of a Brahmin from Gujarat who belonged to the retinue of the Rajput amir Ram Das Kachhwaha and who claimed to have been in the service of the Mughals for twelve years without, however, having received any remuneration in exchange. His coming to the court was therefore a last resort solution to which he was probably compelled by financial straits. Even though Jahangir quickly uncovered the falsity of his claim and therefore dismissed his petition, the emperor lingered as he remembered having met the man eighteen years before and details about his physical appearance (he had no beard) and sartorial preferences (he wore a dhoti and refused pyjamas)[47] sprang to his mind. At this point of the session, a Brahmin called Pathan Mishra[48] stepped into the conversation and said: "Brahmins from Gujarat reproach us for eating meat (*gusht*), and we say [back] to them: 'You abstain from meat but you drink water out of *mashk*, [flasks] which are made of the skin of living beings (*jandar*).'" He added that the Gujarati Brahmins' rejection of trousers derived from mere imitation (*mahz-i taqlid*) and had no rationality (*maʿqulat nadarad*). Whatever the unidentified Gujarati Brahmin had to say in his defense is unfortunately not recorded in the *Majalis-i Jahangiri*, and the discussion thereafter switched to why the Hindus, although they worship the cow (*gaw-ra miparastand*), hold its remains (*nim-khwurda*) to be polluted (*palid*) and consider its mouth the most impure (*napak*) of all its organs. By way

---

dispute concerning a book which had been severely criticized by two leaders of the Tapa Gaccha sect.

47 The dhoti is a long, unstitched clothing which Hindu men traditionally wrapped around their waist, whereas pyjamas refer to a type of trousers that gained popularity during the Sultanate and Mughal periods. For further details on the representations associated with these different types of garments, see Emma Tarlo, *Clothing Matters: Dress and Identity in India*. Chicago: The University of Chicago Press, 1996, 28–29. I am grateful to Catherine Clémentin-Ojha for having pointed out the reference to me.

48 Mentioned as PT(H)AN MSR in the *Majalis-i Jahangiri* and as THYAN MSR in Jahangir's memoirs or *Jahangir Nama* (Nur al-Din Muhammad Jahangir, *Jahangir Nama. The Jahāngīr Nāma. Memoirs of Jahāngīr, Emperor of India*, translated by W. M. Thackston Washington, D. C. and New York: Freer Gallery of Art and Arthur M. Sackler Gallery, Smithsonian Institution & Oxford University Press, 1999, 104), the man is very probably identical to Pathan Mishra Jajipuri, one of the two Sanskrit pandits who assisted Nizam al-din Panipati in the Persian rendition of the *Yogavashista* which he presented to Jahangir (then still known as prince Salim) in 1597. I am grateful to Shankar Nair for having brought to my attention this possible identification.

of answer, Pathan Mishra narrated the following story. In ancient times, when the tyranny (*sitamkari*) of Bala-Vrtra[49] prevailed, the heads of the *devatas* (i. e. devas or deities) came to see Brahma and asked for his help to restore order to the world. Brahma advised them to get hold of the bones of a Brahmin ascetic named Dadhich (the well-known Dadhicha of the *Mahabharata*), from which they would be able to make arms and weapons of war and to destroy the demon (*diw*). The devas found Dadhich in a state of meditation and had a cow lick his back in order to bring him back to consciousness, the animal also serving to protect them from the blaze of the ascetic's splendor. At this point, Pathan Mishra interrupted his narration and emphasized that this was the reason the Brahmins gave to explain why the protection of the cow (*hifz-i gaw*) was mandatory (*wajib*) in their religion (*dar din-i ishan barhama*). When Dadhich woke up, Pathan Mishra continued, he agreed to give his bones to the devas but he added that he should first perform his ablutions in all the *tirthas* ("pilgrimage place") of the earth, which were at once presented to him by the deities. However, before abandoning his body to the devas, Dadhich cursed the cow and said to it: "May your mouth always remain impure (*napak*)." And this is why, Pathan Mishra concluded, the Hindus do not consider the remains of the cow to be pure. But Jahangir was not satisfied with the latter's explanation and he instead suggested that the true reason behind such a belief was that the cow cleaned the filth of its nose with its tongue. The imperial argument brought the discussion to a close, and all the participants in the *majlis*, including Pathan Mishra, approvingly prostrated before the monarch.[50]

If, in this instance, Jahangir does not seem to have been particularly eager to settle the dispute between two competing Brahminical communities and the contrasting sartorial and dietary rules they adhered to, he did not miss the opportunity to discard the mythical explanation offered by Pathan Mishra and stressed instead the hygienic foundations underlying the Hindu ban on beef,[51] thereby

49 I am grateful to Audrey Truschke for her help in identifying these two mythical figures. The story narrated by Pathan Mishra constitutes a late version of the legendary battle between Indra, king of the gods, and the demon brothers Vrtra and Bala, that originally appeared in the Vedas and was subsequently retold in a number of Sanskrit texts, including the *Mahabharata* and some Puranas.

50 'Abd al-Sattar 2006, 95–98. The sources of the section on the cow are difficult to ascertain: while the cow's intervention in Indra's making of the *vajra* out of the bones of Dadhica appears to be mentioned in the *Agni Purana* (Harish Johari, *The Healing Power of Gemstones: In Tantra, Ayurveda, & Astrology*. Rochester (Vermont): Destiny Books, 1988, 8–9), the development on the impurity of the cow and of its mouth bears the unmistakable imprint of *dharmashastras*.

51 Interestingly, a similar hygienic argument was also used by Jahangir to explain the Shiite ban on eating fish without scales ('Abd al-Sattar 2006, 117–118).

making clear to all the present (especially the Brahmin pandits) his supreme expertise in matters of *dharma*. In the end, however, the emperor's intervention on this occasion, as well as in the other discussions concerning Hindu socio-religious norms,[52] was relatively benign and positive, his remarks generally aiming at explaining such rules on a rational and scientific basis and not at discrediting them. If the snapshots provided by the *Majalis-i Jahangiri* are any indication of a larger trend, it seems that, with regard to *dharma* at least, the emperor's arbitrations ultimately resulted in the legitimation of existing norms. An altogether different image emerges from the much more numerous jurisprudential debates pertaining to the sharia whose provisions the monarch considered either inadequate or contradictory. Despite the universal idiom in which the spiritual pretensions of the ruler were formulated and the presence, in the night sessions of the *diwan-i khass*, of representatives of Hinduism, Christianity and Judaism, there is little doubt that Jahangir's efforts to renovate the "world of religion" were primarily directed at Islam and at those ulema who, in his eyes, were trapped in the formalism of the sharia and satisfied with legal conformism (*taqlid*).[53]

It comes out particularly clearly from the ninety-sixth *majlis* during which the monarch bombarded with questions an anonymous *qazi*. The first imperial query was about the validity of a divorce (*talaq*) granted without notifying the spouse. The *qazi* replied that this was permitted and seized the opportunity to lecture Jahangir on the different types of divorce allowed by the sharia. Far from

52 See also ʿAbd al-Sattar 2006, 13–14 for Jahangir's defense of Hindu ritual ablutions during solar and lunar eclipses. On the other hand, the emperor's only mention in the text of Hinduism as a set of metaphysical beliefs is very derogatory (p. 72).

53 Whereas *taqlid* (lit. "imitation", citation or following of a qualified jurist) has long been considered by historians of Islamic law a symbol of the supposed rigidification and stagnation of sharia following the so-called "closing of the gate of *ijtihad*" during the tenth century, it has recently been the object of a thorough historiographical reevaluation emphasizing continuity (rather than opposition) between the once-imagined binaries of *taqlid* and *ijtihad* (for further details, see Ahmed Fekry Ibrahim, Rethinking the *Taqlīd-Ijtihād* Dichotomy: A Conceptual-Historical Approach. *Journal of the American Oriental Society* 136:2 (2016): 285–303, especially 163–169). Such a favorable evaluation of *taqlid* is, however, conspicuously missing from Akbari and Jahangiri imperial sources: in this body of texts, the term is used pejoratively to denote, beyond its technical juridical sense, the idea of blind imitation *vis-à-vis* any kind of transmitted knowledge (*naql*) and is therefore construed as an antithesis of the notion of intellect (*ʿaql*) which the Mughals meant to embody and to promote. The manipulation of the term *taqlid* in official histories is further illustrated by its range of use, chroniclers regularly employing it to discredit the ulema who had voiced scepticism about (if not outright opposition to) the juridical-religious claims of the *padshah*: compare for instance Abu'l Fazl, *Akbar Nama*, translated by H. Beveridge, 3 vols., Calcutta: The Asiatic Society, 2000 (reprint), III: 390–400 with Badaʾuni 1864–1869, II: 211–212 and 272.

being impressed by the *qazi*'s display of his knowledge of *fiqh*, the emperor ruled such a divorce invalid (which is actually standard in Hanafi law): if not informed of the separation, he said, the wife may unwittingly commit all kinds of "forbidden and illegal" (*manhi wa na-mashru*ʿ) acts. In a bid to pacify the monarch, the *qazi* readily agreed with his judgement but was soon put on the spot with another question: what were the provisions of the Islamic law regarding an individual who had taken possession of someone's house by force? Was this person's prayer still valid (*durust*)? In answer, the *qazi* began by stating that there were several opinions on the subject according to the different schools of jurisprudence (*mazhab*) before exposing the one that he deemed the most correct (*asahh*): the prayer of such a person was still valid, he argued, but was considered defective (*naqis*) inasmuch as divine worship required purity of cloth, body, and place. In this case, Jahangir asked half-jokingly, what about the prayer of a monarch who had arbitrarily (*ba-zulm*) seized the house of somebody? Even though the *qazi* rejected outright the very idea that a just emperor (*padshah-i ʿadil*) could thus misbehave, the monarch insisted and cornered the *ʿalim* by reminding him that the conquest of Khandesh by Akbar had been considered illegal by a number of amirs:[54] "emperors," he concluded, "always cause individual wrongs for the common good" (*padshahan daʾim zarar-i khass bara-yi nafʿ-i ʿamm karda-and*). Overcome by the monarch's arguments, the *qazi* had no choice but to acknowledge the illegality of certain royal practices such as execution as a punishment for theft (instead of the amputation of hands dictated by the *hudud* injunctions found in the Qurʾan) or the patronage of singing and music (*naghma wa saz*).[55] If, then, the Islamic law voiced by the ulema is here depicted as ultimately coming up against the ruler's *siyasa* and the reason of state, it is however the sharia's inner contradictions and irrational character that are most often the object of Jahangir's criticisms.

In late August 1611, the emperor for instance challenged the scholars present – Qazi Shukr,[56] Maulana Shukrallah Shirazi[57] and Maulana Taqiyya (Muham-

---

54 Situated in the northwest Deccan, Khandesh was ruled by the Muslim dynasty of the Faruqis from 1370 to 1601.

55 ʿAbd al-Sattar 2006, 236–238.

56 Badaʾuni 1986, II: 191 mentions a Qazi Shukr in charge of Mathura in the time of Akbar. Pending further information and research, it is however impossible to establish whether Badaʾuni's and ʿAbd al-Sattar's Qazi Shukr were one and the same.

57 At the time of the composition of the *Majalis-i Jahangiri*, Shukrallah Shirazi was an Iranian newcomer to the Mughal court, even though he had previously enjoyed the patronage of the amir ʿAbd al-Rahim Khan-i Khanan in Burhanpur. For further details on his life and career (he was later to become one of Shah Jahan's most influential prime ministers under the title of Afzal

mad Taqi al-Din) Shushtari[58] – to answer the following question: to which of her two husbands a remarried widow would be reunited on the day of Resurrection (*qiyamat*)? Considering that the Prophet's wives (several of whom had been widows) would necessarily be at Muhammad's sides on the Day of Judgment, Qazi Shukr argued in favour of the second husband. The monarch, however, immediately discarded his opinion on the grounds that it derived from mere devotion (*taʿabudi*) and instead enjoined him to produce a rational proof (*dalil-i ʿaqli*) in support of his interpretation. Shifting to a legal perspective, the ulema emphasized that since the widow was regarded as a possession (*tasarruf*) of her second husband at the time of her death, she would therefore join him in the hereafter. So what would happen in this case, countered the emperor, if the second husband came to die before her? In these conditions, the scholars replied, she would be reunited with her first spouse. The rest of the debate is unfortunately not recorded in the *Majalis-i Jahangiri*, but ʿAbd al-Sattar's closing remarks leave little doubt as to the identity of its champion: "Each of the Hanafi and Shafiʿi ulema said something [different] according to his knowledge and talent (*danish wa rasaʾi*), but since himself [Jahangir] had fortunately sat on the throne of investigation (*masnad-i tahqiq*), none of them could lay claim to the chair of reason (*kursi-yi maʿqul*)."[59]

While there are plenty of other discussions staging the inability of Muslim jurists to tune up in order to provide a common answer to the monarch's queries or to justify the provisions of the sharia on a rational basis, I would like to conclude the present foray into the *Majalis-i Jahangiri* with one last debate. The latter is especially significant because it indicates that imperial ambitions in matters of religious law went far beyond the sphere of *fiqh* and touched upon its scriptural sources, first among them the Qurʾanic revelation. Carried on during two sessions in early November 1610,[60] the dispute was triggered by the recitation of the Qurʾanic verse "To you your religion, and to us our religion" – a verse which made the monarch wonder why Islam otherwise prescribed the elimination of unbe-

---

Khan), see ʿAbd al-Baqi Nahawandi, *Maʾasir-i Rahimi*, M. Hidayat Husain (ed.), 3 vols., Calcutta: The Asiatic Society of Bengal, 1910–1931, here III: 27–30. Shaikh Farid ibn Maʿruf Bhakkari, *Zakhirat al-khawanin*, S. M. Haq (ed.), 3 vols., Karachi: Pakistan Historical Society, 1961–1974, here II: 255–256.

58 Also a native of Iran, Taqiyya Shushtari entered Mughal service under Akbar. He translated several works of advice from Arabic into Persian, and his deep knowledge of history earned him the title of Muwarrikh Khan ("Lord Chronicler"). According to Nahawandi 1910–1931, III: 682, he held the office of *sadr al-sudur* in 1615, but this statement is not corroborated by any other source.

59 ʿAbd al-Sattar 2006, 265–266.

60 ʿAbd al-Sattar 2006, 121–126.

lievers (*kafiran*).[61] In response to Jahangir's interrogations, the *qazi* of the army (*qazi-yi ʿaskar*) remarked that this verse had been in use (*maʿmul*) only until the time when the order to kill the unbelievers (*hukm ba qatl-i kuffar*) was revealed, following which it was abrogated (*mansukh gasht*). By indirectly acknowledging the existence of contradictions within the Qur'an, the *qazi* had inadvertently opened a breach into which the emperor eagerly stepped. As a matter of fact, the discussion thereafter deviated from legal issues and revolved around the tricky question of the abrogation (*naskh*) of Qur'anic verses, Jahangir questioning the soundness of keeping within the scripture and of carrying on the recitation (*tilawa*) of those verses whose ruling (*hukm*) was no longer deemed binding for the *ʿumma* (community of believers). Even after he had been explained by Maulana Ruzbih Shirazi[62] the three modes of abrogation that the ulema had established since the eighth century to deal with apparent inconsistencies within and between the Qur'an and the Sunna and, beyond, to stabilize the Islamic law, the emperor stuck to his position.[63] In a bold move, he even suggested to expel from the Qur'an those verses whose ruling was no longer binding (*andakhtan-i an az qur'an*), thereby openly challenging the integrity of the sacred text. At this point, Shukrallah Shirazi stepped up in the discussion and sided with his colleague against the monarch, countering the latter's proposal with the theory of

---

61 Reference is here to the sixth verse of the sura 109 known as "The Unbelievers" (*al-Kafirun*): dating from the first Meccan period, the sura "is said to have been revealed in response to a proposal made by the Meccan polytheists to simultaneously or alternatively worship Allah and the idols" (Régis Blachère, *Le Coran. Traduction selon un essai de reclassement des sourates*, 3 vols. Paris: Maisonneuve & Larose, 1947–1950, II: 125). In this respect, sura 109 contrasts with later suras of the Medinan (post-Hegira) period, some of them advocating a more aggressive attitude *vis-à-vis* non-Muslims.

62 Ruzbih Shirazi's career is very poorly documented. Apart from his interventions recorded in the *Majalis-i Jahangiri*, he is credited by a mid-seventeenth biographical dictionary with the composition of an astronomical work (*Kitab-i zij*) together with the better-known Mulla Muhammad of Thatta (Bhakkari 1961–1974, II: 373).

63 The three modes of abrogation are the following: *naskh al-hukm duna l-tilawa* (abrogation of the ruling but not of the recitation); *naskh al-tilawa duna-l hukm* (abrogation of the recitation but not of the ruling); and *naskh al-hukm wa-l-tilawa* (abrogation of the ruling and of the recitation), this last category actually referring to missing verses in the written version of the Qur'an. On the theory of abrogation and its role in Muslim juristic theory and jurisprudence, see Andrew Rippin, Abrogation. In *Encyclopaedia of Islam, THREE*, Kate Fleet, Gudrun Krämer, Denis Matringe, John Nawas, Everett Rowson (eds.), Brill online, 2015, online available under http://referenceworks.brillonline.com/entries/encyclopaedia-of-islam-3/abrogation-COM_0104 (15/06/2015), for a useful introduction and John Burton, *The sources of Islamic law. Islamic theories of abrogation*, Edinburgh: Edinburgh University Press, 1990, for an in-depth analysis.

the inimitability (*i'jaz*) of the Qur'an.[64] Jahangir, however, declared the argument invalid in the case of those verses whose very words (*lafz*) had been abrogated. Driven to the wall, the Maulana had no choice but to invoke "divine wisdom" (*hikmat-i ilahi*) in order to justify the keeping of those verses in the scripture. Resorting to devotion in the midst of a disputation with the Mughal was however, as already suggested above, a particularly clumsy move as Shukrallah was about to discover for himself. Addressing him, Jahangir ordered: "Say: 'I am unable to give a rational explanation and I stand guilty (*ma'qul namitawanam wa mulzam shudam*)." Having confessed to his weakness, the Maulana lowered his head in submission, and the session ended with the amir Mirza 'Aziz Koka's intervention in favour of the ulema who were allowed more time to consult their books (*kitabha*). The discussion resumed the following night along very similar lines, the only new element introduced by the scholars being their equation of the recitation of the Qur'an with a meritorious act (*sawab*) – a line of reasoning that the monarch refuted by pointing out that, in this case, no verse should be abrogated as to recitation. Jahangir further supported his general argument by mentioning a verse whose recitation had, according to him, been abrogated. Ironically, it is precisely the reference to this verse that brought to a close the lengthy debate on abrogation. Ruzbih Shirazi having remarked that the aforementioned verse was actually not part of the Qur'an, the focus of the discussion thereafter shifted on the difference between the Qur'an (the words of God transmitted to Muhammad through the angel Gabriel) and the holy (*qudsi*) *hadis* (the words of God directly transmitted to Muhammad) – a topic on which the emperor does not seem to have been willing or able to impose his views. The debate thus ended in a relatively pacified atmosphere starkly contrasting with the (contained) violence that had presided over most of the monarch's exchanges with the ulema, especially with Shukrallah Shirazi.

Conclusion

What conclusions may be drawn from the *Majalis-i Jahangiri* concerning the Mughals' approach to religious law and its inner diversity? 'Abd al-Sattar's table-talks first and foremost show how important the interactions between messianic

64 For an introduction to the doctrine of inimitability, see Gustav E. von Grunebaum, I'djāz. In *Encyclopaedia of Islam*, Second Edition, Bernard Lewis, Victor L. Ménage, Charles Pellat, Joseph Schacht (eds.), vol. 3, 1018–1020, Leiden: Brill, 1986.

and rationalist elements were in the formulation of the *padshah*'s legal authority. On the one hand, the text unmistakably indicates that, for Jahangir, "presiding over the new post millennial order"[65] involved the implementation of Akbar's messianic program through his own continued efforts to reform religious law and to go beyond existent normative frameworks – missions that were traditionally described as the hallmarks of the Mahdi: under his dispensation, ʿAbd al-Sattar writes unequivocally, "the ancient laws were destroyed and the foundations of justice renewed" (*zabitaha-yi kuhan-ra barham zada wa bina-yi ʿadalat jadid nihadand*).[66] On the other hand, the *Majalis-i Jahangiri* also make clear that the ruler's and, beyond, man's active intellect was thought of as the key instrument of renovation in the juridical-religious sphere (in much the same way as experimentation was used to test authoritative traditions concerning questions of natural philosophy). In other words: while Jahangir's authority was deeply rooted in a sacred and mystic idiom, he simultaneously set out to promote reason as a new universal law and his own person as its chief apostle, in keeping with the contemporary development of rational sciences (*maʿqulat*) and philosophy at work in both Muslim and Hindu intellectual circles.[67] From this perspective, it seems that the monarch took a step further than the Safavid shahs who, until the end of the first quarter of the seventeenth century, were satisfied with patronising the adherents of legal rationalism (*usulis*) at the expense of traditionists (*akhbaris*).[68] In addition to his unswerving support to the "rationalist school" which was by then already well-established in the Mughal empire (notably thanks to the immigration of Iranian scholars trained in the Shirazi philosophical tradition), Jahangir not only did his utmost to be recognized as the leader of that intellec-

---

65 I am here borrowing from Ali Anooshahr's apt phrase (Ali Anooshahr, Review of A. Azfar Moin, The Millennial Sovereign: Sacred Kingship and Sainthood in Islam. *The Medieval History Journal* 18:1 (2015): 183–191).

66 ʿAbd al-Sattar 2006, 247.

67 On the sixteenth-seventeenth-century reinvigoration of rational sciences in the Muslim world, see Rula J. Abisaab, *Converting Persia. Religion and Power in the Safavid Empire*, London, New York: I. B. Tauris, 2004; Ali Anooshahr, Shirazi scholars and the political culture of the sixteenth-century Indo-Persian world. *Indian Economic and Social History Review* 51:3 (2014): 331–352 and Khaled El-Rouayheb, The Myth of "The Triumph of Fanaticism" in the Seventeenth-Century Ottoman Empire. *Die Welt des Islams* 48 (2008): 196–221. On the contemporary development of a "new reason" within Hindu philosophy, see Jonardon Ganeri, *The Lost Age of Reason. Philosophy in Early Modern India 1450–1700*, Oxford: Oxford University Press, 2011.

68 For a useful introduction to the Akhbari-Usuli dispute and further references on the topic, see Robert M. Gleave, Akhbāriyya and Uṣūliyya. In *Encyclopaedia of Islam, THREE*, Kate Fleet, Gudrun Krämer, Denis Matringe, John Nawas, Everett Rowson (eds.), Brill online, 2016, online available under http://dx.doi.org/10.1163/1573-3912_ei3_COM_0029 (16/09/2016).

tual movement but also overstepped the limits that usually constrained Sunni ulema: in the hands of the emperor-*cum-mujaddid* (renewer), reason became an instrument for the renovation and standardization of Islamic law as well as a means to rid the Qur'anic revelation of its contradictions. Needless to say, such reason-based criticism did not apply to the monarch's messianic claims.

Yet, there is no denying that Jahangir's ambitions in the legal domain never translated into any concrete policy of reform. In point of fact, no text comparable to the *A'in-i Akbari* or to the *Fatawa-i 'Alamgiri* – two works that purported to bring some measure of standardization into state legislation and sharia respectively – is known for his reign.[69] Besides, his reformist zeal with regard to sharia does not seem to have had much impact in practice, at least if we are to believe the few notarial and judicial archives that have so far received attention from historians. Among the many seventeenth-century cases of property rights, marriage and divorce brought before the *qazi*s of Surat and Cambay that have been examined by Farhat Hasan, none bears the trace of Jahangir's propositions recorded in 'Abd al-Sattar's text even though, admittedly, none exactly matches the situations described in the *Majalis-i Jahangiri*. Noteworthy is also the fact that the emperor's religious-legal claims are nowhere mentioned in the writings of contemporary ulema and Sufis. Such a silence is particularly remarkable in the case of the Naqshbandi Shaikh Ahmad Sirhindi (d. 1624) who, like the monarch, considered himself to be the "renovator of the second millennium" (*mujaddid-i alf-i sani*) and likewise ambitioned to rejuvenate sharia: unlike the Mughal, however, he advocated a return to the Prophetic example and the exclusion of Hindus from public life.

Even though it remained *lettre morte* in his time, Jahangir's idea to equip the empire with a stable and homogenized juridical framework was not lost on his descendants. Once stripped of its messianic garb and considered as yet another element of the ongoing Mughal centralization, it may be said to presage the legal systematization pursued by his grandson Aurangzeb. If the latter never claimed to be a *mujaddid*, the upper hand his imperial predecessors had struggled to gain over the ulema enabled him to convince a sizeable number of scholars – some of whom were long-time friends and partisans[70] – to produce under his close super-

---

69 In the matter of *zawabit*, mention should nevertheless be made of the twelve edicts Jahangir issued shortly after his accession to the throne in 1605 and of the *farman* he addressed more specifically to provincial governors in 1612 (Jahangir 1999, 26–27 and 127–128): both illustrate the monarch's activity as law-giver and his will to have imperial regulations circulated throughout the realm.

70 Guenther 2003, 218. For further details on the authorial team of the *Fatawa-i 'Alamgiri*, see Khalfaoui 2008, 57–73.

vision what was to become the most comprehensive legal text of Hanafi *fiqh* of the time. Significantly, the compilation of the *Fatawa-i ʿAlamgiri* was recorded in contemporary chronicles in terms strongly reminiscent of Jahangir's dissatisfaction with the confused state of Islamic law. Here is, for instance, how Mustaʿidd Khan explained the composition of the compendium in his *Ma'asir-i ʿAlamgiri*:

> All the aim of his [Aurangzeb's] exalted heart was devoted to making the general Muslim public act according to the legal decisions and precedents of the theological scholars (*ulamā*) of the Hanafi school; but seeing that these rulings as found in the existing law-books were confused (*lit.* mixed) on account of the diversity of opinion among the qāzis and muftis and the weakness (*i.e.*, little weight or authority) of the traditions, and the contradictory nature of the declarations of those ancient authorities [...], the heart of this Emperor, the asylum of the Faith, was set on this that a syndicate of celebrated theologians and well-known scholars of Hindustan should go through the long authoritative books on jurisprudence, which had been collected in the imperial library, extract the rulings of muftis, and compile one comprehensive book out of them all, so that all may find out the authoritative rulings (on their cases) with ease [...]. About two lakhs of rupees were spent in preparing this book, which was entitled the *Fatāwa-i-ʿĀlamgiri*, and which rendered the world independent of all other books of jurisprudence.[71]

As a matter of fact, the *Fatawa-i ʿAlamgiri* quickly "gained a reputation as a crucial Hanafi authority in the larger Muslim community where it was (and still is) known as *Fatāwâ al-Hindiyya*."[72] In a sense, Aurangzeb may therefore be said to have carried out – at least to a certain extent – Akbar's project to transform the Mughal empire into the Islamic world's new *qutb* (or leading pole) through the promotion of the *padshah* as a figure able to transcend legal diversity.

References

ʿAbd al-Sattar ibn Qasim Lahauri, *Majalis-i Jahangiri*, A. Naushahi, M. Nizami (eds.), Tehran: Miras-i Maktub, 2006.

Abisaab, Rula J., *Converting Persia. Religion and Power in the Safavid Empire*, London, New York: I. B. Tauris, 2004.

71 Muhammad Saqi Mustaʿidd Khan, *Ma'asir-i ʿAlamgiri. A History of the Emperor Aurangzib-ʿĀlamgir (Reign 1658–1707 AD) of Sāqi Mus'tad Khan*, translated by J. N. Sarkar, Delhi: Oriental Reprint, 1986 (reprint), 316–317. For the original and longer version of the *ʿAlamgiri Nama* on which Mustaʿidd Khan principally relied for his account of the composition of the *Fatawa-i ʿAlamgiri*, see Muhammad Kazim ibn Muhammad Amin, *ʿAlamgiri Nama*, M. K. Husain, ʿAbd al-Hai (eds.), 2 vols. Osnabrück: Biblio Verlag, 1983 (reprint), here II: 1086–1087.

72 Guenther 2003, 216.

Abu'l Fazl, *Akbar Nama*, translated by H. Beveridge, 3 vols., Calcutta: The Asiatic Society, 2000 (reprint).
Alam, Muzaffar, Subrahmanyam, Sanjay, Introduction. In *The Mughal State (1526–1750)*, Muzaffar Alam, Sanjay Subrahmanyam (eds.), 1–71, Delhi: Oxford University Press, 2000 (reprint).
Alam, Muzaffar, Subrahmanyam, Sanjay, Frank disputations: Catholics and Muslims in the court of Jahangir (1608–11). *Indian Economic and Social History Review* 46:4 (2009): 457–511.
Amin, Muhammad Kazim ibn Muhammad, *'Alamgiri Nama*, M. K. Husain, 'Abd al-Hai (eds.), 2 vols. Osnabrück: Biblio Verlag, 1983 (reprint).
Anooshahr, Ali, Shirazi scholars and the political culture of the sixteenth-century Indo-Persian world. *Indian Economic and Social History Review* 51:3 (2014): 331–352.
Anooshahr, Ali, Review of A. Azfar Moin, The Millennial Sovereign: Sacred Kingship and Sainthood in Islam. *The Medieval History Journal* 18:1 (2015): 183–191.
Bada'uni, 'Abd al-Qadir, *Muntakhab al-tawarikh*, Kabir al-Din Ahmad, M. A. Ahmad 'Ali, W. N. Lees (eds.), 3 vols. Calcutta: Asiatic Society of Bengal, 1864–1869.
Bada'uni, 'Abd al-Qadir, *Muntakhab al-tawarikh*, translated by G. S. A. Ranking, W. H. Lowe, T. W. Haig, 3 vols. Delhi: Renaissance Publishing House, 1986 (reprint).
Barkey, Karen, Aspects of Legal Pluralism in the Ottoman Empire. In *Legal Pluralism and Empires, 1500–1850*, Lauren Benton, Richard J. Ross (eds.), 83–108, New York: New York University Press, 2013.
Benton, Lauren, *Law and Colonial Cultures. Legal Regimes in World History 1400–1900*, Cambridge: Cambridge University Press, 2002.
Benton, Lauren, Ross, Richard J., Empires and Legal Pluralism: Jurisdiction, Sovereignty, and Political Imagination in the Early Modern World. In *Legal Pluralism and Empires, 1500–1850*, Lauren Benton, Richard J. Ross (eds.), 1–17, New York: New York University Press, 2013.
Bhakkari, Shaikh Farid ibn Ma'ruf, *Zakhirat al-khawanin*, S. M. Haq (ed.), 3 vols., Karachi: Pakistan Historical Society, 1961–1974.
Bhatia, M. L., *The Ulama Islamic Ethics and Courts Under the Mughals. Aurangzeb Revisited*, New Delhi: Manak, 2006.
Blachère, Régis, *Le Coran. Traduction selon un essai de reclassement des sourates*, 3 vols. Paris: Maisonneuve & Larose, 1947–1950.
Buckler, Francis W., A New Interpretation of Akbar's 'Infallibility' Decree of 1579. *Journal of the Royal Asiatic Society, New Series* 56:4 (1924): 591–608.
Burton, John, *The sources of Islamic law. Islamic theories of abrogation*, Edinburgh: Edinburgh University Press, 1990.
Chatterjee, Nandini, Reflections on Religious Difference and Permissive Inclusion in Mughal Law. *Journal of Law and Religion* 29:3 (2014): 396–415.
Chatterjee, Nandini, *Mahzar-namas* in the Mughal and British Empires: The Uses of an Indo-Islamic Legal Form. *Comparative Studies in Society and History* 58:2 (2016): 379–406.
Davis, Donald R. Jr., Centres of Law: Duties, Rights and Jurisdictional Pluralism in Medieval India. In *Legalism. Anthropology and History*, Paul Dresch, Hannah Skoda (eds.), 86–113, Oxford: Oxford University Press, 2012.

Duindam, Jeroen, Harries, Jill, Humfress, Caroline, Hurvitz, Nimrod, Introduction. In *Law and Empire. Idea, Practices, Actors*, Jeroen Duindam, Jill Harries, Caroline Humfress, Nimrod Hurvitz (eds.), 1–22, Leiden: Brill, 2013.

El-Rouayheb, Khaled, The Myth of "The Triumph of Fanaticism" in the Seventeenth-Century Ottoman Empire. *Die Welt des Islams* 48 (2008): 196–221.

Fischel, Walter J., Jews and Judaism at the Court of the Moghul Emperors in Medieval India. *Proceedings of the American Academy for Jewish Research* 18 (1948–1949): 137–177.

Ganeri, Jonardon, *The Lost Age of Reason. Philosophy in Early Modern India 1450–1700*, Oxford: Oxford University Press, 2011.

Gleave, Robert M., Akhbāriyya and Uṣūliyya. In *Encyclopaedia of Islam, THREE*, Kate Fleet, Gudrun Krämer, Denis Matringe, John Nawas, Everett Rowson (eds.), Brill online, 2016, online available under http://dx.doi.org/10.1163/1573-3912_ei3_COM_0029 (16/09/2016).

Grunebaum, Gustav E. von, Iʿdjāz. In *Encyclopaedia of Islam*, Second Edition, Bernard Lewis, Victor L. Ménage, Charles Pellat, Joseph Schacht (eds.), vol. 3, 1018–1020, Leiden: Brill, 1986.

Guenther, Alan M., Hanafi *Fiqh* in Mughal India: The *Fatāwá-i ʿĀlamgīrī*. In *India's Islamic Traditions, 711–1750*, Richard M. Eaton (ed.), 209–230, Delhi: Oxford University Press, 2003.

Haidar, Mansura, The Yasai Chingizi (Tura) in the Medieval Indian Sources. In *Mongolia. Culture, Economy and Politics (Indian-Mongolian Assessment)*, S. Bira, M. Haidar, R. C. Sharma, K. Warikoo (eds.), 53–66, Delhi: Khama Publishers, 1992.

Hallaq, Wael B., Model *Shurūṭ* works and the dialectic of doctrine and practice. *Islamic Law and Society* 2:2 (1995): 109–134.

Hasan, Farhat, *State and Locality in Mughal India. Power Relations in Western India, c. 1572–1730*, Cambridge: Cambridge University Press, 2004.

Ibrahim, Ahmed Fekry, The Codification Episteme in Islamic Juristic Discourse between Inertia and Change. *Islamic Law and Society* 22 (2015): 157–220.

Ibrahim, Ahmed Fekry, Rethinking the *Taqlīd-Ijtihād* Dichotomy: A Conceptual-Historical Approach. *Journal of the American Oriental Society* 136:2 (2016): 285–303.

Islam, Zafarul, *Fatāwā Literature of the Sultanate Period*. Delhi: Kanishka, 2005.

Jahangir, Nur al-Din Muhammad, *Jahangir Nama. The Jahāngīr Nāma. Memoirs of Jahāngīr, Emperor of India*, translated by W. M. Thackston Washington, D. C. and New York: Freer Gallery of Art and Arthur M. Sackler Gallery, Smithsonian Institution & Oxford University Press, 1999.

Johansen, Baber, Signs as Evidence: The Doctrine of Ibn Taymiyya (1263–1328) and Ibn Qayyim al-Jawziyya (d. 1351) on Proof. *Islamic Law and Society* 9:2 (2002): 168–193.

Johari, Harish, *The Healing Power of Gemstones: In Tantra, Ayurveda, & Astrology*. Rochester (Vermont): Destiny Books, 1988.

Kane, Pandurang Vaman, *The History of Dharmaśāstra (Ancient and Mediaeval Religious and Civil Law)*, 5 vols. Poona: Bhandarkar Oriental Research Institute, 1930–1962.

Khalfaoui, Mouez, *L'islam indien: pluralité ou pluralisme*. Frankfurt-am-Main: Peter Lang, 2008.

Khalfaoui, Mouez, Together but separate: How Muslim scholars conceived of religious plurality in South Asia in the seventeenth century. *Bulletin of the School of African and Asian Studies* 74:1 (2011): 87–96.

Khan, Hamid al-din, *Ahkam-i ʿAlamgiri*, translated by J. Sarkar, Anecdotes of Aurangzib, Calcutta: M. C. Sarkar & Sons, 1925.
Khan, Reyaz Ahmad, Jahangir and Muslim Theology-Discussions Reported in the *Majalis-i Jahangiri*. In *Proceedings of the Indian History Congress, 71st Session*, 236–242.
Khan, Reyaz Ahmad, Jahangir on *Shias* and *Sunnis* in *Majalis-i Jahangiri*. In *Proceedings of the Indian History Congress, 72nd Session*, 302–307.
Kollatz, Anna, *Inspiration und Tradition. Strategien zur Beherrschung von Diversität am Mogulhof und ihre Darstellung in Maǧālis-i Ǧahāngīrī (ca. 1608–11) von ʿAbd al-Sattār b. Qāsim Lāhōrī*, Berlin: EB-Verlag, 2016.
Lefèvre, Corinne, Recovering a Missing Voice from Mughal India: The Imperial Discourse of Jahāngīr (r. 1605–1627) in his Memoirs. *Journal of the Economic and Social History of the Orient* 50:4 (2007): 452–489.
Lefèvre, Corinne, ʿAbd al-Sattār b. Qāsim Lāhawrī. In *Encyclopedia of Islam, THREE*, Kate Fleet, Gudrun Krämer, Denis Matringe, John Nawas Everett Rowson (eds.), fasc. 1, 6–8, Leiden: Brill, 2015.
Marshall, Dara N., *Mughals in India. A bibliographical survey of manuscripts*. London, New York: Mansell Publishing, 1967.
Moosvi, Shireen, The Conversations of Jahangir 1608–11: Table Talk on Religion. In *Proceedings of the Indian History Congress, 68th Session*, 328–332, Delhi: Indian History Congress, 2008.
Moin, A. Azfar, *The Millennial Sovereign. Sacred Kingship and Sainthood in Islam*, New York: Columbia University Press, 2012.
Mustaʿidd Khan, Muhammad Saqi, *Maʾasir-i ʿAlamgiri. A History of the Emperor Aurang-zib-ʿĀlamgir (Reign 1658–1707 AD) of Sāqi Musʾtad Khan*, translated by J. N. Sarkar, Delhi: Oriental Reprint, 1986 (reprint).
Nahawandi, ʿAbd al-Baqi, *Maʾasir-i Rahimi*, M. Hidayat Husain (ed.), 3 vols., Calcutta: The Asiatic Society of Bengal, 1910–1931.
Nielsen, Jørgen S., Maẓālim. In *Encyclopaedia of Islam, Second Edition*, Charles E. Bosworth, Emeri van Donzel, Wolfhart P. Heinrichs, Charles Pellat (eds.), vol. 6, 933–935, Leiden: Brill, 1986.
O'Hanlon, Rosalind, Letters Home: Banaras pandits and the Maratha regions in early modern India. *Modern Asian Studies* 44:2 (2010): 201–240.
O'Hanlon, Rosalind, Speaking from Siva's temple: Banaras scholar households and the Brahman 'ecumene' of Mughal India. *South Asian History and Culture* 2:2 (2011): 253–277.
Pirbhai, M. Reza, A Historiography of Islamic Law in the Mughal Empire. In *The Oxford Handbook of Islamic Law*, ed. Anver M. Emon and Rumee Ahmed (eds.). Oxford online, 2016, online available under: http://www.oxfordhandbooks.com/view/10.1093/oxfordhb/9780199679010.001.0001/oxfordhb-9780199679010-e-65 (10/04/2016).
Rapoport, Yossef, Royal Justice and Religious Law: *Siyāsah* and Shariʿa under the Mamluks. *Mamlūk Studies Review* 16 (2012): 71–102.
Rippin, Andrew, Abrogation. In *Encyclopaedia of Islam, THREE*, Kate Fleet, Gudrun Krämer, Denis Matringe, John Nawas, Everett Rowson (eds.), Brill online, 2015, online available under http://referenceworks.brillonline.com/entries/encyclopaedia-of-islam-3/abrogation-COM_0104 (15/06/2015).
Strauch, Ingo, Dharma. In *Brill's Encyclopedia of Hinduism*, Knut A. Jacobsen, Helene Basu, Angelika Malinar and Vasudha Narayanan (eds.), vol. 2, 736–743, Leiden: Brill, 2010.

Subrahmanyam, Sanjay, Peasants before the Law: Recent Historiography on Colonial India. *Études rurales* 149–150 (1999): 199–209.
Tarlo, Emma, *Clothing Matters: Dress and Identity in India*. Chicago: The University of Chicago Press, 1996.
Travers, Robert, *Ideology and Empire in Eighteenth-Century India. The British in Bengal*, Cambridge: Cambridge University Press, 2007.

Mia Korpiola

Legal diversity – or the relative lack of it – in early modern Sweden

Introduction

When discussing legal practice in early modern Western Europe, legal diversity is usually mentioned as one of the hallmarks of the era. France resembled a normative mosaic with its roughly 700 local customary laws, most of which were to be found in print before 1600. At the end of the *ancien régime*, there were still 300 local and 60 general customs.[1] Indeed, the French legal system has been described as being of "unbelievable complexity" (*incroyable complexité*).[2] Isabelle Paresys compared the various overlying jurisdictions in Amiens to a mosaic (*mosaïque de juridictions*) that made the functioning of the justice system complex.[3] Similarly, Julie Hardwick has talked about a "patchwork of overlapping and competing jurisdictions in which multiple local legal regimes (customary and Roman) operated alongside the national decrees issued by the crown, and canon law [...] as well as the *arrêts* of the relevant sovereign courts."[4]

Moreover, in France, for example, there was a wide array of feudal or seigneurial courts, due, for example, to partible inheritance, in which real circumstances were very diverse (*grande diversité*) – and consequently, much criticized.[5] In France, jurisdiction over certain types of cases could vary from one town and region to another, and it has been suggested that "juridical inconstancies of this kind were rife in early modern legal systems." In turn, the French case has been

1 Bruce Lenman, Geoffrey Parker, The State, the Community and the Criminal Law in Early Modern Europe. In *Crime and the Law. The Social History of Crime in Western Europe since 1500*, V. A. C. Gatrell, Bruce Lenman, Geoffrey Parker (eds.), 11–48, London: Europe Publications Limited, 1980, here 11, 32–33.

2 Jean-Marie Constant, Prévôtés, vicomtés, vigueries, châtellenies. In *Dictionnaire de l'Ancien Régime. Royaume de France, XVIe–XVIIIe siècle*, Julien Bély (ed.), 1015–1016. Paris: Presses universitaires de France, 1996, here 1016.

3 Paresys, Isabelle, *Aux marges du royaume. Violence, justice et société en Picardie sous François Ier*. Paris: Publications de la Sorbonne, 1998, 136–138: "*La multiplicité des justices dont relèvent les Amiénois rend le fonctionnement judiciaire complexe.*"

4 Julie Hardwick, *Family Business. Litigation and the Political Economies of Daily Life in Early Modern France*. Oxford: Oxford University Press, 2009, 61.

5 Gallet, Jean, Justice seigneuriale. In *Dictionnaire de l'Ancien Régime. Royaume de France, XVIe–XVIIIe siècle*, Julien Bély (ed.), 714–717, Paris: Presses universitaires de France, 1996, here 716–717.

DOI 10.1515/9783110423327-007

claimed to be typical of early modern Europe.[6] In addition, the early modern Spanish court system has been compared to a Cretan labyrinth from which few lawsuits ever emerged. As Henry Kagan has observed, "the labyrinthine state of Castilian law had its bewildering analogue: an array of law courts and legal tribunals so bewildering that lawsuits regularly became lost in a confused jurisdictional morass."[7]

Without attempting the ambitious task to assess the extent to which the alleged representativeness of France really applies to the whole of early modern Europe, as some have claimed, I will conduct here a case study of early modern Sweden. I will argue that, in comparison with countries like Spain and France, there was relatively little legal diversity in Sweden. I will also analyse the reasons for this. The relative simplicity of the system was not the result of one determining factor as this was by no means unique to Sweden. Rather, a mixture of economic and geographical factors (peripheral location, poverty of the country), political factors (turbulence, expensive warfare, rise of royal power after the Lutheran Reformation, the limited role of feudalism and corresponding political representation of the peasantry) and legal factors (lay domination of the judiciary) all contributed to the lack of diversity, as will be discussed below in more detail.

Medieval and early modern Sweden

The century from 1520s to the 1620s, roughly from the accession of the Vasa dynasty and the onset of the Reformation to the German wars, brought with it major cultural and political transformations. As researchers have pointed out, during this period, Sweden developed from a "late medieval, loosely structured state to a centrally governed, militarized monarchy that laid the foundation for the period of Sweden as a Great Power," which came to an end in 1709.[8]

Medieval Sweden was a peripheral country, comprising most of present-day Sweden and Finland. Though vast in area, the kingdom was sparsely inhabited. In 1600, it was estimated to have about one million inhabitants – thus, less than Stockholm County has today (about 1.4 million). In 1700, the mostly agrarian

6 Hardwick 2009, 61, 66.

7 Henry L. Kagan, *Lawsuits and Litigants in Castile 1500–1700*. Chapel Hill: University of North Carolina Press, 1981, 32.

8 See, for example, Ingun Montgomery, *Sveriges kyrkohistoria 4. Enhetskyrkans tid*. Stockholm: Verbum, 2002, 10.

population numbered around 2 million.[9] The towns of early sixteenth-century Sweden were small and politically weak, most having less than 1,000 inhabitants, while Stockholm, one of the biggest towns in Scandinavia, had about 5,000–6,000 inhabitants in 1500. However, Stockholm experienced a period of very rapid growth in the course of the seventeenth century, from about 10,000 inhabitants in 1620 to 50–55,000 at the end of the century. The next largest towns had only 4–6,000 inhabitants in the seventeenth century.[10]

The Swedish nobility was one of the smallest in Europe, comprising only about 0.5 percent of the population at the end of the seventeenth century, while the clergy formed about one percent. Less than two percent of the people were burghers, while the very heterogeneous group of "non-noble persons of rank" (*ståndsperson*) may have amounted to as much as 1.5 percent. The rest of the population, 95 percent, belonged to the peasantry. There was also considerable social mobility due to frequent ennoblements in the seventeenth century, especially of high officials, officers and wealthy entrepreneurs.[11]

The economic development of Sweden also lagged behind that of Central Europe. The characteristics of the economy of medieval Sweden have been assessed as autarkical because of the relatively small role of foreign trade and "overshadowing importance of agriculture", though with "weaker self-sufficiency of households".[12] Before the importance of copper production soared in the early seventeenth century, butter was its main export produce in the later Middle Ages in addition to hides, skins and furs, timber and iron. The main imported goods were salt, hops for ale production, spices, various kinds of cloths, beer and wine. Because of the restricted role of exports, the crown depended for its income on taxes on land, paid by land-owning peasants.[13]

---

9 Maria Sjöberg, Adelns tid. In *Det svenska samhället 800–1720. Klerkernas och adelns tid*, Thomas Lindkvist, Maria Sjöberg, 198–419, Lund: Studentlitteratur, 2013, here 255. Sven Lundkvist, The Experience of Empire: Sweden as a Great Power. In *Sweden's Age of Greatness*, Michael Roberts (ed.), 20–57, London/Basingstoke: Macmillan, 1973, here 21, 60–61.

10 Göran Dahlbäck, The towns. In *The Cambridge History of Scandinavia. Volume I, Prehistory to 1520*, Knut Helle (ed.), 611–634, Cambridge: Cambridge University Press, 2003, here 615–616. Stellan Dahlgren, 1600-talets ståndssamhälle. In *Kultur och samhälle i stormaktstidens Sverige*, Stellan Dahlgren, Allan Ellenius, Lars Gustafsson, Gunnar Larsson (eds.), 9–40, Stockholm: Wahlström & Widstrand, 1967, here 12.

11 Sten Carlsson, *Bonde – präst – ämbetsman. Svensk ståndscirkulation från 1680 till våra dagar*. Stockholm: Prisma, 1962, 15–17, 26–33.

12 Eli Heckscher, *An Economic History of Sweden*. Trans. Göran Ohlin. Cambridge, Mass.: Harvard University Press, 1963, 18–19.

13 Heckscher 1963, 23–24, 42–44, 48, 62.

The Middle Ages had been a period of political instability in Sweden. While the role of the king was not called into question, recurrent *coups d'état* until the seventeenth century made the kings dependent on the support of varying allies. The more independent provinces with their local power bases, including the peasantry, had an important political role. In 1521, Gustav Vasa led the uprising against the Danish king in the final death agony of the Kalmar Union, a personal confederation of the three Scandinavian kingdoms under one Danish ruler founded in 1397. The war was successful, leading to the separation of the Swedish crown from the Union. Vasa was first elected Protector of Sweden, and he later ascended to the throne as King Gustav I Vasa (r. 1521–60), the first ruler of the Vasa dynasty.[14] Sweden had been an elective monarchy until 1544, when the Estates accepted a hereditary monarchy at the Diet of Västerås.[15]

One major feature that distinguishes Sweden from most other European countries – and contributes to its relative lack of legal diversity – was its lack of feudalism. In Denmark, where landownership developed towards serfdom during the Middle Ages, only perhaps 15 percent of the peasantry were freeholders. By contrast, it has been assessed that in 1560 about half of the land in present-day Sweden was owned by peasants. In Finland, the percentage of land owned by peasants was 95 percent on the eve of the Reformation.[16] But even in Sweden, more feudal structures were making inroads in the administrative system. District court judges had been elected locally at first, before the definite power had been given to the king to decide from among locally nominated candidates. In the late fifteenth century, however, these positions were increasingly perceived as feudal and subject to the ruler's unrestricted power to nominate and enfeoff.[17]

---

14 On this see, for example, Jens E. Olesen, Inter-Scandinavian relations. In *The Cambridge History of Scandinavia. Volume I, Prehistory to 1520*, Knut Helle (ed.), 710–770, Cambridge: Cambridge University Press, 2003, here 737–770. Sjöberg 2013, 199–221.

15 Agreement on Succession (*Arfföreningen*), 13 Jan. 1544, *Svenska riksdagsakter jämte andra handlingar som höra till statsförfattningens historia under tidehvarfvet 1521–1718* [hereafter SRA] 1:1, Emil Hildebrand, Oscar Alin (eds.) Stockholm: Riksarkivet, 1887, 378–390.

16 On this see, for example, Eljas Orrman, The condition of the rural population. In *The Cambridge History of Scandinavia. Volume I, Prehistory to 1520*, Knut Helle (ed.), 581–610, Cambridge: Cambridge University Press, 2003, here 600–603. See also Eino Jutikkala, *Bonden – adelsmannen – Kronan. Godspolitik och jordegendomsförhållanden*. Copenhagen, Lund: Nordisk Ministerråd, 1979, esp. 9–19, 42–59.

17 Yrjö Blomstedt, *Laamannin- ja kihlakunnantuomarinvirkojen läänittäminen ja hoito Suomessa 1500- ja 1600-luvuilla (1523–1680). Oikeushallintohistoriallinen tutkimus*. Helsinki: Suomen Historiallinen Seura, 1958, 30–208. Sten Claësson, *Häradshövdingeämbetet i senmedeltidens och Gustav Vasas Sverige*. Stockholm: Institutet för rättshistorisk forskning, 1987, 189–198.

Hereditary noble titles (count, baron) were introduced in Sweden at the coronation of King Erik XIV (r. 1560–68) in 1561, when three counts and nine barons – many of them closely related by blood or marriage to the Vasas – were created. The newly-minted counts and barons were also awarded the right to have their own courts in their domains. In addition, the Swedish nobility lobbied intensively to have more extensive and advantageous privileges in the later sixteenth and early seventeenth centuries. However, the Swedish nobility was unable to obtain such privileges from the king, which would have resulted in a network of patrimonial courts as was the case elsewhere in the Baltic region, for example.[18]

During the reign of Gustav Vasa, the central government developed considerably and the provincial administration was more closely monitored by the crown. Sweden pursued a policy of territorial expansion after the second half of the sixteenth century, and warfare and territorial growth required that the poor country make efficient use of its resources. There were recurrent wars against Russia, Denmark and Poland on Swedish, Finnish and Baltic soil before Sweden embarked on the Thirty Years' War. The peace of Westphalia in 1648 did not end the wars that continued on all fronts until three peace treaties concluded between 1719 and 1721 finished the era of Sweden as a great power.[19]

The laws and courts of Sweden

During this period, the Swedish judiciary was largely in the hands of laymen with only practical experience of the law, although courts of appeal and town courts were increasingly staffed by men who had studies some law, especially in the eighteenth-century.[20] While relatively few high-ranking medieval Swedish clerics, bishops and canons had taken law degrees, the number of formally

18 E.g. Sven A. Nilsson, *Krona och frälse i Sverige 1523 – 1594. Rusttjänst, länsväsende, godspolitik*, Lund: Gleerupska Univ.bokhandeln, 1947, 167–183, 280–373. Sven A. Nilsson, *Kampen om de adliga privilegierna 1526–1594*. Lund: Vetenskaps-Societeten i Lund, 1952. Bo Eriksson, *Svenska adelns historia*. Stockholm: Norstedts, 2011, 138–140. For the Baltic region, see, e.g. Heikki Pihlajamäki, *Conquest and the Law in Swedish Livonia (ca. 1630–1710): A Case of Legal Pluralism in Early Modern Europe*, Leiden: Brill, 2017.

19 Lundkvist 1973.

20 See, for example, Marianne Vasara-Aaltonen, From Well-travelled "Jacks-of-all-trades" to Domestic Lawyers: The Educational and Career Backgrounds of Svea Court of Appeal Judges 1614–1809. In *The Svea Court of Appeal in the Early Modern Period: Historical Reinterpretations and New Perspectives*, Mia Korpiola (ed.), 301–354. Stockholm: Institutet för rättshistorisk forskning, 2014.

trained lawyers plummeted after the Reformation, while clerics seem to have completely given up law studies.[21]

Secular courts in both the towns and the countryside were manned by non-learned laymen – town courts by burghers and district courts by a judge (usually a noble) and twelve local peasant jurors (*nämndemän*). Above the district courts were the *lagman*'s courts, presided over by the *lagman* (pl. *lagmän*), a noble superior provincial judge, together with a peasant jury (*nämnd*). Superior to both local and provincial courts, the king exercised his law-given position as highest judge in the realm. He administered justice in person and through various appointed commissions that were on circuit in the provinces or the provincial capitals. Many different royal assizes – *landsting, räfsteting, rättareting* – were instituted at various times in the later Middle Ages. However, by about 1600, these had been partially replaced in practice by the Council of the Realm supplemented by royal officials, noblemen, officers and burghers, although these ad hoc courts lacked the authority of the law.[22] In addition, the garrison and staff of royal castles and manors were subject to manorial law and courts. In the sixteenth century, manorial law diversified into articles of war (military law for the army and navy) as well as court ordinances (for the functioning of and discipline at the royal court).[23]
While the centralization of the judiciary had to wait until the early seventeenth century, the laws of Sweden had already become less diverse in the course of the Middle Ages. The relatively few extant manuscripts of provincial laws, the oldest

21 Mia Korpiola, On the reception of the *ius commune* and foreign law in Sweden, ca. 1550–1615. *Clio@Thémis* 2 (2009), available online at: http://www.cliothemis.com/On-the-Reception-of-the-Jus (06/06/2017). Mia Korpiola, Lutheran marriage law in sixteenth- and early seventeenth-century Sweden. Authorities and sources of law. In *Law and Religion. The Legal Teachings of the Catholic and Protestant Reformations*, Wim Decock, Jordan J. Ballor, Michael Germann, Laurent Waelkens (eds.), 107–132, Göttingen: Vandenhoeck & Ruprecht, 2014a.

22 For short overviews of this in English, see Mia Korpiola, General Background. From Judicial Crisis to Judicial Revolution through the Svea Court of Appeal? In *The Svea Court of Appeal in the Early Modern Period: Historical Reinterpretations and New Perspectives*, Mia Korpiola (ed.), 21–50, Stockholm: Institutet för rättshistorisk forskning, 2014b, here 36–37. Mia Korpiola, The Svea Court of Appeal: A Fundament of Good Governance and Justice in the Early Modern Swedish Realm (1614–1800). In *Comparative History of the Central Courts of Europe and the Americas, 1200–1800*, Mark Godfrey, Remco van Rhee (eds.), Berlin: Duncker & Humblot, forthcoming 2018.

23 See, for example, the Manorial Law (1544) and Articles of War of King Gustav Vasa (1545). In *Kongl. stadgar, förordningar, bref och resolutioner, ifrån åhr 1528 in til 1701 angående justitiæ och executions-ährender etc.*, Joh. Schmedeman (ed.), Stockholm: Johann Henrich Werner, 1706, 15–27.

layer of Swedish medieval laws, date from the 1280s to 1350s.[24] However, the tiny number of manuscripts strongly suggests that for the most part the provincial laws had been replaced in practice by two laws authorized by King Magnus Eriksson (Magnus IV of Sweden, r. 1319–64) around 1350, one for the towns and another for the rest of the country.[25] Magnus Eriksson's Town Law remained in use until the medieval laws were replaced by the Swedish Code of 1734. However, King Christopher of Bavaria updated the law for the countryside in 1442, although judging by the existing manuscripts his newer version started to replace Magnus Eriksson's version in practice only in the latter half of the sixteenth century.[26] While these laws formed the core of Swedish law before 1736, when the Code of 1734 came into force, they were naturally supplemented and altered by statutes, ordinances and other decrees. The 1734 Code largely unified the law in the Swedish realm even though some differences between towns and the countryside were preserved (for example, different court systems).

Canon law influenced Swedish medieval law through the Catholic Church and its legal system. Most Swedish provincial laws contained chapters on the church that regulated ecclesiastical jurisdiction and the relationship between clergy and secular society on the provincial level based on negotiations on the diocesan level. These chapters in particular contained canon law, which also influenced secular law more generally.[27] In addition, the ecclesiastical courts internally applied canon law that was supplemented by local provincial and

24 The surviving Swedish provincial laws were two versions of the provincial law of West Gothia, law of East Gothia, provincial law of Småland (only one chapter survives), law of Gotland (*Gutalagen*), law of Uppland, law of Hälsingland, law of Dalarna (Dalalagen), law of Södermanland and law of Västmanland.

25 For a concise account of Swedish medieval laws in English, see Thomas Lindkvist, Law and the Making of the State in Medieval Sweden. Kingship and Communities. In *Legislation and Justice*, Antonio Padoa-Schioppa (ed.), 211–228, Oxford: Clarendon Press, 1997, here 213–216.

26 Patrik Åström, *Senmedeltida svenska lagböcker. 136 lands- och stadslagshandskrifter – dateringar och dateringsproblem*. Stockholm: Almqvist & Wiksell, 2003, 177.

27 E.g., Wilhelm Sjögren, De fornsvenska kyrkobalkarna. *Tidsskrift for Retsvidenskap* 17 (1904): 125–176. L. M. Bååth, *Bidrag till den kanoniska rättens historia i Sverige*. Stockholm: 1905. Georg J. V. Ericsson, *Den kanoniska rätten och Äldre Västgötalagens kyrkobalk. En jämförande studie*, Institutet för rättshistorisk forskning: Lund, 1967. Jan Arvid Hellström, *Biskop och landskapssamhälle i tidig svensk medeltid*. Institutet för rättshistorisk forskning: Lund, 1971. Mia Korpiola, On ecclesiastical jurisdiction and the reception of canon law in the Swedish provincial laws. In *How Nordic Are the Nordic Medieval Laws?* Ditlev Tamm, Helle Vogt (eds.), 202–231, Copenhagen: University of Copenhagen Press, 2005. (Reprinted in Copenhagen: DJØF Publishing Press, 2011.). Mia Korpiola, Literary legacies and canonical book collections. Possession of Canon Law Books in Medieval Sweden. In *Law and Learning in Medieval Europe*, Helle Vogt, Mia Münster-Swendsen (eds.), 79–103, Copenhagen: DJØF Publishing Press, 2006.

synodal statutes.[28] The Reformation did not put a stop to the reception and use of canon law in Sweden even though the Reformed Church wanted to emphasize its independence from the papacy.[29]

The impact of Roman law remained very limited in the Middle Ages. However, the roles were reversed after the Reformation, when continental – especially German – law and Roman law were considered useful sources for new legal tools and rules. The extent of this reception should not be exaggerated as it was selective and limited. Moreover, the possibility of using foreign law had been forbidden in the Chapter on the king in the medieval laws, which continued to have an important symbolic role in Swedish society. Roman-German law had also been used, for example, in an attempt to introduce judicial torture in the turbulent period of the early 1600s.[30] While the courts of appeal especially have been seen as conduits for the reception of foreign law, recent research has modified this notion. While Jägerskiöld focused on the use of Latin and Roman law in private law cases, especially in the latter half of the seventeenth century, Trolle Önnerfors and Pihlajamäki have lately criticized this view. They stress quite correctly that Swedish law was the paramount legal source even in the appellate courts.[31]

28 E.g., Sara Risberg, Kirsi Salonen (eds.), *Auctoritate Papae. The Church Province of Uppsala and the Apostolic Penitentiary 1410–1526*, Stockholm: Riksarkivet, 2008. *Statuta synodalia veteris ecclesiæ sveogothicæ*, H. Reuterdahl (ed.). Lund: 1841; *Synodalstatuter och andra kyrkorättsliga aktstycken från den svenska medeltidskyrkan*, Jaakko Gummerus (ed.), Upsala: Wretmans tryckeri, 1902.

29 E.g., Gerhard Schmidt, *Die Richterregeln des Olavus Petri. Ihre Bedeutung im allgemeinen und für die Entwicklung des schwedischen Strafprozeßrechts vom 14. bis 16. Jahrhundert*, Göttingen/Stockholm: Vandenhoeck & Ruprecht/P. A. Norstedt & Söner, 1966. Korpiola, 2009. Korpiola 2014a.

30 Mia Korpiola, Desperately needing lawyers. Contacts in the Baltic Sea region and the rise of diplomacy in Reformation Sweden. In *Migration und Kulturtransfer im Ostseeraum während der Frühen Neuzeit*, Otfried Czaika, Heinrich Holze (eds.), 101–120, Stockholm: Kungliga biblioteket, 2012.

31 See, for example, Stig Jägerskiöld, *Studier rörande receptionen av främmande rätt i Sverige under den yngre landslagens tid* Stockholm: Almqvist & Wiksell, 1963. Mia Korpiola, On the influence of Roman law in medieval Sweden. Books and university studies. In *Liber Amicorum Kjell Å. Modéer*, Bernhard Diestelkamp, Hans-Heinrich Vogel, Nils Jörn, Per Nilsén, Christian Häthén (eds.), 343–355, Lund: Juristförlaget, 2007. Mia Korpiola, Some evidence of the use of Roman law in medieval Sweden. In *Liber amicorum Ditlev Tamm: Law, History and Culture*, Per Andersen, Pia Letto-Vanamo, Kjell Åke Modéer, Helle Vogt (eds.), 173–183, Copenhagen: DJØF Publishing Press, 2011. For recent criticism, see Elsa Trolle Önnerfors, *Justitia et Prudentia. Rättsbildning genom rättstillämpning: Svea hovrätt och testamentsmålen 1640–1690*, Stockholm: Institutet för rättshistorisk forskning, 2014, 47–48, 64–65, 350–351, 356–357. Heikki Pihlajamäki, The court of appeal as legal transfer. The Svea and Dorpat courts compared. In *The Svea Court of Appeal in*

In 1683, King Charles XI (r. 1660–97) forbade all courts to use any legal sources other than Swedish law and statutes. Moreover, only Swedish could be used and no "foreign language" was allowed.[32] Swedish had been used all the time as a court language, but this also curbed the use of Latin expressions. The use of the vernacular was a practical solution, but it was also an ideological choice that made law more understandable and law courts more easily accessible to laymen.

The role of legal science remained very limited all through the early modern period, as first medieval laws and supplementing statutes, and after 1736, the 1734 law became the most frequently used legal source by far.[33] Sweden's adherence to its written laws, which has been called proto-legalism,[34] resulted partly from the lack of competing legal sources, a lay-dominated legal culture and vernacular laws. However, it must be observed that "the law (of Sweden)" had been frequently used an authoritative argument in Swedish political culture by kings and peasants alike ever since the late Middle Ages. The people of Sweden (and Estates) had given their consent to the law and kings had sworn to uphold it. This gave special authority and sanctity to the law.[35] The nexus between the king, popular consent and the law also contributed to the limited legal diversity found in early modern Sweden.

the Early Modern Period: Historical Reinterpretations and New Perspectives, Mia Korpiola (ed.), 217–260. Stockholm: Institutet för rättshistorisk forskning, 2014, here 231–237.

32 King Charles XI to the Göta Court of Appeal, 5 Oct. 1683, *Kongl. stadgar*, Schmedeman (ed.), 856.

33 E.g., Lars Björne, *Patrioter och institutionalister. Den nordiska rättsvetenskapens historia, 1. Tiden före år 1815,* Lund: Institutet för rättshistorisk forskning, 1995. Vepsä, Iisa. Lain ja asian luonteen mukaan – oikeuslähteet 1700-luvulla. *Lakimies* 2012: 499–524.

34 Heikki Pihlajamäki, Positivism before positivism? Royal statutes and early modern Swedish criminal law. In *From the Judge's* Arbitrium *to the Legality Principle. Legislation as a Source of Law in Criminal Trials*, Georges Martyn, Anthony Musson, Heikki Pihlajamäki (eds.), 169–188, Berlin: Duncker & Humblot, 2012.

35 E.g., Mathias Cederholm, *De värjde sin rätt. Senmedeltida bondemotstånd i Skåne och Småland*, Lund: Historiska instutionen vid Lunds universitet, 2007, 449–458. Mia Korpiola, "Not without the consent and goodwill of the common people:" The community as a legal authority in medieval Sweden. *The Journal of Legal History*, 35:2 (2014c): 95–119.

Religion: From an Evangelical reformation to an orthodox Lutheran state church

As Sweden was a peripheral region in Europe, it was Christianised late. The Christianization process was concluded in the central parts of Sweden around 1200, and its church was organized in 1248 in a provincial council presided over by a papal legate. The remoter fringes of the country were only effectively Christianised in the early modern period.[36]

Reformation thought spread to Sweden by 1523. This coincided with the accession of Gustav Vasa to the throne of Sweden after the dissolution of the Kalmar Union. King Gustav quickly profited from the new tenets. There was no upsurge of popular support, but the Reformation is considered to have officially been embraced in 1527, when the Swedish Estates accepted the revocation of property the church had received since 1454. The bishops became accountable to the king for all ecclesiastical incomes, while the king decided how much the Church would keep for itself. All fines from ecclesiastical courts were also to be accounted for to the king. This Reformation from above and following royal supremacy benefitted the king directly as the penniless new regime could dip deep into the ecclesiastical coffers.[37] While the Church had owned more than 20 percent of Swedish agricultural land at the advent of Reformation, this became crown property almost in its entirety, increasing the portion of crown lands by more than 500 percent.[38]

The new Swedish Protestant church went through various stages of confessionalization before 1593. All over Europe, the Reformation had given rulers considerable powers over religious matters and they could enforce religious uniformity in their territories according to the principle *cuius regio, eius religio* ("whose reign, his religion," meaning the ruler could dictate the religion of his subjects). As in other Lutheran territories, the Swedish king came to be the head of the church, which also gave him the ultimate power to hand down both secular and ecclesiastical law, provided that the Law of God was not overstepped.[39] Before the

---

36 Orrman, Eljas, Church and society. In *The Cambridge History of Scandinavia. Volume I, Prehistory to 1520*, Knut Helle (ed.), 421–436, Cambridge: Cambridge University Press, 2003. Pentti Laasonen, *Suomen kirkon historia 2. Vuodet 1593–1808*, Porvoo, Helsinki, Juva: WSOY, 1991, 97–101.
37 Ordinance of Västerås, 24 June 1527, *SRA* 1:1, Hildebrand, Alin (eds.), 89–95. For the Swedish Reformation in general, see James L. Larson, *Reforming the North. The Kingdoms and Churches of Scandinavia, 1520–1545*, Cambridge: Cambridge University Press, 2010, 227–266.
38 Heckscher 1963, 67.
39 Åke Andrén, *Sveriges kyrkohistoria 3. Reformationstid*. Stockholm: Verbum, 1999, 116–118.

Reformation, Rome had been the pivot of a supranational ecclesiastical administration with its own independent jurisdiction and hierarchical court system with the pope on top. This parallel legal system claiming superiority by virtue of divine authority was a force no secular ruler could ignore. However, the Reformation signified a fundamental change here as the ruler became the supreme authority in both the secular and ecclesiastical jurisdictions within his territories.

In Sweden, after the Reformation had been initiated in economic, political and legal matters in 1527, the new religious doctrine had largely been left undefined. The Estates had proclaimed an "Evangelical" faith in 1544. The "word of God and the Holy Gospels were generally to be used in the Christian parishes" of Sweden, but the tenets of the Evangelical doctrine were not defined.[40] In their coronation oaths and declarations as custodians of the Church, the kings now promised to protect the "true religion, God's pure word and Christian faith" as well as "the offices of the Church and all their incumbents." Religious matters remained unsettled in the latter half of the sixteenth century, with doctrine vacillating according to the policy of the ruler.[41] This slow process of the top-down Reformation probably made its onset more moderate than in many parts of the continent and England. Heretics burned at the stake were not seen in Sweden and, while they were not allowed to practice in public, other Protestant believers were tolerated. However, the jurisdiction of ecclesiastical courts in criminal cases became supplementary to that of the secular courts and pertained only to church discipline. Ecclesiastical courts continued to function. The early modern consistory courts also had jurisdiction over university students and teachers – a limited *privilegium fori*.

However, in 1593 there was some urgency to break with the principle of *cuius regio, eius religio* due to the succession of the son of John III (r. 1568–92), Sigismund Vasa, who had been raised a Catholic and was king of Catholic Poland. When John III died, Swedish clerics put aside their doctrinal squabbles and united against the common enemy, the perceived Catholic threat. A provincial council was quickly convened to define and confirm the Lutheran faith, while the medieval university of Uppsala was resurrected as a future bastion of the true Lutheran religion and educator of its clergy. At Uppsala, the clergy, more than 300 priests and four bishops, defined the Lutheran faith and made it the only permitted religion. The decision of the Council of Uppsala was ratified by the Council of the Realm and the Estates, while the confirmation of the document was a precondition for the coronation of Sigismund Vasa as king of Sweden. The

---

40 Note on the decisions of the Diet of Västerås (1544), *SRA* 1:1, Hildebrand, Alin (eds.), 390.
41 Coronation oath of John III, 10 July 1569, *SRA* 2, Emil Hildebrand (ed.). Stockholm: Riksarkivet, 1899, 399. Andrén 1999, 160–185.

1593 Council and its decision marked the consolidation of the Lutheran Reformation in Sweden.[42] Yet, Sigismund's reign dissolved in internal strife, plotting and peasant revolt. Civil war followed, and Duke Karl of Södermanland, Sigismund's Machiavellian uncle, finally emerged triumphant as the protector of the Lutheran faith against his tyrannical Papist nephew and ascended the throne as Charles IX (r. 1599–1611). Many political purges also followed. By the early 1600s, Catholicism was identified with the deposed King Sigismund and his allies, and it became associated with treason.[43]

As in other Reformed regions, the new faith with its social norms had to be translated into novel legislation. The Church started to make Protestant canon law by diocesan and provincial councils and Church Ordinances. Secular police legislation supplemented it.[44] These changes made themselves known in ordinary parish life around 1600.[45] Church architecture changed to reflect Reformatory changes, and the pulpit became more important to correspond to the emphasis on preaching and teaching the laity. Since the early 1600s, the importance of the pulpit also grew as an important local node of the official information system. The crown used increasingly the clergy as means of mass communication.[46]

In the seventeenth century, the links between the Lutheran church and the crown were tightened even more and the church became an integrated and integral part of the state machinery. Religious unity, represented by the Swedish Lutheran Church, was safeguarded by the state in the spirit of strict Lutheran Orthodoxy. The Church Law of 1686 became a monument of this, dictating that all the inhabitants of the country were to confess the Lutheran faith.[47] The clergy denounced and investigated crime on a local level together with crown officials, which made control of the people more efficient than ever before.[48] For ordinary

---

42 Decision of the Council of Uppsala, 20 March 1593, *SRA* 3, Emil Hildebrand (ed.). Stockholm: Riksarkivet, 1894–1910, 86–90. Andrén 1999, 212–228.

43 See, for example, Michael Roberts, *Gustavus Adolphus. A History of Sweden 1611–1632*, 1, London/New York/Toronto: Longmans, Green and Co, 1953, 20–38, 93–111.

44 For Swedish police legislation in the early modern period, see Toomas Kotkas, *Royal Police Ordinances in Early Modern Sweden. The Emergence of Voluntaristic Understanding of Law*, Leiden: Brill, 2014.

45 Montgomery 2002, 16–19.

46 Bill Widén, *Predikstolen som massmedium i det svenska riket från medeltiden till stormakttidens slut*, Åbo: Åbo Akademi, 2002, esp. 56–61.

47 Montgomery 2002, 9–12. I Chapter (On the True Christian Doctrine) in: Lahja-Inkeri Hellemaa, Anja Jussila, Martti Parvio (eds.), *Kircko-Laki Ja Ordningi 1686*, Helsinki: Suomalaisen Kirjallisuuden Seura, 1986, 1–6.

48 E.g., Seppo Aalto, *Kirkko ja kruunu siveellisyyden vartijoina. Seksuaalirikos, esivalta ja yhteisö Porvoon kihlakunnassa 1621–1700*, Helsinki: SHS, 1996.

sedentary people, it was difficult to evade the law when both church and crown worked in unison to bring all sinners and criminals to account. The Swedish system offered few possibilities to play ecclesiastical against secular jurisdiction, or vice versa, as the king was at the top of both hierarchies and was the ultimate arbiter of any jurisdictional disputes. In practice, the jurisdiction of ecclesiastical courts was clipped even further in the later seventeenth century when King Charles XI clarified the boundaries between ecclesiastical and secular courts to the advantage of the latter.[49]

The centralizing and standardizing "legal revolution" in the seventeenth century

The Swedish need to make the administration of the country more effective was largely driven by fiscal considerations. The process had been started by Gustav Vasa, who had recruited German chancellors to remodel the central administration, but progress in other fields was slow. Around 1600, there was no uniformity of law because all the law manuscripts included a variety of supplementing statutes and other material. There was no one standardized version of the law, nor was there any authoritative collection of statutes. King Erik XIV had proposed to have the laws of Sweden "corrected" and printed and the Estates had consented to this in 1566. However, the project was never realized.[50] King Charles IX (r. 1599–1611) also proposed to the Estates in 1602 that a new law book be drafted and printed. According to the king, there was such confusion that hardly no two identical copies of the law could to be found in all the realm. Despite initial consent by the Estates and the work of a law committee, apparently no consensus could be achieved about the content of the law, and in the end, the project was aborted.[51]

As a new law proved too complicated a project, King Christopher's Law of the Realm of 1442 was finally printed in 1608 and confirmed by the king so that there would be one standardized and "certain" copy of the law. Having a printed law book would enable people to observe a common source, which, it was thought,

49 5 May 1684, *Kongl. stadgar*, Schmedeman (ed.), 864.

50 15 March 1566, *Erik XIV:s almanacks-anteckningar, hans dagböcker, ritningar och musiknoter i urval utgifvna*, Carl Magnus Stenbock (ed.), Stockholm: Personhistoriska Samfundet, 1912, 10.

51 *Lagförslag i Carl den Niondes tid*, J. J. Nordström (ed.). Stockholm: Norstedt, 1864, vii–xxii and passim.

would lead "to general well-being and to a significant increase in justice".[52] Magnus Eriksson's Town Law was published and confirmed by King Gustav II Adolf in 1618, as were some of provincial laws with mainly antiquarian value. The printed law books replaced the law manuscripts within a decade or two, which contributed to the unification of Swedish law.

There had also been attempts to improve the control of the judiciary ever since 1563, when King Erik XIV had insisted that all district court judges deliver their court records for annual inspection.[53] In 1602, the notion of a yearly inspection of all court records by "good men" was repeated, but to what extent the royal mandate was followed, remains unclear.[54]

What really put Sweden on the path to more coherent legal practice was the financial and political crisis of the early 1610s. Recurrent warfare since the 1550s had strained the Swedish economy. In addition, the ransoming of the Swedish fortress of Älvsborg from the Danish for the exorbitant sum of a million silver *dalers* between 1613 and 1619 pushed Sweden to the verge of bankruptcy. This coincided with constant needs to levy funds and soldiers, which required the consent of the Estates.[55]

To cement the regime's position and appease the Estates, which had expressed its concern for the unsatisfactory state of the judiciary and the king's supreme judgement, King Gustav II Adolf (r. 1611–32) established a royal Court of Appeal with the consent of the Estates and the hereditary dukes in 1614. It would sit in Stockholm and hear appeals from all over the country as the 1614 Ordinance of Judicial Procedure prescribed. The ordinance confirmed the court hierarchy: decisions of district courts were to be appealed to the *lagman*'s courts, which, in turn – together with the decisions of town courts – were to be appealed to the Court of Appeal. In addition, the court would annually inspect all court records from the lower courts and accept any complaints from people claiming that they had been denied justice. The new Court would manage all justice-related business during the king's absence – he was about to embark on a campaign against Russia – but the exact powers of the court after his return were left unspecified.

52 Stadfästelse på Landz-Lagen, 20 Dec. 1608, *Kongl. stadgar*, Schmedeman (ed.), 128.

53 Instruction of King Erik XIV for crown officials, 1 Nov. 1563, in *Handlingar rörande Skandinaviens historia* 27. Stockholm: Kungl. Samfundet för utgivande av handskrifter rörande Skandinaviens historia, 1845, 27.

54 Summary of the decisions of the Diet of Linköping, 19 March 1600, in *Kongl. stadgar*, Schmedeman (ed.), 117–118. Mandate on Review Assizes in Uppsala, 4 Dec. 1602, in *Kongl. stadgar*, Schmedeman (ed.), 118–119.

55 Roberts 1953, 122–129, 141–145.

As no appeals from the new court were allowed, only the extraordinary remedy of *beneficium revisionis* could be petitioned from the king for a high sum.[56]

The string of other courts of appeal established in the provinces – Turku (in Finland 1623), Dorpat (Tartu in Estonia 1630) and Göta (in Jönköping 1634) – demonstrate that the appellate court model was considered an effective means of controlling the judiciary in its jurisdiction and of providing justice to the locals. The monarch then further unified the practice within the realm by answering queries from the Courts of Appeal, which then were made known to all.

Thus, during the so-called "age of empire" (*stormaktstiden*), when Sweden became a European great power, all the human and economic resources of Sweden became subservient to the war state. It also required a reform and centralization of the crown administration expressed in the board (*kollegium*, ministry) system in the 1634 Instrument of Governance.[57]

The centralizing of the royal administration that became a precondition for the seventeenth-century Swedish military state also took place in the field of law. As a result, all the boards – including the Svea Court of Appeal and its sister appellate courts – were subject to regular inspections by the government. While the Boards of Admiralty and War had their own judiciaries in the form of military courts, the first inspection in 1636 levelled some serious criticism at their activities.[58]

Despite some more diversity of law, as fiscal cases or the revenues of the Crown did not pertain to the ordinary courts but rather to the Royal Treasury (*Kammarkollegium*) and cases involving mining to the Board of Mining (*Bergskollegiet*),[59] the new appellate courts inspected and unified the legal practice in the courts under their supervision. The monarch and the Council of the Realm, in their turn, started to harmonize the practice between the different appellate court jurisdictions. Considering that all towns followed King Magnus Eriksson's Town Law, and the rest of Sweden and Finland proper (the Baltic and German provinces

56 Mia Korpiola, A safe haven in the shadow of war? The founding and the raison d'être of the new court, based on its early activity. In *The Svea Court of Appeal in the Early Modern Period: Historical Reinterpretations and New Perspectives*, Mia Korpiola (ed.), 51–102. Stockholm: Institutet för rättshistorisk forskning, 2014d. For a classical study on the Svea Court, see Sture Petrén, Stig Jägerskiöld, Tord O:son Nordberg, *Svea hovrätt. Studier till 350-årsminnet*. Stockholm: Norstedt, 1964.

57 Sjöberg 2013, 3, 199–221.

58 Rådsprotokoller angående Collegiernas redogörelse inför Kongl. Regeringen. In *Handlingar Rörande Skandinaviens Historia*, 33. Stockholm: Kungl. Samfundet för utgivande av handskrifter rörande Skandinaviens historia, 1852, 196–197, 230–233, 262–267, 275–281.

59 David Nehrman, *Inledning Til Then Swenska Processum Civilem. Efter Sweriges Rikes Lag och Stadgar författad*, Stockholm,Upsala: Gottfried Kiesewetter, 1751, 74–75.

excluded) the 1442 law for the countryside, there was rather limited space for diversity in the early modern Swedish realm.

Patrimonial jurisdictions in Sweden during the long seventeenth century: An interlude of potentially greater diversity

King Gustav I Vasa first gave duchies as fiefs for his younger sons and later (1560) divided his kingdom in his will between his sons, each of whom received a hereditary duchy. The donation letter talked about "a princely jurisdiction" (*furstelige jurisdiction*), but what this meant in practice was not defined. However, they were to receive all the royal fines (*cronones årlige [...] sakörer*) of the duchy.[60] The agreement between the new King Erik XIV and his brothers in 1561 clarified the matter. The dukes were allowed to nominate district judges but not *lagmän* in their duchies. The court hierarchy in the duchies allowed appeals from the local level either to the *lagman*'s court or the duke/ducal court. Appeals from the *lagman*'s court or the duke were to go to the king or his court, whereas decisions of the duke could not be appealed to the *lagman* or vice versa.[61] All fines from the duchies were to be collected and criminals tried by the dukes "reasonably and according to the written law of Sweden and nothing else," except for lese-majesty, which pertained to the royal jurisdiction alone. In addition, the king was entitled to arrange his royal correctional assizes (*konungs räffst*) every three years in the whole realm, the duchies included.[62] Thus, the king remained the supreme judge in his reign as the law of Sweden decreed.

The ideology remained largely the same in the early seventeenth century. When Duke Johan of East Gothia (1589–1618, Sw. Östergötland), younger son of King John III, gave up all his claims to the throne, he received in return very extensive privileges in 1604; these increased in 1611.[63] At the succession of Gustav II Adolf to the throne of Sweden in 1611, his younger brother Duke Karl Filip of Söder-

60 King Gustav Vasa's donation letter to Duke Johan, 7 Sep. 1557, *SRA* 1:2, Hildebrand (ed.), 750–756, see esp. 751. King Gustav Vasa's will, 1 July 1560, ibidem, 675–695.

61 Agreement on the princely privileges *SRA* 2, Hildebrand (ed.), 17.

62 Agreement on the princely privileges *SRA* 2, Hildebrand (ed.), 17–18.

63 Folke Lindberg, Hertig Johan av Östergötland och hans furstendöme. *Historisk Tidskrift* 61 (1941): 113–149, here 115–118. Folke Lindberg, Johan av Östergötland. In *Svenskt biografiskt lexikon 20*, Erik Grill (ed.), 199–201, Stockholm: Norstedt, 1973–1975, here 199.

manland (1601–22) was guaranteed more or less the same rights in his duchy as had been granted to his cousin Duke Johan. Therefore, when King Gustav II Adolf established the first royal court of appeal (Svea Court of Appeal) in the capital city of Stockholm in 1614, the establishing documents observe the existence of ducal courts of appeal as well. This could have resulted in the considerable diminishing of the king's jurisdiction, but it did not. Sentences of the ducal appellate courts could be appealed to the royal court of appeal in Stockholm.[64] Thus, the judiciary of the duchies largely stayed under the control of the king.

The ducal courts of appeal were probably first organized as ad hoc panels of judges of the closest officials of the ducal court. However, the existence of the organized royal court of appeal and its monitoring of the lower courts – including the ducal courts of appeal – brought about a standardization of even the ducal courts. At least the activity of the ducal court of appeal in East Gothia was modelled after the royal Svea Court of Appeal in 1618 after the Svea Court had reprimanded the ducal court in hearing an appellate case from the duchy. Duke Johan himself had been forced to explain the sentence.[65]

Ever since the latter part of the sixteenth century, the nobility had attempted to have their privileges expanded so that all noblemen would be allowed to have a third of the fines owed by their tenants, that is, the third due to the judge, except in cases of lese-majesty. Counts, barons, knights and members of the Council of the Realm had already been granted the third of the fines, that is, the third due to the king, again lese-majesty excepted. Moreover, they wanted all counts to be allowed to nominate district judges in their counties. In addition, all positions as district judges were to be monopolized by the nobility.[66] King John III granted some of these requests in the 1569 privileges of the nobility. Counts were allowed to nominate the district judges in their own counties provided the judges were righteous and fair and were to grant ordinary people "law and justice" (*lagh och rätt*). The legal practice was to be similar in similar cases and in accordance with the law of Sweden in the territories of the counts as in the rest of the realm. The king also reserved for himself an exclusive prerogative of pardon in certain severe crimes.[67] In his confirmation of the fief of the county of Visingsborg to Count Per Brahe the Elder (1520–1590), his first cousin, King John III defined the court hier-

64 *Rättegångs-Ordinantie* 1614, *Kongl. stadgar*, Schmedeman (ed.), 138.
65 Lindberg 1941, 123–124.
66 Proposal for privileges of the nobility, sine dato, *SRA* 2, Hildebrand (ed.), 376–377. Nilsson 1952. For many crimes, the fines were ordinarily equally divided between the king, the injured party and the judicial district.
67 King John III's privileges of the nobility, 9 July 1569, *SRA* 2, Hildebrand (ed.), 380–382.

archy in the county in 1569. All appeals (*appellation*) were to go from the district court to the count, then to the Council of the Realm and ultimately, to the king.[68]

In the seventeenth century, Sweden moved towards more feudal structures because the continuous wars in Karelia, the Baltic Region and on the Continent required considerable funds and the Swedish crown lacked the wherewithal to pay regular salaries to its servants, officials and civil servants alike. The sale, donation, enfeoffment or mortgage of crown lands was the solution. By 1654, about two-thirds of all farms were in noble hands, which made the peasants – regardless of whether their lands were owned by themselves or by the Crown – subservient to the discipline of their noble masters. In the course of the century, this went on to the extent that the Crown received the taxes from less than 30 per cent of the peasantry.[69] This trend towards more feudal structures also influenced the Swedish jurisdictional system as more patrimonial courts were correspondingly established. The territorial lord had the power to nominate the surrogate judge (*lagläsare*) and collect many of the fines.[70]

Yet, the peasant estate was represented together with the nobility, clergy and burghers in parliament, and the local peasantry elected its representatives to travel to the diets, increasingly convening in Stockholm. Even if the political role of the peasant estate remained limited, parliamentary representation was a way of having its grievances of voiced and discussed publicly. Moreover, kings could and did seek support for their policies from the commoner estates. Indeed, the peasants eagerly supported – even demanded – a reversal of alienated crown lands in 1655 and in the Great Reduction of 1680.[71] The latter ended almost completely the activities of the patrimonial courts.

The rise of patrimonial courts from the 1580s to the 1680s could have resulted in greater diversity of law practiced in Sweden proper. However, royal control of patrimonial courts was considered important, because the kings were adamant about retaining their position as supreme judge and guarantor of justice to all subjects. First, the sentences of the patrimonial courts could be appealed to the Council of the Realm, and, after 1614, to the royal appellate courts, which also

68 King John III's confirmation of the County of Visingsborg, 9 July 1569, *SRA* 2, Hildebrand (ed.), 394.

69 Carlsson 1962, 9–10. Dahlgren 1967, 15, 18.

70 Mauno Jokipii, *Suomen kreivi- ja vapaaherrakunnat* 2. Helsinki: Suomen Historiallinen Seura, 1960, 32–68. Lars-Olof Larsson, Borgrätt och adelsjurisdiktion i medeltidens och 1600-talets Sverige. In *Historia och samhälle. Studier tillägnade Jerker Rosén*, 49–67, Lund: Studentlitteratur, 1975.

71 On the reductions, see, for example, Kurt Ågren, The *reduktion*. In *Sweden's Age of Greatness*, Michael Roberts (ed.), 237–264, London and Basingstoke: Macmillan, 1973, here 242–244.

inspected their court records yearly. In this sense, there is a certain parallel in France, where the sentences of feudal courts could always be appealed to royal justice, which allowed the king to enhance his own judicial authority in his reign.[72] The move towards feudalism proved a relative short-term interlude that did not alter the relatively uniform Swedish legal landscape.

Conclusion

The early modern Swedish legal system was much less complicated than those of several other countries in Continental Europe. The laws and norms were written in vernacular Swedish: the small and politically rather insignificant towns followed King Magnus Eriksson's Town Law (ca. 1350) and the rest of the country King Christopher's Law of 1442. Later, the Code of 1734 did a great deal to unify the law across the whole country. The "law of Sweden", consented to by the Estates – including the peasantry – had an important practical, political and ideological role in medieval and early modern Sweden. Consequently, other sources of law – customary law, legal science, precedents, canon, Roman or other foreign law – had a relatively minor role to play in the Swedish legal system before the nineteenth century.

The judiciary was in the hands of laymen who usually had neither studied at university nor attained degrees in law. In the seventeenth century, the role of universities in producing legal learning was modest, but growing. After the Reformation, the monarch was the supreme arbiter of both the secular and ecclesiastical court systems. In secular jurisdiction, the first Court of Appeal came to be on top of the court hierarchy as confirmed by the Ordinance of 1614, second only to the king. He was the supreme judge in his realm in all matters ecclesiastical and secular.

A major factor limiting the legal diversity of Sweden was its lack of feudalism. Patrimonial jurisdictions were first introduced in the 1560s with the establishment of the first hereditary noble titles. After a modest beginning, patrimonial courts gained momentum during the seventeenth century until the Great Reduction of 1680. However, the patrimonial courts were almost without exception subordinated to royal control: appeal to the royal courts was possible and the records of the patrimonial courts were to be reviewed yearly by the royal appellate courts.

72 Gallet 1996, 716.

Efforts were made to ensure that people all over the realm could expect standard procedure and punishments in similar cases regardless of the type of court. Even if there was a tendency to create special fora for matters like mining and military and naval legal affairs, these were rather marginal. There were few possibilities for them to encroach upon the jurisdiction of ordinary courts because of regular inspections and the active role of the courts of appeal in defending their position. The king would quickly resolve any jurisdictional dispute.

None of the factors mentioned in my essay were unique to Sweden in early modern Europe, and while Sweden was a peripheral country, it was by no means immune to European trends. Although the notion of path dependence[73] should not be taken as unavoidable destiny, however, many of Sweden's economic and political *longue durée* structures, based on geography and climate, came to precondition its future development. In combination, all these factors made Sweden a country with relatively little legal diversity in comparison with many other European territories. Even if the Swedish territorial expansion in the Baltic regions, Germany and Denmark introduced some different legal and judicial models into the Swedish realm,[74] these had relatively little effect on Sweden proper.

Thus, it seems safe to conclude by claiming that early modern Swedes did not have "a dazzling array of overlaid jurisdictions with multiple and sometimes conflicting legal regimes"[75] at their disposal, and the possibility of forum-shopping were limited. Whether this was beneficial or detrimental to Swedish early-modern litigants remains another matter.

References

Aalto, Seppo, *Kirkko ja kruunu siveellisyyden vartijoina. Seksuaalirikos, esivalta ja yhteisö Porvoon kihlakunnassa 1621–1700*, Helsinki: SHS, 1996.

Ågren, Kurt, The *reduktion*. In *Sweden's Age of Greatness*, Michael Roberts (ed.), 237–264, London and Basingstoke: Macmillan, 1973.

Andrén, Åke, *Sveriges kyrkohistoria 3. Reformationstid*. Stockholm: Verbum, 1999.

73 On path dependence, see, for example, James Mahoney, Path dependence in historical sociology. *Theory and Society* 29:4 (2000): 507–548.

74 E.g., Kjell Åke Modéer, *Gerichtsbarkeiten der schwedischen Krone im deutschen Reichsterritorium. 1. Voraussetzungen und Aufbau 1630–1657*, Lund: Institutet för rättshistorisk forskning, 1975. Bernard Diestelkamp, Kjell Åke Modéer (eds.), Integration durch Recht. Das Wismarer Tribunal (1653–1806), Berlin: Böhlau Verlag, 2003. Pihlajamäki 2017.

75 Hardwick 2009, 61.

Åström, Patrik, *Senmedeltida svenska lagböcker. 136 lands- och stadslagshandskrifter – dateringar och dateringsproblem*. Stockholm: Almqvist & Wiksell, 2003.
Bååth, L. M., *Bidrag till den kanoniska rättens historia i Sverige*. Stockholm: 1905.
Björne, Lars, *Patrioter och institutionalister. Den nordiska rättsvetenskapens historia, 1. Tiden före år 1815*, Lund: Institutet för rättshistorisk forskning, 1995.
Blomstedt, Yrjö, *Laamannin- ja kihlakunnantuomarinvirkojen läänittäminen ja hoito Suomessa 1500– ja 1600-luvuilla (1523–1680). Oikeushallintohistoriallinen tutkimus*. Helsinki: Suomen Historiallinen Seura, 1958.
Carlsson, Sten, *Bonde – präst – ämbetsman. Svensk ståndscirkulation från 1680 till våra dagar*. Stockholm: Prisma, 1962.
Cederholm, Mathias, *De värjde sin rätt. Senmedeltida bondemotstånd i Skåne och Småland*, Lund: Historiska instutionen vid Lunds universitet, 2007.
Claësson, Sten, *Häradshövdingeämbetet i senmedeltidens och Gustav Vasas Sverige*. Stockholm: Institutet för rättshistorisk forskning, 1987.
Constant, Jean-Marie, Prévôtés, vicomtés, vigueries, châtellenies. In *Dictionnaire de l'Ancien Régime. Royaume de France, XVIe–XVIIIe siècle*, Julien Bély (ed.), 1015–1016, Paris: Presses universitaires de France, 1996.
Dahlbäck, Göran, The towns. In *The Cambridge History of Scandinavia. Volume I, Prehistory to 1520*, Knut Helle (ed.), 611–634, Cambridge: Cambridge University Press, 2003.
Dahlgren, Stellan, 1600-talets ståndssamhälle. In *Kultur och samhälle i stormaktstidens Sverige*, Stellan Dahlgren, Allan Ellenius, Lars Gustafsson, Gunnar Larsson (eds.), 9–40, Stockholm: Wahlström & Widstrand, 1967.
Diestelkamp, Bernhard, Modéer, Kjell Åke (eds.), Integration durch Recht. Das Wismarer Tribunal (1653–1806), Berlin: Böhlau Verlag, 2003.
Ericsson, Georg J. V., *Den kanoniska rätten och Äldre Västgötalagens kyrkobalk. En jämförande studie*, Institutet för rättshistorisk forskning: Lund, 1967.
Erik XIV:s almanacks-anteckningar, hans dagböcker, ritningar och musiknoter I urval utgifvna, Carl Magnus Stenbock (ed.), Stockholm: Personhistoriska Samfundet, 1912.
Eriksson, Bo, *Svenska adelns historia*. Stockholm: Norstedts, 2011.
Gallet, Jean, Justice seigneuriale. In *Dictionnaire de l'Ancien Régime. Royaume de France, XVIe–XVIIIe siècle*, Julien Bély (ed.), 714–717, Paris: Presses universitaires de France, 1996.
Handlingar rörande Skandinaviens historia 27. Stockholm: Kungl. Samfundet för utgivande av handskrifter rörande Skandinaviens historia, 1845.
Handlingar rörande Skandinaviens Historia, 33. Stockholm: Kungl. Samfundet för utgivande av handskrifter rörande Skandinaviens historia, 1852.
Hardwick, Julie, *Family Business. Litigation and the Political Economies of Daily Life in Early Modern France*. Oxford: Oxford University Press, 2009.
Heckscher, Eli, *An Economic History of Sweden*. Trans. Göran Ohlin. Cambridge, Mass.: Harvard University Press, 1963.
Hellemaa, Lahja-Inkeri, Jussila, Anja, Parvio, Martti (eds.), *Kircko-Laki Ja Ordningi 1686*, Helsinki: Suomalaisen Kirjallisuuden Seura, 1986.
Hellström, Jan Arvid, *Biskop och landskapssamhälle i tidig svensk medeltid*. Institutet för rättshistorisk forskning: Lund, 1971.
Jägerskiöld, Stig, *Studier rörande receptionen av främmande rätt i Sverige under den yngre landslagens tid* Stockholm: Almqvist & Wiksell, 1963.
Jokipii, Mauno, *Suomen kreivi- ja vapaaherrakunnat* 2. Helsinki: Suomen Historiallinen Seura, 1960.

Jutikkala, Eino, *Bonden – adelsmannen – Kronan. Godspolitik och jordegendomsförhållanden.* Copenhagen, Lund: Nordisk Ministerråd, 1979.
Kagan, Henry L., *Lawsuits and Litigants in Castile 1500–1700.* Chapel Hill: University of North Carolina Press, 1981.
Kongl. stadgar, förordningar, bref och resolutioner, ifrån åhr 1528 in til 1701 angående justitiæ och executions-ährender etc., Joh. Schmedeman (ed.), Stockholm: Johann Henrich Werner, 1706.
Korpiola, Mia, On ecclesiastical jurisdiction and the reception of canon law in the Swedish provincial laws. In *How Nordic Are the Nordic Medieval Laws?* Ditlev Tamm, Helle Vogt (eds.), 202–231, Copenhagen: University of Copenhagen Press, 2005 (Reprinted in Copenhagen: DJØF Publishing Press, 2011.).
Korpiola, Mia, Literary legacies and canonical book collections. Possession of Canon Law Books in Medieval Sweden. In *Law and Learning in Medieval Europe*, Helle Vogt, Mia Münster-Swendsen (eds.), 79–103. Copenhagen: DJØF Publishing Press, 2006.
Korpiola, Mia. On the influence of Roman law in medieval Sweden. Books and university studies. In *Liber Amicorum Kjell Å. Modéer*, Bernhard Diestelkamp, Hans-Heinrich Vogel, Nils Jörn, Per Nilsén, Christian Häthén (eds.), 343–355, Lund: Juristförlaget, 2007.
Korpiola, Mia, On the reception of the *ius commune* and foreign law in Sweden, ca. 1550–1615. *Clio@Thémis* 2 (2009), available online at: http://www.cliothemis.com/On-the-Reception-of-the-Jus (29/03/2017).
Korpiola, Mia, Some evidence of the use of Roman law in medieval Sweden. In *Liber amicorum Ditlev Tamm: Law, History and Culture*, Per Andersen, Pia Letto-Vanamo, Kjell Åke Modéer, Helle Vogt (eds.), 173–183, Copenhagen: DJØF Publishing Press, 2011.
Korpiola, Mia, Desperately needing lawyers. Contacts in the Baltic Sea region and the rise of diplomacy in Reformation Sweden. In *Migration und Kulturtransfer im Ostseeraum während der Frühen Neuzeit*, Otfried Czaika, Heinrich Holze (eds.), 101–120, Stockholm: Kungliga biblioteket, 2012.
Korpiola, Mia, Lutheran marriage law in sixteenth- and early seventeenth-century Sweden. Authorities and sources of law. In *Law and Religion. The Legal Teachings of the Catholic and Protestant Reformations*, Wim Decock, Jordan J. Ballor, Michael Germann, Laurent Waelkens (eds.), 107–132, Göttingen: Vandenhoeck & Ruprecht, 2014a.
Korpiola, Mia, General Background. From Judicial Crisis to Judicial Revolution through the Svea Court of Appeal? In *The Svea Court of Appeal in the Early Modern Period: Historical Reinterpretations and New Perspectives*, Mia Korpiola (ed.), 21–50, Stockholm: Institutet för rättshistorisk forskning, 2014b.
Korpiola, Mia, "Not without the consent and goodwill of the common people:" The community as a legal authority in medieval Sweden. *The Journal of Legal History*, 35:2 (2014c): 95–119.
Korpiola, Mia, A safe haven in the shadow of war? The founding and the raison d'être of the new court, based on its early activity. In *The Svea Court of Appeal in the Early Modern Period: Historical Reinterpretations and New Perspectives*, Mia Korpiola (ed.), 51–102, Stockholm: Institutet för rättshistorisk forskning, 2014d.
Korpiola, Mia, The Svea Court of Appeal: A Fundament of Good Governance and Justice in the Early Modern Swedish Realm (1614–1800). In *Comparative History of the Central Courts of Europe and the Americas, 1200–1800*, Mark Godfrey, Remco van Rhee (eds.), Berlin: Duncker & Humblot, forthcoming 2018.

Kotkas, Toomas, *Royal Police Ordinances in Early Modern Sweden. The Emergence of Voluntaristic Understanding of Law*, Leiden: Brill, 2014.
Laasonen, Pentti, *Suomen kirkon historia 2. Vuodet 1593–1808*, Porvoo,Helsinki,Juva: WSOY, 1991.
Lagförslag i Carl den Niondes tid, J. J. Nordström (ed.). Stockholm: Norstedt, 1864.
Larson, James L., *Reforming the North. The Kingdoms and Churches of Scandinavia, 1520–1545*, Cambridge: Cambridge University Press, 2010.
Larsson, Lars-Olof, Borgrätt och adelsjurisdiktion i medeltidens och 1600-talets Sverige. In *Historia och samhälle. Studier tillägnade Jerker Rosén*, 49–67, Lund: Studentlitteratur, 1975.
Lenman, Bruce, Parker, Geoffrey, The State, the Community and the Criminal Law in Early Modern Europe. In *Crime and the Law. The Social History of Crime in Western Europe since 1500*, V. A. C. Gatrell, Bruce Lenman, Geoffrey Parker (eds.), 11–48, London: Europe Publications Limited, 1980.
Lindberg, Folke, Hertig Johan av Östergötland och hans furstendöme. *Historisk Tidskrift* 61 (1941): 113–149.
Lindberg, Folke, Johan av Östergötland. In *Svenskt biografiskt lexikon 20*, Erik Grill (ed.), 199–201, Stockholm: Norstedt, 1973–1975.
Lindkvist, Thomas, Law and the Making of the State in Medieval Sweden. Kingship and Communities. In *Legislation and Justice*, Antonio Padoa-Schioppa (ed.), 211–228. Oxford: Clarendon Press, 1997.
Lundkvist, Sven, The Experience of Empire: Sweden as a Great Power. In *Sweden's Age of Greatness*, Michael Roberts (ed.), 20–57, London/Basingstoke: Macmillan, 1973.
Mahoney, James, Path dependence in historical sociology. *Theory and Society* 29:4 (2000): 507–548.
Modéer, Kjell Åke, *Gerichtsbarkeiten der schwedischen Krone im deutschen Reichsterritorium. 1. Voraussetzungen und Aufbau 1630–1657*, Lund: Institutet för rättshistorisk forskning, 1975.
Montgomery, Ingun, *Sveriges kyrkohistoria 4. Enhetskyrkans tid*. Stockholm: Verbum, 2002.
Nehrman, David, *Inledning Til Then Swenska Processum Civilem. Efter Sweriges Rikes Lag och Stadgar författad,* Stockholm,Upsala: Gottfried Kiesewetter, 1751.
Nilsson, Sven A., *Krona och frälse i Sverige 1523 – 1594. Rusttjänst, länsväsende, godspolitik*, Lund: Gleerupska Univ.bokhandeln, 1947.
Nilsson, Sven A., *Kampen om de adliga privilegierna 1526–1594*. Lund: Vetenskaps-Societeten i Lund, 1952.
Olesen, Jens E., Inter-Scandinavian relations. In *The Cambridge History of Scandinavia. Volume I, Prehistory to 1520*, Knut Helle (ed.), 710–770, Cambridge: Cambridge University Press, 2003.
Orrman, Eljas, Church and society. In *The Cambridge History of Scandinavia. Volume I, Prehistory to 1520*, Knut Helle (ed.), 421–436, Cambridge: Cambridge University Press, 2003.
Orrman, Eljas, The condition of the rural population. In *The Cambridge History of Scandinavia. Volume I, Prehistory to 1520*, Knut Helle (ed.), 581–610, Cambridge: Cambridge University Press, 2003.
Paresys, Isabelle, *Aux marges du royaume. Violence, justice et société en Picardie sous François Ier*. Paris: Publications de la Sorbonne, 1998.

Petrén, Sture, Jägerskiöld, Stig, Nordberg, Tord O:son, *Svea hovrätt. Studier till 350-årsminnet.* Stockholm: Norstedt, 1964.

Pihlajamäki, Heikki, Positivism before positivism? Royal statutes and early modern Swedish criminal law. In *From the Judge's* Arbitrium *to the Legality Principle. Legislation as a Source of Law in Criminal Trials*, Georges Martyn, Anthony Musson, Heikki Pihlajamäki (eds.), 169–188, Berlin: Duncker & Humblot, 2012.

Pihlajamäki, Heikki, The court of appeal as legal transfer. The Svea and Dorpat courts compared. In *The Svea Court of Appeal in the Early Modern Period: Historical Reinterpretations and New Perspectives*, Mia Korpiola (ed.), 217–260. Stockholm: Institutet för rättshistorisk forskning, 2014.

Pihlajamäki, Heikki, *Conquest and the Law in Swedish Livonia (ca. 1630–1710): A Case of Legal Pluralism in Early Modern Europe*, Leiden: Brill, 2017.

Risberg, Sara, Salonen, Kirsi (eds.), *Auctoritate Papae. The Church Province of Uppsala and the Apostolic Penitentiary 1410–1526*, Stockholm: Riksarkivet, 2008.

Roberts, Michael, *Gustavus Adolphus. A History of Sweden 1611–1632*, 1, London/New York/ Toronto: Longmans, Green and Co, 1953.

Schmidt, Gerhard, *Die Richterregeln des Olavus Petri. Ihre Bedeutung im allgemeinen und für die Entwicklung des schwedischen Strafprozeßrechts vom 14. bis 16. Jahrhundert*, Göttingen/Stockholm: Vandenhoeck & Ruprecht/P. A. Norstedt & Söner, 1966.

Sjöberg, Maria, Adelns tid. In *Det svenska samhället 800–1720. Klerkernas och adelns tid*, Thomas Lindkvist, Maria Sjöberg, 198–419, Lund: Studentlitteratur, 2013.

Sjögren, Wilhelm, De fornsvenska kyrkobalkarna. *Tidsskrift for Retsvidenskap* 17 (1904): 125–176.

Svenska riksdagsakter jämte andra handlingar som höra till statsförfattningens historia under tidehvarfvet 1521–1718 [hereafter SRA] 1:1, Emil Hildebrand, Oscar Alin (eds.) Stockholm: Riksarkivet, 1887.

Statuta synodalia veteris ecclesiæ sveogothicæ, H. Reuterdahl (ed.). Lund: 1841.

Synodalstatuter och andra kyrkorättsliga aktstycken från den svenska medeltidskyrkan, Jaakko Gummerus (ed.), Upsala: Wretmans tryckeri, 1902.

Trolle Önnerfors, Elsa, *Justitia et Prudentia. Rättsbildning genom rättstillämpning: Svea hovrätt och testamentsmålen 1640–1690*, Stockholm: Institutet för rättshistorisk forskning, 2014.

Vasara-Aaltonen, Marianne, From Well-travelled "Jacks-of-all-trades" to Domestic Lawyers: The Educational and Career Backgrounds of Svea Court of Appeal Judges 1614–1809. In *The Svea Court of Appeal in the Early Modern Period: Historical Reinterpretations and New Perspectives*, Mia Korpiola (ed.), 301–354. Stockholm: Institutet för rättshistorisk forskning, 2014.

Widén, Bill, *Predikstolen som massmedium i det svenska riket från medeltiden till stormaktidens slut*, Åbo: Åbo Akademi, 2002.

Part III: **Transitions to modernity**

Sanjog Rupakheti

Beyond *dharmashastras* and Weberian modernity

Law and state making in nineteenth-century Nepal

Introduction

> It is in Nepal alone, of all Hindu states, that two-thirds of the time of the judges is employed in the discussion of cases better fitted for the confessional, or the tribunal of public opinion… than for a King's Court of Justice. Not such, however, is the opinion of the Nepalese; who while they are forcing confession from young men and young women, by dint of scolding and whipping, in order to visit them afterwards with ridiculous penances or savage punishments…glorify themselves in that they are maintaining the holy will of BRAHMA, enforcing from the judgment-seat those sacred institutes which elsewhere the magistrate (shame upon him!) neglects through fear, or despises as an infidel.[1]

Brian Hodgson,[2] who ostensibly catalogued the supposedly arbitrary, cruel, and scripture-driven justice for violations of bodily and ritual purity in Nepal, popularized the image of its legal system being exclusively rooted in Shastric injunctions.[3] This interpretation has left such an enduring imprint in the scholarship

I would like to thank Gijs Kruijtzer and Thomas Ertl for their critical suggestions on the earlier drafts of this paper. I am also grateful to an anonymous reviewer whose comments were very helpful in reworking some of my ideas here. Especial thanks to Paul Buhler, Lincoln Paine, and Rian Thum for their valuable feedbacks in allowing me to sharpen my arguments.

1 Brian H. Hodgson, On Law and Legal Practices of Nepal as Regards Familiar Intercourse Between a Hindu and an Outcast. *Journal of the Royal Asiatic Society of Great Britain and Ireland*, vol. 2 (1834): 47–48.

2 Brian Hodgson was an ethnologist working for the East India Company. After the conclusion of the Anglo-Gorkha War (1814–1816), he went to Kathmandu as an Assistant British Resident in 1820. He later assumed the post of Resident in 1833 and served in that capacity till 1844. A detailed discussion of his life and work can be found in William Wilson Hunter, *Life of Brian Houghton Hodgson: British Resident at The Court of Nepal*, 1896, reprint, New Delhi: Asian Educational, 1991. David Waterhouse (ed.), *The Origins of Himalayan Studies: Brian Houghton Hodgson in Nepal and Darjeeling 1820–1858*, London, New York: Routledge Curzon, 2004.

3 Though some of the earliest western accounts on Nepali legal system are interspersed in the works of Francis Hamilton, *An Account of the Kingdom of Nepal*, Edinburgh: Archibald Constable, 1819. William Kirkpatrick, *An Account of the Kingdom of Nepaul: Being the Substance of Observations Made During a Mission to that Country, in the Year 1793*, 1811, London: Miller, 1971. None

DOI 10.1515/9783110423327-008

that most modern-day scholars writing about Nepal accept the fixation with ritual purity and arbitrary power as the defining hallmarks of nineteenth-century Nepali justice administration.[4] Perhaps nowhere has this influence been more problematic than in the study of the 1854 Nepali legal codification, popularly also known as the *Ain*.

At slightly over fourteen hundred pages, the *Ain* brought almost all aspects of socio-economic life under the disciplinary gaze of the new Rana family power.[5] The text's temporal origin is also significant. It preceded the official British legal codification of 1861. Beyond the comprehensive nature of social regulation envisioned by the document, specific features set the *Ain* apart from other precolonial legal practices.[6] Offering a rationale for its promulgation in its preamble, the *Ain* emphasized that the "wide disparity in punishment for the same offense across regions and social ranks had led to great inconsistency in the administration of justice." It sought to remedy the existing system by highlighting that "no two individuals committing a similar crime should hereafter receive separate punishments." With few notable exceptions, this applied consistently in most criminal cases. As far as civil issues (marriage, commensality, adoptions) were concerned, the "nature of the offense and the *jati* [caste] of the offender" continued to weigh heavily in the administration of justice administration, which highlights the centrality of political and social hierarchy in the Himalayan kingdom.[7]

The chief goal of the *Ain* was not to equalize justice for everyone. Instead, it was aimed at bringing about uniformity and standardization while upholding dif-

---

match the details offered by Hodgson in Brian Hodgson, *Miscellaneous Essays Relating to Indian Subjects*, vol. 2, London: Trubner, 1880, 211–250.

4 See Andras Hofer, *The Caste Hierarchy and the State in Nepal: A Study of the Muluki Ain of 1854*. 1979, reprint, Kathmandu: Himal, 2005. Axel Michaels, *The Price of Purity: The Religious Judge in 19th Century Nepal*, Torino: Comitato Corpus iuris sanscriticum et fontes iuris Asiae meridianae et centralis, 2005, 11–60. An exception to this is Daniel Edwards, *Patrimonial and Bureaucratic Administration in Nepal: Historical Change and Weberian Theory*, PhD. diss., University of Chicago, 1977.

5 I use the Romanized transliteration of the text done by Jean Fezas in Jean Fezas (ed.), *Le Code Nepalais (Ain) De 1853*, Tornino, Italy: Comitato per la pubblicazione del Corpus juris sanscriticum, 2000. Here to after referred as *Ain*.

6 Nowhere in the region had indigenous rulers issued comprehensive code as envisaged by the Nepali codification of 1854. For discussion on some of the earlier regional justice administrations see, Vithal T. Gune, *The Judicial System of the Marathas: A Detailed Study Based on Original Decisions called Mahzars, Nivadpatras, and Official Orders*, Poona: Deccan College, 1953. A. R. Kulkarni (ed.), *Explorations in the Deccan History*, New Delhi: Pragati, 2006. Wahed Husain, *Administration of Justice During the Muslim Rule in India*, Delhi: Idarah-I Adabiyat-I Delhi, 1977.

7 *Ain*, "Lalmohar", 3–5.

ferences. Other significant innovations championed by the *Ain* included replacement of corporal punishment with monetary fines, a prohibition on ordeals and torture to extract confessions, checks on the arbitrary power of state officials, and greater use of written evidence. Despite the extensive coverage of diverse socio-economic relations in the *Ain*, modern scholarship curiously remains focused only on the caste question to draw authoritative claims about the Nepali past.[8]

Frustrated by their search for civil rights in the *Ain*, some have even described it as 'codification of tradition', thus implying that only the Occident could codify modernity.[9] But is a search for civic equality a sound method for evaluating the *Ain* in a period when equalization of justice was rarely a desirable goal anywhere in the world?[10] This kind of presentist approach obscures the broader historical context leading to the creation and implementation of the *Ain* and forecloses possibilities for comparing Nepal to other polities both in South Asia and beyond.[11] Instead of locating the *Ain* on a preconceived continuum of modernity or seeing it as a variation on *dharmashastras*, I propose to interrogate the aim, scope, and workings of the text to offer an alternative narrative of law and power in Nepal. In doing so, I hope to steer the existing debates away from categorizing nine-

---

8 The most influential in this genre is the work of Hofer 2005.

9 This theme comes up regularly in many works. See for example, M. S. Jain, *The Emergence of a New Aristocracy in Nepal*, Agra: Sri Ram Mehta, 1972. Saphalya Amatya, *Rana Rule in Nepal*, Delhi: Nirala, 2004. Krishna Kant Adhikari, *Nepal Under Jung Bahadur, 1846–1877*, Kathmandu: Buku, 1984. Satish Kumar, *Rana Polity in Nepal: Origin and Growth*, Bombay: Asia Pub. House, 1967, 63. The initial impetus to this theme of modernity vs. tradition was laid out by Lloyd Rudolph, Susanne Rudolph, Barristers and Brahmans in India: Legal Cultures and Social Change, *Comparative Studies in Society History* 8 (1965): 24–49, here 25. Notwithstanding variations in this debate, all seem to agree that the lack of impersonal and universal values pervasive in the indigenous legal system makes it incomparable to the modern western legal system.

10 On the discussion of status-differentiated law in the US south, see Annette Gordon-Reed, *Race on Trial: Law and Justice in American Society*, New York: Oxford University Press, 2002. Thomas D. Morris, *Southern Slavery, and Law, 1619–1860*, Chapel Hill: University of North Carolina, 1996. For a similar discussion on racialized justice administration in India under the British, see Radhika Singha, *Despotism of Law: Crime and Justice in Early Colonial India*, Delhi; New York: Oxford University Press, 1998. Elizabeth Kolsky, *Colonial Justice in British India*, Cambridge: Cambridge University Press, 2010. Jordanna Bailkin, The Boot and the Spleen: When Was Murder Possible in British India, *Comparative Studies in Society and History*, 48:2 (2006): 462–493.

11 Regional scholars too have paid scant attention to the *Ain*. Nepal was conspicuously absent from an important edited volume that explored themes of rights and justice in "South Asia". See Michael Anderson, Sumit Guha (ed.), *Changing Concepts of Rights & Justice in South Asia*, New Delhi: Oxford University Press, 2000.

teenth-century Nepal as either a Dharmashastric playground or a 'traditional' polity devoid of the trappings of 'modernity'.

Whither religion and modernity?

Hodgson's records on the Nepali judicial system were informed by the larger eighteenth-century imperial discourse on the putative relationship between Hindu religious texts and law in India.[12] This discussion had origins in earlier Oriental scholarship that projected South Asia "without rule and law" led by despotic "will and caprices."[13] The colonial project in greater South Asia was constructed on the foundation of this alleged difference between rule-bound British governance as against the arbitrary power of precolonial regimes.[14] Though East India Company (EIC) officials did not wield the comparable power to remake the Nepali society through direct military interventions, in stressing the religious-magical elements and arbitrary court proceedings as the operating logic of Nepali system, they made it incomparable to genealogies of law elsewhere. This was most evident in Hodgson's strong suggestion on the religious roots undergirding confession and "savage punishment" rampant in the Nepali justice system.[15]

12 There is a vast literature on this topic. For a succinct review and useful bibliography, see Marc Galanter, *Law and Society in Modern India,* Delhi: Oxford University Press, 1989. On the relationship between Hinduism and law in India, see J. Duncan Derrett, *Religion, Law and the State in India,* New York: The Free Press, 1968. A concise discussion of Anglo-Muslim law is explored by Michael Anderson in Michael Anderson, Islamic Law and the Colonial Encounter in British India. In *Institutions and Ideologies: A SOAS South Asia Reader*, David Arnold, Peter Robb (eds.), 165–185, London: RoutledgeCurzon, 1993. For recent and updated bibliography and debates on these themes see Timothy Lubin, Donald R. Davis, Jr., Jayanth K. Krishnan, *Hinduism and Law: An Introduction.* Cambridge: Cambridge University Press, 2010.
13 For a more focused discussion on this theme, see Nasser Hussain, *The Jurisprudence of Emergency: Colonialism and the Rule of Law,* Ann Arbor: University of Michigan Press, 2003, 44–55.
14 For some of the earlier and relevant works, see Bernard Cohn, *Colonialism and Its Forms of Knowledge: The British in India,* Princeton: Princeton University Press, 1996. Anand Yang, *Crime and Criminality in British India,* Tucson: University of Arizona Press, 1985. On the role of colonial law in the re-making of family and gender relations see, Indrani Chatterjee, *Gender, Slavery, Law in Colonial India,* New Delhi: Oxford University Press, 1999. Chandra Mallampalli, *Race, Religion, and Law in Colonial India: Trials of Interracial Family,* Cambridge: Cambridge University Press, 2011. Durba Ghosh, *Sex and Family in Colonial India: The Making of Empire,* Cambridge: Cambridge University Press, 2006.
15 Hodgson 1880, 223.

Historical evidence tells us a different story. Ordeals were rarely practiced in the Nepali courts and even when they were, they were far more humane compared to the ones that prevailed in Europe.[16] Here Hodgson seemed to be reading the European experience of confession and ordeals into his Nepali materials. As scholars have shown, confession "as modes of establishing truth and as techniques for dealing with dangers of transgression" was perfected in clerical institutions and practices of late medieval Christianity that became an integral aspect of the European legal system.[17] Confession extracted through elaborate judicial torture lay at the heart of the new inquisitorial system in Europe, conjoining legal and religious spheres in the making of the early modern state.[18] The manifestly disciplinary power exercised by religious institutions to shape normative behaviour in the European population equally problematizes the Foucauldian location of discipline on a modern temporal map.[19]

There is a big void in our current knowledge regarding the administration of justice in eighteenth- and early nineteenth-century Nepal, yet surprisingly enough scholars have repeatedly accepted it as being inferior to the Western system. Interrogating the process leading up to the British codification in India, David Skuy has pointed out the fallacy built into such assumptions. English criminal law in the eighteenth century, as Skuy shows, was no more modern than the Indian ones, as almost every criminal act in England at the time was punished with death.[20] English

---

16 Even the trial described by Hodgson does not seem to involve any bodily coercion or punishment. See Hodgson 1880, 211–250. On the discussion of the European ordeals see, Robert Barlett, *Trial by Fire and Water,* New York: Oxford University Press, 1986.

17 See Talal Asad, *Genealogies of Religion: Discipline and Reasons of Power in Christianity and Islam,* Baltimore: Johns Hopkins University Press, 1993, 97.

18 See Robert I. Moore, *The Formation of a Persecuting Society,* Cambridge; Oxford: Blackwell, 1987. Peter Brown, *Society and the Holy in Late Antiquity,* Berkeley: University of California Press, 1982. Morris S. Arnold (ed.), *On the Laws and Customs of England: Essays in Honour of Samuel E. Thorne,* Chapel Hill: University of North Carolina Press, 1981. Moore argues that confession began to replace ordeal when public participation in heresy trials compounded their unpredictability and risked undercutting the disciplinary power of both church and state in the period of rapid socio-economic transformation enveloping Europe. See Moore 1987, 102–106, 140–146. For specific discussion on the relationship between church and early modern states in Europe see Philip S. Gorski, *The Disciplinary Revolution: Calvinism and the Rise of State in Early Modern Europe,* Chicago: University of Chicago Press, 2003.

19 See Thomas Tentler, *Sin and Confession on the Eve of the Reformation,* Princeton: Princeton University Press, 1977. For a more recent critique on this topic see Gorski 2003, 22–26.

20 Skuy argues that the British codification "was rooted in the English experience, and not in India's supposed primitiveness." See David Skuy, Macaulay and the Indian Penal Code of 1862: The Myth of the Inherent Superiority and Modernity of the English Legal System Compared to India's Legal System in the Nineteenth Century, *Modern Asian Studies*, 32:3 (1998): 513–557.

criminal law likewise lacked uniformity and was rife with judicial discretion.[21] In many ways, nineteenth-century Nepali treatment of property crimes was far more humane.[22] England lacked a uniform criminal law well into the 1870s, that is, after a comprehensive criminal law codification was implemented in India in 1861. The nature of the relationship between law and religion is also ambiguous in European history. Rationalization and secularization – the celebrated twin pillars of modernity, as new scholarship has demonstrated – seem to have originated in theological innovations rooted in Christianity rather than from a cathartic divorce from religion.[23] In that regard, religious-secular boundaries appear more porous than Max Weber otherwise believed.[24] A gradual withdrawal of judicial torture to extract confession at the turn of the nineteenth century was less a result of enlightenment ideals and more guided by the imperatives of efficiency and state building.[25] A singular focus on rationality – the rule of law – granted to one system (Western), or the lack thereof – the rule of force – in the other (Eastern), occludes the way in which truth and power are socio-historically determined. Could it be that similar concerns for state building might have shaped the development of the Nepali legal system during the nineteenth-century push towards codification? How would the *Ain* and nineteenth-century Nepal look if we were to shift our perspective so that religion and caste are not seen as the only forces shaping state power?

21 For instance, "Stealing and killing a horse, cow or sheep was a capital offense; stealing a deer from an enclosed ground was a simple felony; and, child-stealing carried the same sentence as stealing a deer." And, in a similar fashion, "five different definitions of larceny were listed from five reputable legal digests." See Skuy 1998, 530–533.

22 Property violations in Nepal, unlike that of England, did not lead to capital punishment. On the discussion related to capital punishments for property crimes in England see E. P. Thompson, *Whigs and Hunters: The Origin of the Black Act,* New York: Pantheon, 1975. For a more detailed historical exploration of this topic see Douglas Hay (ed.), *Albino's Fatal Tree: Crime and Society in Eighteenth-Century England,* New York: Pantheon, 1975.

23 Harold Berman has forcefully argued that the secularization of law across Europe was derived from the various religious beliefs generated in the wake of reformation and post-reformation theological innovations. See Harold J. Berman, *Faith and Order: The Reconciliation of Law and Religion,* Atlanta: Emory University Press, 1993, especially chapter 3 and 5.

24 Weber's Protestant beliefs, Caroll argues, informed a particular idea of secularism and law in his works. See Anthony Caroll, *Protestant Modernity: Weber, Secularization, and Protestantism,* Scranton: University of Scranton Press, 2007.

25 John Langbein links the declining reliance on Roman law of Proof to the growing ambitions of the states. He mainly argues that the imperatives of administrative efficiency that circumstantial evidence provided made confession extracted through judicial torture less attractive. See John Langbein, *Torture and the Law of Proof: Europe and England in the Ancien Regime,* Chicago: University of Chicago Press, 1977.

Taking these into consideration, let us return to nineteenth-century Nepal. The Anglo-Gorkha War (1814–16) had halted the Gorkhali imperial ambitions and fixed the Gorkhali territorial boundaries.[26] However, this hardly led to the application of a unitary state sovereignty in Gorkhali domains. Since the House of Gorkha had gained a foothold in the region by exploiting and managing local conflicts, it remained deeply embedded in the existing relations of power. When Hodgson arrived in Kathmandu in 1820 as a part of the post-war settlement (Sugauli Treaty), the nascent Nepali kingdom was struggling to govern a domain marked by bewilderingly heterogeneous systems of religious beliefs, political structures, cultural practices, and legal systems.[27] Time and again, the Shah ruling family in Kathmandu was compelled to share its sovereignty with many different powerholders across Nepal. This was most evident in the administrative and juridical power granted to many former vanquished chiefs and local power holders in return for nominal fees.[28] While local customs and practices continued to flourish under such arrangements, allowing the centre to operate with a minimal administrative footprint, it prevented the state from maintaining direct control over a vast majority of the people residing in its domain.

After the mid-eighteenth century, the Gorkhali state gradually began to expand its power to regulate aspects of socio-economic life, but uniformity and consistency were conspicuously absent.[29] For instance, an order from 1834 instructed Narsingh Thapa to oversee *nisaf* (justice) to the best of his ability.[30] The vagueness of the term *nisaf* gave officeholders considerable leeway in overseeing administrative affairs. Unless cases of violations were extreme, local rulers were mostly let go with warnings when implicated in embezzlement and were often reinstated after a temporary termination. Many administrative regulations issued from Kathmandu were peculiarly region-specific. For example, one about non-interference with the postal service.[31] The 1809 order banning slavery likewise lacked uniformity as is evident in

---

26 The territorial dispute between the House of Gorkha and the East India Company (EIC) leading to the Anglo-Gorkha War has been explored by Bernardo Michael in Bernardo Michael, *Statemaking and Territory in South Asia: Lessons from the Anglo-Gorkha War, 1814–1816*, London: Anthem Press, 2012.

27 See Sanjog Rupakheti, Reconsidering State-Society Relations in South Asia: A Himalayan Case Study, *Himalaya* 35:2 (2015): 73–86.

28 See Dhanvajra Vajracharya, Gyanmani Nepal, *Aitihasik Patra Sangraha*. Vol.1, Kathmandu: Nepal Sanskritik Parishad, 2014 VS, 25.

29 Jagdish C. Regmi, *Nepalko Vaidhanik Parampara*, Kathmandu: Tribhuvan University, 1978, 247–253.

30 *Regmi Research Collection*, Vol. 19, 509.

31 LM/1826/ BN. 58 Packet. 16, Serial No. 79, f. 4.

another order from 1825, which let the institution of slavery go on so long as those involved in the trade "registered slave transactions at the local court."[32]

The nineteenth-century Gorkhali kingdom was far from the despotic power described by the colonial officers.[33] At the very least, the Gorkhali kings certainly did not enjoy absolute property rights of the whole kingdom, which was in hereditary possession of various social groups.[34] New transfers of unclaimed property to groups or individuals carried a clear title of proprietorship so long as the area remained cultivated. The absence of an organized administrative apparatus in the countryside made it equally difficult to collect arrears.[35] A large portion of the revenue, in fact, went to various intermediaries, rural magnates and local elites who were often also delegated to oversee the maintenance of law and order.[36] It reflected, as in the context of eighteenth-century Maratha state making, a "state that held only a major and fluctuating measure of power conjointly with many powerful and resilient social groups, and one at all times compelled to be aware of the constraints on its abilities."[37] Thus, when a member of a dominant ethnic group in the Eastern region of the Gorkhali territory raped the wife of a Brahmin, his life was spared.[38] When a slave was found guilty of having committed a similar crime, he was executed.[39] One could again draw a close parallel between the eighteenth-century Maratha and the early 1800s Gorkhali penal system. Both were characterized by broad discretion and considerable latitude that was "diffused among a variety of institutions and shared by many different persons".[40]

The increasing volume of property and labour disputes arriving at the centre from the rural areas overwhelmed the barebones administrative system.[41] It produced a massive backlog of petitions in Kathmandu.[42] These rural petitioners

---

32 See *LM/* 1825, Serial No. 2473.

33 Sanjog Rupakheti, *Leviathan or Paper Tiger: State-Making in the Himalayas, 1740–1900*. PhD. diss., Rutgers University, 2012.

34 B. R Grover in his influential work has shown this in the case of Maharashtra. See Amrita Grover (ed.), *Land Rights, Landed Hierarchy and Village Community During Mughal Age*, Vol. 1, Delhi: Originals, 2006, chapter 1.

35 See Mahesh C. Regmi, *Landownership in Nepal*, Berkeley: University of California Press, 1976.

36 Rupakheti 2015, 73–86.

37 Sumit Guha, An Indian Penal Regime: Maharashtra in the Eighteenth Century, *Past and Present* 147 (1995): 101–126.

38 LM/1826/BN. 58, Packet. 16, Serial No. 79, f. 36.

39 LM/1826/BN. 58, Packet. 16, Serial No. 79, f. 36

40 Guha 1995.

41 Available archival evidence suggests an unusual increase in petitions related to property and labour disputes after 1846. Most of these were complaints against local excesses.

42 LM/1853/BN. 8, Packet. 2, Serial No. 6.

demanded justice from kings, who historically played a crucial role as lawgivers across South Asia.[43] Jang Bahadur, who had been entrusted by the king in 1845 to look into the large volume of petitions filed by the peasantry against excesses committed in rural areas, was well aware of the challenges awaiting Rana rule beyond Kathmandu.[44]

Having come to power in the wake of political instability in the Durbar, the Ranas were particularly troubled by the rise of intermediaries in rural Nepal that threatened their ability to access resources and labour. The application of outright force to discipline rural potentates was ineffective. After all, one of the chief complaints of the peasantry was also against the excesses committed by military personnel traveling through rural regions.[45] Realizing that the long-term consolidation of Rana power was not possible without reigning in rural excesses, Jang Bahadur pushed for the centralization of information, resources, and loyalty through administrative and legal innovations. The origins of the 1854 legal code are rooted in this fluid nineteenth-century landscape in the competition for labour and resources, not in the pages of ancient religious texts.

Familial consolidation, legal codification

Two methodological issues in particular have overshadowed critical scholarly understandings of the period under discussion. First is the assumption regarding the existence of the state system almost immediately after the first wave of the Gorkhali territorial consolidation in 1768.[46] Second is a tendency to view Nepali history through a particular narrative of progress and decay. Nationalist historians prefer to read the periods of direct Shah rule in a positive light and associate era of the non-Shah rule with decay. Not surprisingly, we find the period between 1846 and 1951 (when the Rana family dominated politics) being frequently described as a 'dark age'.[47] One prominent historian extends the temporal boundary of the dark

43 See Patrick Olivelle, *King, Governance, and Law in Ancient India*, New Delhi: Oxford University Press, 2013.

44 Bishal Khanal, *Nepalko Naya Prasasan Yak Aitihasik Simbhalokan*, Kathmandu: Ram Prashad Khanal, 1987, 208.

45 These involved forced labour and demand for goods by the military.

46 Even the most astute economic historian of Nepal fell victim to this methodological error. See Mahesh C. Regmi, *A Study in Nepali Economic History, 1768–1846*, New Delhi: Manjushri, 1971.

47 For few exceptions, see Ghanshyam Bhattarai, *Ranakalin Jilla Prasasan ma Badahakimharuko Bhumika*, Kathmandu: Center for Nepal and Asian Studies, 2059 VS, 38. Rajesh Gautam, *Ranakalin Nepal ko Prasasanik, Shaichik ra Samajik Sudharharu*, Delhi: Adroit, 2004, esp. ch. 2.

ages even further back, to the emergence of the Thapa family in 1806.[48] Another holds the Pandey family responsible for the internecine conflicts that ultimately led to the emergence of the Ranas in 1846.[49] A broad consensus holds the Ranas primarily responsible for ruthless exploitation, tyranny, and the general backwardness of Nepal. Thus, the grand narrative of the Nepali nation begins with the emergence of a unified state under the tutelage of the Shah family, which in the hands of the Ranas becomes despotic, and finds a new life only after 1951.[50] There is obviously an acknowledgment of one or the other family being the central actors at different points in Nepali history, but other than blaming individual families for this or that problem, no systematic attempt is made to interrogate the familial nature of state formation.

Even post-1990 scholarship that problematizes the aforementioned narrative arc accepts the Nepali state as a monolithic and fully formed system as early as 1768.[51] These rise-and-fall narratives uncannily echo past strands of Mughal-Maratha historiography that were heavily influenced by Western European theoretical paradigms of absolutist and feudal states.[52] Indeed, Mughal and Maratha scholarship has since undergone several revisions, but the intersection between familial power and state formation has not been systematically studied.[53] Ques-

---

Bhabeshwor Pangeni, *Nepal ko Prasasanik Ithihas 1825–1903 VS*, Kathmandu: Bidhyarthi Pustak Bhandar, 2064 VS.

48 Ludwig F. Stiller, *The Silent Cry: The People of Nepal, 1816–1839*, Kathmandu: Sahayogi Prakashan, 1976.

49 See Chittaranjan Nepali, *General Bhimsen Thapa ra Tatkalin Nepal*, Kathmandu: Ratna Pustak Bhandar, 2022 VS.

50 With the emergence of mass politics after 1990, the old narrative underwent a radical revision wherein all period of Nepali history before the abolition of Shah monarchy in 2008 is seen as regressive, marked by Shah-Rana feudal order and despotism. For two representative works on this latest periodization, see Mahendra Lawoti, *Looking Back, Looking Forward: Centralization, Multiple Conflicts, and Democratic State Building in Nepal*, Washington, D.C.: East-West Center, 2007. Ali Riaz, Subho Basu, *Paradise Lost?: State Failure in Nepal*, Lanham: Lexington, 2007.

51 The only difference now being the state in the post-nationalist literature appears in feudal and despotic form throughout the Shah and Rana rule.

52 W.H. Moreland provided the initial impetus to this historiography when he portrayed the Mughal state as a classic example of Oriental Despotism. The 'Aligarh School' with slight variations took up this model. In both analyses, society and people were seen to be suffering silently while meeting the exorbitant revenue demands. See Irfan Habib, *The Agrarian System of Mughal India 1556–1707*, 1963 revised edition, New Delhi: Oxford University Press, 1999. W.H. Moreland, *The Agrarian System of Moslem India*, 1929 rpntd, Delhi: Oriental Books, 1968.

53 The revisionist work on Mughal-Maratha historiography is vast and expanding. I cite here some of the most influential works in the debate. Muzaffar Alam, Sanjay Subrahmanyam, *The Mughal State, 1526–1750*, Delhi: Oxford University Press, 1998. Stewart Gordon, *Marathas, Ma-*

tioning orientalist models is not sufficient if our theoretical assumptions do not problematize the idea of the state itself. I, therefore, put family and hierarchized society at the centre of our narrative, and trace the progressive development of the Rana clan into a centralized state. Most importantly, I argue that the substance of Rana familial power was built on legal and administrative innovations that codified social hierarchy on the one hand while inaugurating regulatory uniformity and the rationalization of justice administration on the other.

It is a well-known fact amongst historians that politics in the premodern period was an aggregate of family feuds. Andre Wink's seminal work sheds particular light on one such intimate relationship between family feud and state formation in precolonial South Asia.[54] His framework is also applicable in the Himalayan region, where ambitious rulers had succeeded in projecting power by exploiting existing family disputes and alliances within their own households as well as that of their rivals. Since its inception, the House of Gorkha had been embroiled in a series of interfamily struggles for power. When a long tussle for power between Thapa, Pandey, and Basnet clans, and various factions within the royal family culminated in the Kot Massacre of 1846, it propelled a new group (Rana) to the centre stage of Nepali politics.[55] Jang Bahadur Rana, the patriarch of the clan, sought to institutionalize the familial gains achieved in the wake of the tectonic shifts in the Nepali political landscape. This, he envisioned, was possible only through a centralization of information, resources, and loyalty that could be achieved by putting checks on rival families, officials, and local potentates alike.

The *Ain* became the most useful tool in the Rana quest for power. First, it brought together disparate practices and laws into a single document and made them applicable to the whole of the Gorkha territory. In this, it subordinated local elites to the administrative and judicial rules crafted at the centre. Second, a structured deployment of rewards and summary dismissals helped to entrench Rana power vis-à-vis local governors in rural areas. Third, the *Ain* held individ-

---

rauders and State Formation in Eighteenth-Century India, Delhi: Oxford University Press, 1994. Richard M. Eaton, *The Rise of Islam and the Bengal Frontier, 1204–1760,* Berkeley: University of California Press, 1993.

54 Andre Wink, *Land, and Sovereignty in India: Agrarian Relations and Politics Under the Eighteenth-century Maratha Svarajya,* Cambridge: Cambridge University Press, 1986.

55 This has been discussed in Baburam Acharya, Madhav Acharya, *The Blood Stained Throne: Struggles for Power in Nepal, 1775–1914,* New Delhi: Penguin Books India, 2013. For the particular discussion on the Kot Massacre see Ludwig F. Stiller, *Letters from Kathmandu: The Kot Massacre,* Kathmandu: Research Center for Nepal and Asian Studies, Tribhuvan University, 1981. On Thapa-Pandey politics see Kumar Pradhan, *Thapa Politics in Nepal: With Special Reference to Bhimsen Thapa, 1806–1839,* New Delhi: Concept , 2012.

uals and groups responsible for reporting of wrongdoing and punished them for suppressing information of violations of provisions of the *Ain*. The *Ain* shifted the burden of regulating many spheres of social life onto the people by turning communities and family members into informants for the state.

Unfortunately, we do not have much documentation on the process surrounding the composition of the *Ain*. One of the earlier Rana ambitions to standardize the justice system can, however, be glimpsed from a series of letters written by Jang to his brother Bam Bahadur. Writing from London, Jang registered his adamant opposition to the decision of the Kausal,[56] when he found out that the latter had granted immunity to Ramu Ale for murder.[57] Kausal had set Ramu free after a fine of Rs. 2000, while another state official, Chandrabir, was dismissed from office and imprisoned even though both had committed a similar offense. Ramu Ale was a trusted associate of Jang Bahadur and had played a key role during the Kot Massacre. Despite this, Jang demanded stringent punishment for Ale. If capital punishment was not forthcoming, Jang stressed, Ale should be dismissed and imprisoned. Jang reminded Bam Bahadur that for committing a similar crime, he had earlier ordered the execution of Bhairav Singh, a state official who had also been his trusted worker. In another set of letters, Jang defended his dismissal of high-ranking officials for their grave and unpardonable violations of offices.[58] Some of their misdeeds involved appropriation of state funds, forging tax records, and local excesses. Jang's letters are replete with ideas of impartiality and speedy justice. They offer us rare glimpses into Jang's view of rule-based governance as integral to his centralization objective. The Rana patriarch showed a remarkable penchant for uniformity and standardization. So, for instance, Jang Bahadur secured royal permission to employ *jhara* (compulsory labour) to renovate a bridge across the Bagmati River, originally built by his father, even though he could have effortlessly mobilized the needed labour.[59]

In repeatedly alluding to the idea of the rule of law as a source of legitimacy, Jang reminded his brother to keep the population happy.[60] Jang argued that all previous regimes had sown the seeds of their demise by failing to rein in local potentates, and he likened the latter to "ravenous tigers" set against the vulnerable

56 Kausal was the central judiciary-legislative body that passed the final verdicts on cases brought to them. They often oversaw appeals and presided over cases involving significant punishments.

57 See Kamal Dixit, *Janga-Gita*, Lalitpur: Jagadamba Prakashan, 1984, 38.

58 Dixit 1984, 39–41.

59 *Regmi Research Collection*, Vol. 62, pp: 617–618.

60 Dixit 1984, 40.

rural populace.[61] The Rana family considered such intermediaries the greatest threat to their access to resources, information, and power in rural Nepal. Thus, in prioritizing the "welfare" of the peasantry as the paramount goal of the Rana family, Jang even interpreted the unprecedented violence of 1846 as an attempt to free defenceless peasants from the clutches of the "tigers". Much of the discussion in the *Ain* related to court proceedings, evidence gathering, modalities of punishment was thus designed to limit such local excesses. Justice administration through codification also allowed the Ranas to eclipse the traditional role the Shah kings had enjoyed as the ultimate authority of law. This usurpation of legal power through the codification process completed the Rana political consolidation of 1846. The Ranas also reinvented their social rank and status though equally innovative innovations in genealogy.

Family, law, and making of caste

As kinship and caste formations through systematic deployment of genealogies and claims to higher status had been crucial to consolidation of political power in the region,[62] Jang Bahadur too commissioned a hitherto non-existent family genealogy by linking his clan to the illustrious Rajputs of fourteenth-century Northern India.[63] The cultural and political saliency accorded by the Rajput status allowed the Rana family to recast the Kot Massacre as recovering dharmic grounds by "cleansing" the social order of the corruptions in the body politic. Soon after, the new genealogical claims were translated into actual practice through a series of marital alliances.[64] To prevent similar iterations by rival families, Jang Bahadur engineered official rolls of succession, according to which only members of the extended Rana clan were ranked into different groups in relation to their hered-

61 Dixit 1984, 41.

62 For the most recent historical work on the role of genealogies in consolidating power in pre-colonial India, see Ramya Sreenivasan, *The Many Lives of a Rajput Queen: Heroic Pasts in India c. 1500–1900*, Seattle: University of Washington Press, 2007. For other important works on this theme see Surajit Sinha, *Tribal Polities and State Systems in Pre-colonial Eastern and North Eastern India*, Calcutta: K. P. Bagchi, 1987. Sumit Guha, *Environment and Ethnicity in India, 1200–1991*, Cambridge: Cambridge University Press, 1999. Dirk H. A. Kloff, *Naukar, Rajput and Sepoy: The Ethnohistory of the Military Labor Market in Hindustan, 1450–1850*, Cambridge: Cambridge University Press, 1990.

63 See John Whelpton, The Ancestors of Jung Bahadur Rana: History, Propaganda and Legend, *Contribution to Nepal Studies* 14:3 (1987): 161–191.

64 *Nepal National Archives/Foreign Ministry Documents*/1/106.

itary rights to the post of prime minister.[65] Brahmins who helped to cleanse Jang Bahadur of the violence surrounding the Kot Massacre, and who solemnized his purported Rajput status were awarded handsome land grants.[66] In returning the favour, the prime minister reinstated the earlier confiscated landed property of several hundred Brahmin families.[67] The new Rana patronage system gave Brahmins, who had seen their power diminish following the land confiscation of 1805, a new role in Nepali politics. Leading among them was Vijay Raj, who was awarded the position of chief state priest. The remarkable rise of Vijay Raj and the growing importance of neo-orthodox ideas parallel the seventeenth-century rise of Shivaji and Maratha state power, which also witnessed an increasing collaboration between the Brahmins and the new elites. The import of neo-orthodoxy was most visible in the Ranas' elaborate attempt to regulate caste hierarchy in a resolutely political fashion to preserve their own status while being able to access a broad range of labour for the project of state making. Therein emerged the conundrum of modernity in Nepal. Far from precluding familial relations, the coming of modernity in nineteenth-century Nepal led to unique ways of building power that were at once deeply religious and secular, problematizing the Weberian notion of modernity.

The *Ain* allowed a higher-caste freeborn male who had a child by a slave woman to grant the child freedom and give it the right to wear the sacred thread and thereby belong to the higher caste, regardless of the caste of the slave woman, so long as she belonged to the clean caste groups.[68] Male slaves who married higher caste women did not, however, enjoy the same right, and the caste ranking of their offspring was that of the father, not the mother. In other words, while slave women were deployed as a reproductive vehicle for the construction of lineage and family, male slaves were prevented from moving up in the caste ranking. Following promulgation of the *Ain*, higher-caste individuals were exempted from slavery as a penal measure. The law protected members of the upper caste from being reduced to slavery even if they had been relegated to enslavable caste status for criminal offenses.[69]

---

65 See Naya Raj Panta, Devi Prashad Bhandari, Rana Rajya Byabastha, *Purnima*, 87 (2051 VS): 1–22.

66 On the relationship between Vijay Raj and Jung Bahadur, see Prakash A. Raj, *Vijayraj Pandit: Jivani*, Kathmandu: Navin Prakashan, 1996.

67 For a discussion of the 1805 land confiscation, see Chittaranjan Nepali, *Sri Panch Rana Bahadur Shah: Vyaktitva ra Shasankal*, Kathmandu: Mary Rajbhandari, 1965.

68 *Ain*, "Janai Dinyako", 478–480.

69 *Ain*, "Danda Kaida Garnako", 262–274.

Lower-caste individuals and groups enslaved through judicial interventions, on the other hand, became the property of the state. Such persons and groups became an important source of productive and reproductive labour for the Rana state. Many such slaves were often handed out to state officials as salary or gifts.[70] The linking of caste ranking and legal regulations of slavery allowed the state to eventually bring the practice under its exclusive control away from the domain of households and that of the local power holders. The *Ain* outlined a detailed pricing structure for different age groups of slaves.[71] All transactions in slaves had to be registered with the state and extensive details on cases involving the recovery of runaway slaves, disciplining non-compliant slaves, inheriting slaves, rights over slave children, and sexual relations between slaves and members of the master's families were meticulously outlined in the *Ain*. The *Ain* prohibited local officials and family members from selling people by assigning the individual a lower-caste status.[72] In cases where deeds of sale had been facilitated by the local courts, they were revoked, and the enslaved individuals were freed. If local court officials themselves had resorted to the extrajudicial enslavement of lower-caste people, they were fined Rs. 100 each.[73] Neither the family nor the officials were allowed to enslave people by manipulating caste identity. Only the state reserved the ultimate right to do so under particular administrative arrangements. Sexual relations between individuals and castes were redefined in the *Ain* in ways that made members of lower-caste groups most vulnerable to enslavement, under the pretext of maintaining moral order in society. In that respect, the mid-nineteenth-century consolidation of state power at the centre was as much a building of rank and status as it was a strengthening of territory. Rana ambitions to craft and shape family and status were ultimately spelled out in the *Ain*.

Despite the linking of slavery to more inferior caste, slave status itself was not fixed and did not follow Shastric precedence. Instead, it was contingent on the changing matrix of labour needs. A prominent example was that experienced by the Limbu people. Eastern Nepal, like many other regions that became a part of the larger Gorkhali domain, had remained outside the direct control of Kathmandu up to the second half of the nineteenth century. After the initial attempts to take over the region by force ended unsuccessfully, the Gorkhalis brokered an agreement with the Limbus. In return for loyalty to the Gorkhali state, the Limbus were granted considerable autonomy, including the authority to regulate and

70 *Lal Mohar* 1906–1907 VS [1849–1851] Packet 2, Serial No. 3, f. 89.

71 *Ain*, "Jui Masnya Bechanyako", 408–413.

72 *Ain*, "Kamara Kamari Becatako", 405–407.

73 *Ain*, "Ghati Badi Sanjaya Garnyako".

oversee internal societal order.[74] When the *Ain* was promulgated, the Limbus were categorized as an enslavable group. During the Gorkha-Tibet War (1856) a large number of Limbus were recruited in the military and fought on the Gorkhali side. Upon return from the battlefield, the Limbus became vulnerable to enslavement by moneylenders and local potentates, and many fled to Sikkim. But as they had become a valuable prop to the centralizing Rana power, their elevation in caste ranking followed. After 1860, the Limbus were elevated to the non-enslavable category.[75] The order cited the bravery displayed by the Limbus during the Nepal-Tibet War of 1856 as the principal reason for their elevation in caste ranking. Interestingly, no appeal was made to religious ethos, nor were the Brahmins called on to corroborate the new rank. The administrative power of the rulers was sufficient to change the caste ranking of an entire group. What we have here essentially is evidence of the Ranas securing access to a pool of significant military labour. By transforming the Limbus into a non-enslavable group, the centre ended the prevalent practice of slavery and used the group as a conduit for state expansion into the region, which had otherwise remained subject to divided, decentralized powers.

The regulation of cast rank through administrative-judicial provisions was guided by the various labour needs of the powerful families at the centre. But instead of fixity of law, whose provisions were to be uniformly applied to all social groups, this created a situation in which rules could be manipulated by one particular group of households to further the development of its lands or fields or orchards. So, when the Rana family members acquired large tracts of land in Tarai after 1860[76], slaves fleeing to this "Naya Muluk" were protected from being extradited to their owners, provided the former agreed to settle there. This did not, however, apply to those slaves who fled to India or any privately-owned land held by other subjects. In such cases, the *Ain* explicitly categorized runaway slaves as private property of their owners and outlined specific provisions to recover them.

---

74 See Nepal National Archives/*DNA Series*/7/60. Some of the key parts in the Royal Order dated 1831 VS [1774–1775] read: Enjoy the land from generation to generation and in case we confiscate your lands, may our ancestral gods destroy our kingdom (Translation mine).

75 The royal order stressed the various positions occupied by the Limbus since 1851 in the Gorkhali army as a further evidence of their unwavering loyalty to the Gorkhali state. See Yogi Naraharinath, *IP*, 611.

76 Naya Muluk, which includes the present district of Banke, Bardia, Kailali and Kanchanpur, was given back to Nepal as a token of gift in return for Jang Bahadur's assistance to British in suppressing the Indian Rebellion of 1857. Nepal had lost this land to the British during the Anglo-Gorkha War (1814–1816). For the relevant historical documents on this, see C. V. Aitchison, *A Collection of Treaties, Engagements, Sunnuds Relating to India and Neighbouring Countries*, Calcutta: Bengal Printing Co., 1863, 223–224.

A case from the year 1855 is noteworthy in this regard.[77] One slave woman named Chamya had fled from her master's home. After eleven years, she was found to be residing in a village near Helambu. When the slave owner approached the court with this information, the latter dispatched soldiers to bring back Chamya so she could be rightfully restored to her original owner, even though a decade had elapsed since she first fled.[78] Individuals who stole slaves and transferred them to India or kept them in their houses were likewise prosecuted. The *Ain* required that those sent to India be recovered and restored to their rightful owner. If recovery was not successful, the accused was to be arrested and released only after paying the price of the slave to the original owner.[79] Individuals and families were also held accountable for accepting runaway slaves in their households without a proper background check.

The law was thus meant to further expand and consolidate the power of the Rana family while curbing that of competing power holders by granting the former unhindered access to labour and resources in rural areas. Strategies of rule got linked to a great modernizing moment, which is also very perverse. The dispensation of justice remained differentiated according to status, with exemptions and privileges granted to ruling families and their dependents. While previous regimes had allowed a relatively flexible system of slave-free marriages, with administrative exemptions being given without reference to Brahminical codes, the *Ain* began to link slave status directly to the Hindu caste order. The marriage rules and property inheritance laws charted out in the *Ain* also signalled that marriage boundaries were specifically deployed to prevent the transfer of property to women and children born of lower castes.[80] Though widow remarriage was encouraged by the state, when it came to widows' property rights, the laws were explicitly drawn along the gender lines. Regardless of her caste, no widow was allowed to take ownership of her deceased husband's property if she chose to remarry or live with another man. Nor were the children born of a widow granted the caste status of the mother.[81] Evidently, various kinds of households

---

77 See *Regmi Research Collection, Vol.* 29, 232–233.

78 The document does not indicate whether she was living in another household since she came to Helambu or just by herself.

79 *Ain*, "Bandha Kamara Bhagaunyako". In the case of slaves being recovered the person accused of transferring slaves was responsible for paying the expenses involved in the recovery (to the state) in addition to paying one ana (per day) to the slave owner. The state additionally also collected ten percent from the proprietor as a winning fee.

80 *Ain*, "Amsa Bandako", 127–136.

81 For example, if a Brahmin male married a widow Upadhyaya, the children born out of such alliance were not allowed a Upadhyaya status and were accorded a Jaisi rank.

and family relations were simultaneously refashioned at the same time that the Ranas refashioned their power into that of a centralized state.

From Norms to Practice

Scholars have sought to link the origins of the *Ain* to different geographic locations. Some have taken Jang Bahadur's exposure to Western laws in England and France as a precursor to the Nepali codification.[82] Others highlight the text as an indigenous venture.[83] A letter of Jang Bahadur dispatched from London in 1851, prompting Bam Bahadur to respect the *Ain* when passing verdicts, only compounds this enigma.[84] We do not know whether the term *Ain* in the letter referred to the same 1854 codification, but the choice of the word to classify the eventual 1854 codification is particularly revealing. Also, if we take Jang Bahadur's allusion to the rule of law in his letters from London as preparing the stage for the ambitious codification upon his return, our knowledge as to whether he composed those letters after becoming aware of western codifications is very limited. While the Rana rulers after 1850 increasingly adopted European dress and architecture, the administrative-legal framework they built borrowed heavily from the Mughal-Maratha system.[85] As such, the Rana genealogical and legal advancement remained decidedly embedded in sub-continental dharmic-political models. Unlike Thailand, which under threat of colonialism opted to westernize its legal system,[86] Nepal under the Ranas turned to the old power centres of South Asia to model their new polity. The choice of the Persian word *Ain* is very telling in this regard. Regardless of what the sources were, the Rana codification was a part of

82 See Daniel Wright, *History of Nepal with an Introductory Sketch of the Country and People of Nepal*, 1877, reprint, New Delhi: Rupa, 2007, 59–60. Henry A. Oldfield, *Sketches from Nipal: Historical and Descriptive with Anecdotes of the Court Life and Wild Sports of the Country in the Time of Maharaja Jang Bahadur, G.C.B*, 1880, reprint, New Delhi: Cosmo, 1974, 244. Gautam 2004, 10.
83 See Adhikari 1984, 276.
84 Dixit 1984, 7.
85 A brief history of Rana orientation to Western consumption trend is explored in Mark Liechty, *Suitably Modern: Making Middle-Class Culture in a New Consumer Society*, Princeton: Princeton University Press, 2003. Stefanie Lotter, Distinctly Different Everywhere: Politics of Appearance Amongst Rana Elites Inside and Outside of Nepal, *Comparative Sociology* 10 (2011): 508–527.
86 For two fascinating accounts on the success and failure of Western influence in the Siamese legal codification see David Engel, *Law and Kingship in Thailand During the Reign of King Chulalongkorn*, Ann Arbor: University of Michigan, 1975. Apirat Petschsiri, *Eastern Importation of Western Criminal Law: Thailand as a Case Study*, Colorado: Fred B. Rothman, 1987.

the global legal innovations of the nineteenth century. Perhaps the Ranas, taking cues from the EIC push to create Anglo-Hindu and Anglo-Muslim law, too were turning to Brahmins and classical texts to mould their newly acquired power.

Like many previous rulers on the Himalayan foothills, the Ranas took lawgiving as the central tenet of state making.[87] However, unlike the earlier attempts at codification, both the thematic and geographic coverage of the *Ain* were unparalleled. The Ranas ensured that the normative aspects of written laws were translated into real practice. Their emphasis on the depersonalization of law through codification tied both the rulers and the subjects to a textual practice. So, for instance, Jang Bahadur paid a large sum of money (Rs. 125,000) when he bought some state-owned land, signalling to others the Rana commitment to the rule of law.[88]

In taking a positivist view of law, most scholars have dismissed the importance of such clauses by suggesting that very few cases involving high-status individuals were prosecuted after 1854. High-status people in many western societies have frequently escaped prosecution even in the twentieth century, but that has rarely made the law ineffective in those places. The effectiveness of law lies in its "independence from gross manipulation" and must relatively appear "to be just".[89] Granted that the Rana codification and its attendant legal innovation remained embedded in hierarchy and a status-differentiated concept of justice, it would be too simplistic to overlook its profound effect in building a relatively impartial system of rule and state sovereignty. In most civil and criminal cases, the law did take a neutral stance. When three Brahmin brothers confiscated the property of a Magar (ranked lower in the caste hierarchy), citing the *Ain*, the state ruled in favour of the subaltern member.[90] If the vast majority of the rural population had perceived the system to be arbitrary and partial, they would not have frequently travelled great distances to seek justice in Kathmandu. In the absence of that deep engagement with the rural population, the Rana state would not have succeeded in expanding its administrative arms to check the power of the local magnates. A systematic implementation of justice deliverance was the key to building Rana authority in the hinterland. It is for this reason that the Ranas stressed uniformity and impartiality as two rationales for the codification of 1854.

87 The two earlier notable attempts at legal codifications in the region are discussed in Dinesh Raj Pant (ed.), *Nayabikashini: Manavnayashastra,* Kathmandu: Kanoon Byabasahi Club, 2065 VS [2008]. Theodore Riccardi, The Royal Edicts of King Rama Shah of Gorkha, *Kailash* 5:1 (1977): 29–65.

88 *Regmi Research Collection, Vol.* 47, 130.

89 Thompson 1975, 263.

90 LM/1854/BN. 8, Packet. 2, Serial No. 6.

In other words, the struggle to define "moral law" through the codification was designed to establish the sovereignty of the emergent state.

By encompassing administrative and legal uniformity, the *Ain* brought together manifold existing customs and practices into a single document, thereby granting the Rana state power in all adjudications. The *Ain* shifted the role of administrative and judicial functions from traditionally powerful local rulers to state-appointed and state-trained bureaucrats dispatched from the centre.[91] Judges and magistrates stationed at different courts across the Gorkhali kingdom were instructed to look into complaints and deliver justice as per the guidelines outlined in the *Ain*. In 1857, Jang Bahadur abolished the post of *jimmawal* (revenue collector) in the western region.[92] The earlier practice of giving out two-thirds of fines to *jimmawals* and one-third to village heads was now made null, and henceforth the incomes from such fines were to be deposited with the court.

Over time, the responsibility of collecting revenue and overseeing judicial and general administrative affairs in rural areas was transferred from traditional functionaries to state-appointed, salaried civil servants. These salaried officials were barred from obtaining land and engaging in trade in the region where they were assigned.[93] The *Ain* put in place a fairly sophisticated administrative and judicial system that functioned with a reasonable degree of autonomy. The expansion of the administrative-cum-bureaucratic power together with a systematic collection of information after 1854 allowed the regime to maintain a firmer grip in areas previously left to local power holders. Anyone found or reported to have taken to financial mismanagement was dismissed immediately from office and fined the amount he had appropriated. Failure to pay was punishable by imprisonment.[94] This, coupled with the state's encouraging locals to report violations, allowed even greater control of information, loyalty, and funds after 1854. The state devised different methods of encouraging local people to come forward and file complaints against local officials.[95] A clause included in the *Ain* assured individuals who informed of officials' irregularities were to be rewarded. So, for instance, when Gambhir Singh Majhi Chhetri petitioned against irregularities committed by village head Ballav Dhoj Basnet Chhetri, Gambhir was appointed to the post.[96]

---

91 *LM* 1860–1863, Packet. 12, Serial No. 2093.

92 *LM* 1857–1860, Packet. 28, Serial No. 3251.

93 *Regmi Research Collection, Vol. 10*, 245.

94 *Ain*, "Rakam Bandobasta Ko".

95 *Ain*, "Adalati Badibastko".

96 *LM* 1860–1863, Serial No. 2089.

After 1854, key administrative offices were established to deepen the judicial power of the state.[97] The establishment of the various offices facilitated local people's ability to file complaints and report abuses without having to travel all the way to the capital. The institution of *daudaha* (inspection tours) further ensured that officials carried out their duties as prescribed. The individuals performing *daudaha* had to prepare detailed reports. Complaints and reports of grievances brought through the tours were sent as directives to the local administrators.[98] The widespread application and growing familiarity with the *Ain* offered the Kathmandu Durbar (royal palace) entrée into spheres historically dominated by competing powers and interests. So, when the widow of Fateh Singh Karki requested that the central power assist her in collecting the money owed to her deceased husband by the local people, she framed it as a legal case.[99] She invoked the *Ain* in her petition and argued that the refusal of the local residents to return the loan in spite of the contractual papers they had earlier signed was in violation of the clause outlined in the *Ain*. In appealing to the centre to intervene on her behalf she was, however, not asking the ruler to render a personal verdict, but to ensure that the laws laid down in the *Ain* be implemented.

The bulk of the *Ain*, in fact, dealt with curbing the power of the local rulers and bringing people in direct relationship to the state through a strict regulation of individual as well as collective social relations.[100] To prohibit local rulers from unlawfully extracting labour, the *Ain* transformed work into a voluntary employment contract. The rule did not apply to the regime and its households, which still reserved the exclusive right to mobilize labour in rural areas. But in demanding that labour be utilized in exchange for a fixed daily wage, the Rana rulers made it difficult for others to challenge what it regarded as its exclusive prerogatives.[101]

The *Ain* made tenancy rights in state-owned lands permanent and heritable, even allowing the widow (provided she did not remarry) or the daughter (until her marriage) to inherit the rights.[102] The extended discussions in the *Ain* protecting the tenurial rights in state-owned lands were specifically designed to limit local power holders from expanding their holdings by pushing tenants off the land. When such land became vacant after residents emigrated, fled, or died without leaving anyone to inherit the tenurial rights, local officials were instructed to find

---

97 See Adhikari 1984.
98 *LM* 1861–1862, Packet.17, Serial No. 79.
99 *LM* 1861–1862, Packet.17, Serial No. 79.
100 *Ain*, "Rakam Bandobasta Ko".
101 *Ain*, "Jhara Khetala Ko".
102 *Ain*, "Jagga Pajani Ko".

new tenants immediately. The protection of tenurial security enabled the state to cultivate loyalty and check local irregularities. An example from 1857 illustrates this.[103] When the widow of Nanda Ram Upadhyaya petitioned that the land assigned to her husband had been taken away by one Lila Dhar Koirala on the grounds that she had become a widow, citing a clause from the *Ain*, the state directed the concerned officials to return the property to the widow.[104]

The decision in itself was not an innovation, because previous regimes had also respected the property rights of widows. What is remarkably different here is that the state was using a legal text as a reference point to exercise its authority and enforce a depersonalized system of rule. It was not merely a decision guided by the whim of an individual ruler, but one led by the concrete formulations of codes that defined the parameters of punishment and fines. The periodic tours of inspection, rigorous implementation of *pajani* (annual reappointment of all official positions) together with the establishment of different administrative offices enabled the Rana rulers to gather a vast cache of information that allowed them to recast the entire socio-economic order and build a state on a somewhat rational and bureaucratic grounds.

Conclusion

The *Ain* put in place a fairly sophisticated administrative and judicial system that was given a reasonable degree of functional autonomy. Much of the routine administrative tasks were overseen by junior staff without the direct supervision of the Rana prime minister. Nor were provisions of the *Ain* fixed. A group of administrators was entrusted to amend the text as deemed appropriate in light of new cases and disputes not already covered in it. In that respect, the Ranas did not see much conflict between developing a highly rational legal and administrative system and preserving patrimonial rule. Detailed instructions were laid out for the execution of official duties.[105] An officer ordered to prepare a formal document was required to always consult the relevant laws, charters, and regulations. In situations where a new directive conflicted with existing legislation, the *Ain Kausal* (law council) had to resolve the issue before it could be implemented.

---

103 *LM* 1857–1859, Packet. 28, Serial No. 3251.

104 In its verdict, the state stressed that Koirala had no right to take away the widow's land as the *Ain* guaranteed tenurial security even to the widows.

105 *Prashasan*, 4 (19730): 71–75.

Apparently, the Rana regime not only appealed to officials to "stay faithful to the salt," or act simply on their conscience in doing *nisaf* (justice), as previous rulers had done, but they also subordinated them to a system of written regulations and guidelines. These meticulously delineated office and official functions even included provisions for punishing kings and prime ministers if they were found to have overstepped their power. The *Ain* disallowed even the Rana prime minister from intervening in an ongoing case or demanding the release of a suspect implicated in a grave crime unless the evidence to the contrary was forthcoming. Even the brothers and sons of Jang Bahadur were expected to follow the established rule.[106] If Rana family members deputed in high offices failed to punish those accused of bribery, they were fined three times the amount of that bribe.

To prevent cases from being dragged on for a prolonged time, a thirty-five–day limit was put in place for petitioners to present their respective documents once their case was initiated. If either party failed to appear within that time, the case was dismissed. The *Ain* particularly barred local judges and even state officials from inflicting severe punishments. Such decisions had to be secured from the *Kausal* after presenting relevant documents about the case.[107] Even state-appointed judges were penalized for overstepping their authority.

Nor were the laws about slavery, marriage, and property inheritance specifically Hindu practices. South Asian scholars have shown that the colonial state in India used rules to similarly remake property and familial relationships.[108] During this same period, from America to Africa, new states shaped gender and property relations in ways that saw a redefinition of status and ownership rights increasingly along patrilineal and racial lines.[109] European states both in the metropole and in colonies were equally preoccupied with notions of sexual and blood purity.[110] In Nepal, such rigidification of social relations should be seen as taking place at a particular moment in history rather than as being a histori-

106 "Order to General Jagat Shumsher Rana".
107 *Ain*, "Danda Sanjaya Garnyako Ko".
108 For some of the most recent works see Indrani Chatterjee, *Forgotten Friends: Monks, Marriage, and Memories of Northeast India*, Delhi: Oxford University Press, 2013. Rochisha Narayan, *Caste, Family and Politics in Northern India During the Eighteenth and Nineteenth centuries*. PhD. diss., Rutgers University, 2011.
109 See Philippa Levine, *Gender and Empire*, Oxford: Oxford University Press, 2004. Glen Evelyn Nakano, *Unequal Freedom: How Race and Gender Shaped American Citizenship*, Cambridge: Harvard University Press, 2002.
110 See Guillame Aubert, *Constructing Race in the French Atlantic World: The Blood of France*, Basingstoke: Palgrave Macmillan, 2012. Ghosh 2006.

cal inevitability. As such, it seems to have been driven by a widely-shared nineteenth-century need for labour and the centralization of state power.

Outlining the distinction between traditional (arbitrary) and modern (lawful) forms of governance, Max Weber argued that the latter emerged only on European soil.[111] Two defining features of the Weberian notion of modernity were the rationalization of offices and consistency in the application of law.[112] The *Ain* problematizes this binary. The Rana state simultaneously exhibited traditional and modern orientations, marked by status-differentiated conceptions of justice, but also by the secularization of offices, administrative uniformity, and rule by law. Historical sensitivities to family as an important locus of power offer us a way out of the Weberian paradigm. The neat distinction between private households and secular officials, with the latter as a marker of transition to modernity, was neither a foregone conclusion nor a universal outcome of modernity.[113] As this essay illustrates, far from precluding familial relations, the coming of modernity reconfigured them and led to new modes of power and domination, most visibly in the sphere of law.

Instead of continuing as a traditional Hindu state that scholars have misperceived it to be, Nepal in the nineteenth century grew into both its "Hinduness" and "state" power as a result of very rational politico-legal manoeuvres that were neither fully patrimonial or traditional, nor yet entirely bureaucratic or modern in the Western European sense. But was there ever a singular path to modernity and/or rationality?

References

Acharya, Baburam, Acharya, Madhav, *The Blood Stained Throne: Struggles for Power in Nepal, 1775–1914,* New Delhi: Penguin Books India, 2013.

Adams, Julia, *The Familial State: Ruling Families and Merchant Capitalism in Early Modern Europe,* Ithaca: Cornell University Press, 2005.

Adhikari, Krishna Kant, *Nepal Under Jung Bahadur, 1846–1877,* Kathmandu: Buku, 1984.

Aitchison, C. V., *A Collection of Treaties, Engagements, Sunnuds Relating to India and Neighbouring Countries,* Calcutta: Bengal Printing Co., 1863.

111 See Max Weber, *Economy and Society*, Vol. 2, 1968, Translated by Guenther Roth and Claus Wittich, Berkeley and London: University of California Press, 1978, 1006–1069.

112 Weber 1968, 844–848.

113 For the limit of this model in the context of the early modern European state formations, see, Julia Adams, *The Familial State: Ruling Families and Merchant Capitalism in Early Modern Europe,* Ithaca: Cornell University Press, 2005.

Alam, Muzaffar, Subrahmanyam, Sanjay, *The Mughal State, 1526–1750,* Delhi: Oxford University Press, 1998.
Amatya, Saphalya, *Rana Rule in Nepal,* Delhi: Nirala, 2004.
Anderson, Michael, Islamic Law and the Colonial Encounter in British India. In *Institutions and Ideologies: A SOAS South Asia Reader*, David Arnold, Peter Robb (eds.), 165–185, London: RoutledgeCurzon, 1993.
Anderson, Michael, Guha, Sumit (ed.), *Changing Concepts of Rights & Justice in South Asia,* New Delhi: Oxford University Press, 2000.
Arnold, Morris S. (ed.), *On the Laws and Customs of England: Essays in Honour of Samuel E. Thorne,* Chapel Hill: University of North Carolina Press, 1981.
Asad, Talal, *Genealogies of Religion: Discipline and Reasons of Power in Christianity and Islam,* Baltimore: Johns Hopkins University Press, 1993.
Aubert, Guillaume, *Constructing Race in the French Atlantic World: The Blood of France,* Basingstoke: Palgrave Macmillan, 2012.
Barlett, Robert, *Trial by Fire and Water,* New York: Oxford University Press, 1986.
Bailkin, Jordanna, The Boot and the Spleen: When Was Murder Possible in British India, *Comparative Studies in Society and History*, 48:2 (2006): 462–493.
Berman, Harold J., *Faith and Order: The Reconciliation of Law and Religion,* Atlanta: Emory University Press, 1993.
Bhattarai, Ghanshyam, *Ranakalin Jilla Prasasan ma Badahakimharuko Bhumika,* Kathmandu: Center for Nepal and Asian Studies, 2059 VS.
Caroll, Anthony, *Protestant Modernity: Weber, Secularization, and Protestantism,* Scranton: University of Scranton Press, 2007.
Chatterjee, Indrani, *Gender, Slavery, Law in Colonial India,* New Delhi: Oxford University Press, 1999.
Chatterjee, Indrani, *Forgotten Friends: Monks, Marriage, and Memories of Northeast India,* Delhi: Oxford University Press, 2013.
Cohn, Bernard, *Colonialism and Its Forms of Knowledge: The British in India,* Princeton: Princeton University Press, 1996.
Derrett, J. Duncan, *Religion, Law and the State in India,* New York: The Free Press, 1968.
Dixit, Kamal, *Janga-Gita,* Lalitpur: Jagadamba Prakashan, 1984.
Eaton, Richard M., *The Rise of Islam and the Bengal Frontier, 1204–1760,* Berkeley: University of California Press, 1993.
Edwards, Daniel, *Patrimonial and Bureaucratic Administration in Nepal: Historical Change and Weberian Theory*, PhD. diss., University of Chicago, 1977.
Engel, David, *Law and Kingship in Thailand During the Reign of King Chulalongkorn,* Ann Arbor: University of Michigan, 1975.
Fezas, Jean (ed.), *Le Code Nepalais (Ain) De 1853,* Tornino, Italy: Comitato per la pubblicazione del Corpus juris sanscriticum, 2000.
Galanter, Marc, *Law and Society in Modern India,* Delhi: Oxford University Press, 1989.
Gautam, Rajesh, *Ranakalin Nepal ko Prasasanik, Shaichik ra Samajik Sudharharu,* Delhi: Adroit, 2004.
Gordon, Stewart, *Marathas, Marauders and State Formation in Eighteenth-Century India,* Delhi: Oxford University Press, 1994.
Gordon-Reed, Annette, *Race on Trial: Law and Justice in American Society,* New York: Oxford University Press, 2002.

Gorski, Philip S., *The Disciplinary Revolution: Calvinism and the Rise of State in Early Modern Europe,* Chicago: University of Chicago Press, 2003.
Ghosh, Durba, *Sex and Family in Colonial India: The Making of Empire,* Cambridge: Cambridge University Press, 2006.
Grover, Amrita (ed.), *Land Rights, Landed Hierarchy and Village Community During Mughal Age*, Vol. 1, Delhi: Originals, 2006.
Guha, Sumit, An Indian Penal Regime: Maharashtra in the Eighteenth Century, *Past and Present* 147 (1995): 101–126.
Guha, Sumit, *Environment and Ethnicity in India, 1200–1991,* Cambridge: Cambridge University Press, 1999.
Gune, Vithal T., *The Judicial System of the Marathas: A Detailed Study Based on Original Decisions called Mahzars, Nivadpatras, and Official Orders,* Poona: Deccan College, 1953.
Hamilton, Francis, *An Account of the Kingdom of Nepal,* Edinburgh: Archibald Constable, 1819.
Hay, Douglas (ed.), *Albino's Fatal Tree: Crime and Society in Eighteenth-Century England,* New York: Pantheon, 1975.
Hodgson, Brian H., On Law and Legal Practices of Nepal as Regards Familiar Intercourse Between a Hindu and an Outcast. *Journal of the Royal Asiatic Society of Great Britain and Ireland*, Vol.1 (1834): 47–48.
Hodgson, Brian, *Miscellaneous Essays Relating to Indian Subjects,* vol. 2, London: Trubner, 1880.
Hofer, Andras, *The Caste Hierarchy and the State in Nepal: A Study of the Muluki Ain of 1854.* 1979, reprint, Kathmandu: Himal, 2005.
Hunter, Willian Wilson, *Life of Brian Houghton Hodgson: British Resident at The Court of Nepal,* 1896, reprint, New Delhi: Asian Educational, 1991.
Husain, Wahed, *Administration of Justice During the Muslim Rule in India,* Delhi: Idarah-I Adabiyat-I Delhi, 1977.
Hussain, Nasser, *The Jurisprudence of Emergency: Colonialism and the Rule of Law,* Ann Arbor: University of Michigan Press, 2003.
Habib, Irfan, *The Agrarian System of Mughal India 1556–1707,* 1963 revised edition, New Delhi: Oxford University Press, 1999.
Jain, M. S., *The Emergence of a New Aristocracy in Nepal,* Agra: Sri Ram Mehta, 1972.
Khanal, Bishal, *Nepalko Naya Prasasan Yak Aitihasik Simbhalokan,* Kathmandu: Ram Prashad Khanal, 1987.
Kirkpatrick, William, *An Account of the Kingdom of Nepaul: Being the Substance of Observations Made During a Mission to that Country, in the Year 1793*, 1811, London: Miller, 1971.
Kloff, Dirk H. A., *Naukar, Rajput and Sepoy: The Ethnohistory of the Military Labour Market in Hindustan, 1450–1850,* Cambridge: Cambridge University Press, 1990.
Kolsky, Elizabeth, *Colonial Justice in British India,* Cambridge: Cambridge University Press, 2010.
Kulkarni, A. R. (ed.), *Explorations in the Deccan History*, New Delhi: Pragati, 2006.
Kumar, Satish, *Rana Polity in Nepal: Origin and Growth,* Bombay: Asia Pub. House, 1967.
Langbein, John, *Torture and the Law of Proof: Europe and England in the Ancien Regime,* Chicago: University of Chicago Press, 1977.
Lawoti, Mahendra, *Looking Back, Looking Forward: Centralization, Multiple Conflicts, and Democratic State Building in Nepal,* Washington, D.C.: East-West Center, 2007.
Levine, Philippa, *Gender and Empire,* Oxford: Oxford University Press, 2004.

Liechty, Mark, *Suitably Modern: Making Middle-Class Culture in a New Consumer Society,* Princeton: Princeton University Press, 2003.
Lotter, Stefanie, Distinctly Different Everywhere: Politics of Appearance Amongst Rana Elites Inside and Outside of Nepal, *Comparative Sociology* 10 (2011): 508–527.
Lubin, Timothy, Davis Jr., Donald R., Krishnan, Jayanth K., *Hinduism and Law: An Introduction,* Cambridge: Cambridge University Press, 2010.
Mallampalli, Chandra, *Race, Religion, and Law in Colonial India: Trials of Interracial Family,* Cambridge: Cambridge University Press, 2011.
Michael, Bernardo A., *Statemaking and Territory in South Asia: Lessons from the Anglo-Gorkha War, 1814–1816,* London: Anthem Press, 2012.
Michaels, Axel, *The Price of Purity: The Religious Judge in 19th Century Nepal,* Torino: Comitato Corpus iuris sanscriticum et fontes iuris Asiae meridianae et centralis, 2005.
Moore, Robert I., *The Formation of a Persecuting Society,* Cambridge; Oxford: Blackwell, 1987. Peter Brown, *Society and the Holy in Late Antiquity,* Berkeley: University of California Press, 1982.
Moreland, W. H., *The Agrarian System of Moslem India,* 1929, reprint, Delhi: Oriental Books, 1968.
Morris, Thomas D., *Southern Slavery, and Law, 1619–1860,* Chapel Hill: University of North Carolina, 1996.
Nakano, Glen Evelyn, *Unequal Freedom: How Race and Gender Shaped American Citizenship,* Cambridge: Harvard University Press, 2002.
Narayan, Rochisha, *Caste, Family and Politics in Northern India During the Eighteenth and Nineteenth centuries.* PhD. diss., Rutgers University, 2011.
Nepal National Archives/Foreign Ministry Documents.
Nepali, Chittaranjan, *Sri Panch Rana Bahadur Shah: Vyaktitva ra Shasankal,* Kathmandu: Mary Rajbhandari, 1965.
Nepali, Chittaranjan, *General Bhimsen Thapa ra Tatkalin Nepal,* Kathmandu: Ratna Pustak Bhandar, 2022 VS.
Oldfield, Henry A., *Sketches from Nipal: Historical and Descriptive with Anecdotes of the Court Life and Wild Sports of the Country in the Time of Maharaja Jang Bahadur, G.C.B,* 1880, reprint, New Delhi: Cosmo, 1974.
Olivelle, Patrick, *King, Governance, and Law in Ancient India,* New Delhi: Oxford University Press, 2013.
Pangeni, Bhabeshwor, *Nepal ko Prasasanik Ithihas 1825–1903 VS*, Kathmandu: Bidhyarthi Pustak Bhandar, 2064 VS.
Pant, Dinesh Raj (ed.), *Nayabikashini: Manavnayashastra,* Kathmandu: Kanoon Byabasahi Club, 2065 VS [2008].
Panta, Naya Raj, Bhandari, Devi Prashad, Rana Rajya Byabastha, *Purnima*, 87 (2051 VS): 1–22.
Petschsiri, Apirat, *Eastern Importation of Western Criminal Law: Thailand as a Case Study,* Colorado: Fred B. Rothman, 1987.
Pradhan, Kumar, *Thapa Politics in Nepal: With Special Reference to Bhimsen Thapa, 1806–1839,* New Delhi: Concept, 2012.
Raj, Prakash A., *Vijayraj Pandit: Jivani,* Kathmandu: Navin Prakashan, 1996.
Regmi, Jagdish C., *Nepalko Vaidhanik Parampara,* Kathmandu: Tribhuvan University, 1978.
Regmi, Mahesh C., *A Study in Nepali Economic History, 1768–1846,* New Delhi: Manjushri, 1971.
Regmi, Mahesh C., *Landownership in Nepal,* Berkeley: University of California Press, 1976.
Regmi Research Collection.

Riaz, Ali, Basu, Subho, *Paradise Lost?: State Failure in Nepal,* Lanham: Lexington, 2007.
Riccardi, Theodore, The Royal Edicts of King Rama Shah of Gorkha, *Kailash* 5:1 (1977): 29–65.
Rudolph, Lloyd, Rudolph, Susanne, Barristers and Brahmans in India: Legal Cultures and Social Change, *Comparative Studies in Society History* 8 (1965): 24–49.
Rupakheti, Sanjog, Reconsidering State-Society Relations in South Asia: A Himalayan Case Study, *Himalaya* 35:2 (2015): 73–86.
Rupakheti, Sanjog, *Leviathan or Paper Tiger: State-Making in the Himalayas, 1740–1900*. PhD. diss., Rutgers University, 2012.
Singha, Radhika, *Despotism of Law: Crime and Justice in Early Colonial India,* Delhi; New York: Oxford University Press, 1998.
Sinha, Surajit, *Tribal Polities and State Systems in Pre-colonial Eastern and North Eastern India,* Calcutta: K. P. Bagchi, 1987.
Skuy, David, Macaulay and the Indian Penal Code of 1862: The Myth of the Inherent Superiority and Modernity of the English Legal System Compared to India's Legal System in the Nineteenth Century, *Modern Asian Studies*, 32:3 (1998): 513–557.
Sreenivasan, Ramya, *The Many Lives of a Rajput Queen: Heroic Pasts in India c. 1500–1900,* Seattle: University of Washington Press, 2007.
Stiller, Ludwig F., *The Silent Cry: The People of Nepal, 1816–1839,* Kathmandu: Sahayogi Prakashan, 1976.
Stiller, Ludwig F., *Letters from Kathmandu: The Kot Massacre,* Kathmandu: Research Center for Nepal and Asian Studies, Tribhuvan University, 1981.
Tentler, Thomas, *Sin and Confession on the Eve of the Reformation,* Princeton: Princeton University Press, 1977.
Thompson, E. P., *Whigs and Hunters: The Origin of the Black Act,* New York: Pantheon, 1975.
Vajracharya, Dhanvajra, Nepal, Gyanmani, *Aitihasik Patra Sangraha*. Vol.1, Kathmandu: Nepal Sanskritik Parishad, 2014 VS.
Waterhouse, David (ed.), *The Origins of Himalayan Studies: Brian Houghton Hodgson in Nepal and Darjeeling 1820–1858*, London, New York: Routledge Curzon, 2004.
Weber, Max, *Economy and Society*, Vol. 2, 1968, Translated by Guenther Roth and Claus Wittich, Berkeley and London: University of California Press, 1978.
Whelpton, John, The Ancestors of Jung Bahadur Rana: History, Propaganda and Legend, *Contribution to Nepal Studies* 14:3 (1987): 161–191.
Wink, Andre, *Land, and Sovereignty in India: Agrarian Relations and Politics Under the Eighteenth-century Maratha Svarajya,* Cambridge: Cambridge University Press, 1986.
Wright, Daniel, *History of Nepal with an Introductory Sketch of the Country and People of Nepal,* 1877, reprint, New Delhi: Rupa, 2007.
Yang, Anand, *Crime and Criminality in British India,* Tucson: University of Arizona Press, 1985.

Daniel Schönpflug

Constitutional law and diversity in the French Revolution

National and imperial perspectives

The night of August 4, 1789 saw one of the most memorable sessions of the National Assembly in the entire course of the French Revolution. The session started at five o'clock in the afternoon with a motion made by the Comte de Noailles to abolish all the privileges of the feudal system in France. After that, one by one, representatives of the nobility and the clergy stood up and raised their voices in front of the assembly. Every speaker seemed to try to outdo the previous ones with an even higher degree of generosity: hunting rights, seigneurial jurisdiction, regional privileges, and even the tithe of the Church were proposed for abolition. And every proposal was acclaimed loudly and enthusiastically by an assembly that contemporaries described as being in a state of "drunkenness". The newspaper *Courrier de Versailles à Paris* commented: "This unforgettable night [...] The Representatives of the nation were all animated by the same spirit. By trampling down ancient prejudices, they seemed to have only one regret: not to be able to make even more sacrifices for the public good."[1]

The term "privileges", the stumbling block of August 1789, designated private or corporate laws. From its outset, the French Revolution was inspired by the ambitious idea to fit a society characterized by social, cultural, and legal diversity into a new unified legal framework. A few weeks later, on August 26, 1789, the Declaration of the Rights of Man laid the cornerstone for a new constitution – a constitution that came into effect in September 1791 and that guaranteed equality before the law to every Frenchman.[2]

In this article, I will analyze the vicissitudes of the revolutionary process of constitutionalization, understood as the project of introducing legal equality in a society built on diversity. After a brief introduction to revolutionary concepts

1 Transl. from "*Cette nuit à jamais memorable [...] Les Représentants de la Nation animés du même esprit, et foulant aux pieds d'antiques préjugés, sembloient n'avoir plus qu'un seul regret, celui de ne pas pouvoir faire de nouveaux sacrifices pour le bien public*", in: *Courrier de Versailles à Paris, et de Paris à Versailles*, no. 30 of Aug. 6, 1789.

2 La Constitution de 1791, Préambule, Art. 6: "*La loi est l'expression de la volonté générale. (...) Elle doit être la même pour tous.*", in: Maurice Duverger, *Les constitutions de la France*, Paris: Univ. de France, 1993, p. 34.

DOI 10.1515/9783110423327-009

of legal equality, I will look into two particularly telling regional cases: on the one hand, I will present the case of Alsace, where local and regional autonomy, religious pluralism, and bilingualism were integrated quite successfully into a new constitutional order. On the other hand, I will outline the very different situation on the Caribbean island *Saint-Domingue*, once the "pearl" of the French colonial empire, where a new territorial order, based on elected administrations of municipalities, was introduced, but where a vast majority of the inhabitants remained excluded from the new realm of equal law. Even after the formal abolition of slavery in 1794 and after the full inclusion of the island into the French Republic in 1795, the degree to which former slaves could profit from equal legal status varied greatly. In my analysis, I will focus on the tensions between privileges and legal equalities for citizens in the early years of the revolution. The question of the equality of territorial entities, which is a related but distinct subject, will not be treated. My aim is to reformulate the question of diversity and law, which is at the heart of this volume, by asking: to what degree did a context shaped by traditions of heterogeneity limit the introduction of legal equality in the French Revolution? Why and how was legal diversity renewed during the birth of a modern political system in France, despite all the rhetoric of "*une loi*" ("one law")?

I From "privilege" to "equality" – the constitutional process 1789–1791

The elaboration of the first French constitution took more than two years, from June 1789 until September 1791. The National Assembly worked successively on the constitutional text, decree by decree, article by article – often driven by pressing circumstances that needed quick solutions. The composition of the fundamental legal text took place in the middle of violent struggles and under strong tensions, during which the leading figures and guiding principles continuously changed. Pressure groups tried to exercise their influence: on the one hand, there were individuals and groups that insisted on maintaining former privileges; on the other hand, the assembly had to deal with demands from individuals and groups who were excluded from the benefits of the new constitution.[3]

3 Denis Richet, L'esprit de la constitution 1789–1791, in *The French Revolution and the Creation of Modern Political Culture*, Colin Lucas (ed.), vol. 2, 63–68, Oxford: Pergamon Press, 1987. Wolfgang Schmale, Constitution, constitutionnel, in *Handbuch politisch-sozialer Grundbegriffe in*

In the language of most revolutionaries, the term "privilege" had very negative connotations. The abbot and pamphleteer Emmanuel Sieyès characterized specific individual and corporate rights as the origin of the corruption of the Old Regime. He underlined the psychological consequences of exceptional legislation, which to his mind caused frustration and feelings of exclusion and thus deflated engagement for the common good. To his mind, this form of injustice had to be overcome, just like "tyranny", "despotism", and "fanaticism".[4] On the other hand, *égalité* was a concept that was as dear to the Enlightenment philosophers and to the patriotic movement as *liberté*. In the debates of the time, "equality" had a particular meaning: equal rights were the precondition of equal chances for every citizen and of equal reward for achievement. "Equality" in this sense thus did not describe the levelling of cultural or social differences.[5]

This meritocratic understanding of equality played a crucial role in the revolutionary creation of a new regime. After the memorable night of August 4, 1789, it took only one week before the National Assembly passed a decree that started with the general claim: "The National Assembly hereby completely abolishes the feudal system." What follows is a pragmatic, in some respects even timid, realization of the revolutionary verve of the night of August 4. The majority of feudal dues were not simply abolished, but could only be redeemed if the subjects were able to afford to pay the necessary sums.[6]

If the August decrees meant, at least symbolically, the end of the Old Regime, the Declaration of the Rights of Man of August 26, 1789 laid the cornerstone for a new regime. Liberty and equality were the leading principles of the declaration, which started with the basic statement that "men were born and stay free and equal in rights". Article VI clarified that "the law (...) has to be the same for all [...] All citizens, being equal in its eyes, shall be equally eligible for all high offices,

---

Frankreich 1680–1820, Rolf Reichardt, Eberhard Schmitt (eds.), vol. 12, 31–64, Munich: Oldenbourg, 1992. Keith Michael Baker, Constitution, in *Critical Dictionary of the French Revolution*, by François Furet, Mona Ozouf (eds.), vol. 2, 4474–479, Cambridge, Mass.: Harvard University Press, 1989. Michael Fitzsimmons, *The Remaking of France. The National Assembly and the Constitution of 1791*, Cambridge: Cambridge University Press, 1994. François Furet, Ran Halévi, *La Monarchie républicaine. La constitution de 1791*, Paris: Fayard, 1996.

4 Emmanuel Sieyès, *Essai sur les privileges*, s.l. 1788.

5 Otto Dann, Gleichheit, in *Geschichtliche Grundbegriffe*, vol. 2, 1014–1018, Stuttgart: Klett-Cotta, 1975. Mona Ozouf, Equality, in *Critical Dictionnary of the French Revolution*, François Furet, Mona Ozouf (eds.), 669–683, Cambridge: Harvard University Press, 1989.

6 J. H. Robinson (ed.), *Readings in European History*, vol. 2, Boston: Ginn, 1906, 404. John Markoff, *The Abolition of Feudalism. Peasants, Lords, and Legislators in the French Revolution*, University Park: Pennsylvania State University Press, 1996. Gail Bossenga, *The Politics of Privilege. Old Regime and Revolution in Lille*, Cambridge: Cambridge University Press, 1991.

public positions and employments, according to their ability, and without other distinction than that of their virtues and talents."[7]

The final draft of the Constitution of 1791 re-emphasizes these fundamental orientations by stating in its opening paragraphs: "There is no privilege, neither for any part of the nation, nor for any individual, and no exception to the common law of all the Frenchmen."[8]

Equality before the law was thus a guiding principle of the new regime. But the major challenge for equality were not revolutionary principles and general declarations, it was their application on the ground. Generally speaking, there were two major problems in putting these principles into practice: first, to introduce this equality in the context of a society that was diverse and stayed diverse; and second, a much more basic problem: to define which of the subjects of the French King would be entitled to the rights of the constitution in the first place. The former status of "subject" was mainly one of submission and thus attributed very generously to as many human beings as possible; but the status of "citizen" entitled one to rights and services and thus those who profited from these rights had to be carefully chosen. While the term "subject" was common in the vocabulary of the Old Regime, "citizen" was a catchword of the revolutionaries that programmatically claimed the reinvention of political man. After 1789, it was not only used in constitutional and legal texts, but Frenchmen also addressed each other with pride as *citoyen*.[9]

7 "*Les hommes naissent et demeurent libres et égaux en droits*"; art. VI. "*La loi* [...] *doit être la même pour tous* [...] *Tous les citoyens étant égaux à ses yeux, sont également admissibles à toutes dignités, places et emplois publics, selon leur capacité, et sans autre distinction que celle de leurs vertus et de leurs talents*" (Déclaration des droits de l'homme et du citoyen, art. I, in *Les declarations des droits de l'homme de 1789*, Christine Fauré (ed.), Paris: Payot & Rivage, 1988, 11. Marcel Gauchet, *La Révolution des droits de l'homme*, Paris: Gallimard, 1989. Antoine de Baecque (ed.), *L'an I des droits des l'homme*, Paris: CNRS, 1988. Philippe Raynaud, La declaration des droits de l'homme, in *The French Revolution and the Creation of Modern Political Culture*, Colin Lucas (ed.), 139–160, Oxford: Pergamon Press, 1988.

8 "*Il n'y a plus, pour aucune partie de la Nation, ni pour aucun individu, aucun privilege, ni exception au droit commun de tous les Français.*" (Constitution du 3 septembre 1791, in: Jacques Godechot (ed.), *Les constitutions de la France depuis 1789*, Paris: Flammarion, 1995, 35.

9 Pierre Rétat, Citoyen, sujet, civisme, in *Handbuch politisch-sozialer Grundbegriffe in Frankreich 1680–1820*, Rolf Reichardt, Eberhard Schmitt (eds.), vol. 9, 75–105, Munich: Oldenbourg, 1988. William H. Sewell, Le citoyen / la citoyenne: Activity, Passivity, and the Revolutionary Concept of Citizenship, in *The French Revolution and the Creation of Modern Political Culture*, Colin Lucas (ed.), 105–123, Oxford: Pergamon Press, 1988. Shanti Marie Singham, Betwixt Cattle and Men: Jews, Blacks, and Women, and the Declaration of the Rights of Man, in *The French Idea of Freedom. The Old Regime and the Declaration of Rights of 1789*, Dale van Kley (ed.), 114–153, Stanford: Stanford University Press, 1994.

For the historical actors, it went without saying that not everybody in France was entitled to equality – that is: equal opportunities for free development and equal possibilities of participation in the political process in the full sense. From the beginning, the new regime created dividing lines: first between different ranks of citizens, and second between citizens and non-citizens. Women, to relate to the subject addressed in the Vienna conference by my colleague Indrani Chatterjee, were considered citizens, but not entitled to all the citizens' rights. They were included in basic constitutional warrants, but important liberties, such as voting and being elected, were not given to them.[10] The male citizens of France were divided into different groups: there were those excluded from the vote, those entitled to vote, and finally those with the right to vote and to be elected. The latter group, defined by higher income, constituted the elite of so-called "active citizens." Many of the "foreigners" living on French soil were excluded from citizenship altogether.[11]

More than 150 years ago, Alexis de Tocqueville already stated that the French Revolution, by trying to overcome the diversity of the old regime, created "equality" and "inequalities" at the same time: "The Revolution burst these ties [of the feudal system], and substituted no political bonds in their stead; it thus paved the way for both equality and servitude." [12] While "privilege" was a basic and unchallenged principle of the Old Regime and thus widely accepted, "inequality" was seen as illegitimate under the new order. The fact that it still existed, even though it was not supposed to, led to political conflict and, in the long run, to a cascade of further revolutions. It was, again, Tocqueville who claimed that "the passion for equality has retained its place at the bottom of the hearts [...] it [...] has remained uniformly the same, striving for its object with obstinate and often blind ardor, willing to sacrifice everything to gain it, and ready to repay its grant from government by cultivating such habits, ideas, and laws as a despotism may require."[13] During the French Revolution, the tensions stemming from the partial realization of ideas of equality grew stronger the further one moved away from the Parisian center of the new order to its peripheries.

---

10 Olwen Hufton, *Women and the Limits of Citizenship in the French Revolution*, Toronto: University of Toronto Press, 1992. Gisela Bock, *Women in European History*, Oxford: Blackwell, 2002, 32–81.

11 Michael Rapport, *Nationality and citizenship in revolutionary France, the treatment of foreigners 1789–1799*, New York, Oxford: Oxford University Press, 2000. Sophie Wahnich, *L'impossible citoyen. L'étranger dans le discours de la Révolution française*, Paris: Albin Michel, 1997.

12 Alexis de Tocqueville, *The Old Regime and the Revolution*, New York: Harper, 1858, 318.

13 de Tocqueville 1858, 253.

II Equality by integration – the case of Alsace

The province of Alsace was added to the kingdom of France in the second half of the 17th century, under Louis XIV. In 1648, the peace settlement of Westphalia declared the Habsburg territories of Alsace a property of the King of France. In 1679, the French crown annexed ten free German cities on the left bank of the Rhine River. In 1680, the "reunions", that is, the military eastward expansion of France, began. The results of this campaign were fixed in 1697, when the Treaty of Ryswick confirmed the Rhine River as France's eastern border. The Alsatians, who had formerly been subjects of the princes of the Holy Roman Empire, now became subjects of the King of France. But in many respects, the region remained a foreign body within the *Royaume de France*. To make his rule of the region acceptable, Louis XIV guaranteed far-reaching exclusive rights to the newly conquered region. First, the King gave the economic privileges of a "*province à l'instar d'étranger effectif*" to Alsace, which meant in practice that, in order to keep the Alsatian economy open to the Reich, the French customs boundary was not established along the Rhine but along the Vosges mountains. Second, the particular rights of the former Free Imperial Cities were maintained, so that these could continue to function in accordance with their often medieval constitutions. Third, far-reaching privileges were given to the Protestants of Alsace: the Edict of Fontainebleau that, in 1685, ended almost a hundred years of religious tolerance in France and was in vigorous effect until 1787, was never applied to Alsace. While Protestants in the rest of the French kingdom faced prosecution, the Alsatian Lutherans, Calvinists, and Zwinglians were granted free exercise of their confession.

This did not mean, though, that the French kings did not try to re-Catholicize the region. By encouraging Catholics to move to the east and by reserving access to the royal administration to them, by establishing churches for service in both denominations, and by insisting on a quota of Catholics in formerly exclusively Protestant municipal administrations, the balance was slowly re-established in a region where the Reformation had been particularly strong since the 16th century.[14]

The specific status of Alsace also had linguistic aspects: Alsatians traditionally spoke German, and the royal policy of integration was very slow to change

14 Lucien Sittler, *L'Alsace terre d'histoire*, Strasbourg: Alsatia, 1988, 164–206. Jean Claude Streicher, Georges Fischer, Pierre Blèze, *Histoire des alsaciens*, vol. 1, Paris: Nathan, 1979, 165–231. Francis L. Ford, *Strasbourg in Transition 1648–1789*, Cambridge, Mass.: Harvard University Press, 1958. David A. Bell, Nation Building and Cultural Particularism in Eighteenth-Century France: The Case of Alsace. *Eighteenth-Century Studies* 21:4 (1988): 472–490.

that. On the eve of the revolution, in bigger cities like Strasbourg, half of the burghers had French and the other half German as their mother tongue. In the Alsatian countryside, only a few understood the language of their King.[15]

Particular rights were also granted to the approximately 20,000 Jews of Alsace, who accounted for 3% of the overall population of Alsace. The Jews in this region had the status of *étrangers* (foreigners); their presence was legalized by individual letters of protection on the base of personal taxation. Their domiciles, their claims to property, and their professions were regulated. Like the Protestants, Jews were not only distinct because of their religion, but also because of their idiom, Yiddish.[16]

In the summer of 1789, the Revolution reached the east of France. Urban revolts in big cities like Strasbourg and Colmar took up the Parisian impulses of July 14. The night of August 4 meant an end to most of Alsace's privileges. From this moment on, the specific conditions in the region were seen as a challenge to the principle of "equality" promised so vociferously by the French revolutionaries. Could a province with populations of a different faith, language, traditions, daily routines, and laws be integrated into the new realm of legal equality?

This question was not only asked by the Parisian government and lawmakers, but also by local elites who called themselves *patriotes* or *amis de la constitution* (friends of the constitution).[17] In these circles, which existed not only in Alsace, but all over France, another concept was extremely widespread, one that resonated with the idea of constitutional "equality" but had slightly different connotations: the concept of *unité*. It meant first and foremost the harmonious and concerted action of the revolutionary movement, and was based on Rousseau's concept of the *volonté générale* (general will).[18]

"Today, one has to cease to be French, or cease to be it only half," the local baron Jean de Turckheim claimed.[19] Accordingly, the local revolutionary elites collaborated with the Parisian center to bring equality before the law and revolutionary unity into a region shaped by its distinctness and diversity. The opera-

---

15 Paul Lévy, *Histoire linguistique d'Alsace et de Lorraine*, vol. 1, Paris, Les belles lettres, 1928, 345.

16 Paula Hyman, *The Emancipation of the Jews of Alsace*, New Haven, London: Yale University Press, 1991, 11–30.

17 Daniel Schönpflug, *Der Weg in die Terreur. Radikalisierung und Konflikte im Straßburger Jakobinerclub 1790–1795*, Munich: Oldenbourg, 2002, 29–47.

18 Patrice Higonnet, *Goodness beyond Virtue: Jacobins during the French Revolution*, Cambridge, Mass.: Harvard University Press, 1998, 240–258.

19 "*Il faut aujourd'hui cesser d'être Français ou cesser de l'être à demi*", cit. in: Jean Claude Streicher, Georges Fischer, Pierre Blèze, *Histoire des alsaciens*, vol. 2, Paris: Nathan, 1979, 11.

tion started very successfully in December 1789. Two days before Christmas, the National Assembly passed a decree establishing a new administrative system, organized in departments, cantons, and municipalities. The administrators on all three levels were democratically elected by the active citizens. A second decisive step was the granting of the full rights of citizenship to the Protestants of Alsace on December 24, 1789, which also meant – for the first time since annexation – access for the Protestants to all offices from the municipal to the national level, and even to the National Assembly. The Protestants, often wealthy urban merchants, profited widely from this integration into the sphere of equal rights. They embraced the new order even more enthusiastically when the new constitution granted religious freedom to all Protestants in France.[20]

Moreover, germanophone Alsatians realized with great satisfaction that the new regime was willing to accept even their diverging language practices. The key decision of the National Assembly was the decree of January 14, 1790. Taking into consideration that the vast majority of Alsatians were unable to read French, the new regime established translation offices that prepared German versions of all legislative texts and advised all administrations to function bilingually.[21] This decree sheds light on the revolutionary understanding of "equality" in this particular context: it meant equality before the law for formerly divergent groups of society, not reduction of cultural diversity by assimilation. Later that same year, in October of 1790, the economic integration of Alsace advanced when the customs frontier of France was moved forward from the Vosges to the Rhine River.

The integration of the Alsatian Jews into the realm of equality took a longer time. In July 1789, there was a wave of violence against Jews in the Alsatian countryside. It was related to the fall of the Bastille, as the waning of the Old Regime liberated hidden antisemitic aggressions. The pogroms of 1789 in the beginning of the Revolution served as a pretext to withhold citizenship from this particular group as a means of protecting them from further violence. First impulses for a new integrative interpretation of equality came from the decree of January 28, 1790, which gave citizenship to the Sephardic Jews of southern France. One and a half years later, after long and heated debates in Paris and the east of France, the Jews of Alsace were finally accepted as full citizens of the new regime.[22]

---

20 Bernard Vogler, Les protestants et la Révolution. *Revue d'Alsace* 116 (1989/90): 197–205.

21 Martyn Lyons, Politics and Patois: The Linguistic Policy of the French Revolution. *Australian Journal of French Studies* 18 (1981): 264–281. Erich Pelzer, Sprachpolitik und Propaganda in Straßburg während der Französischen Revolution, in *Revolution und konservatives Beharren. Das alte Reich und die Französische Revolution*, Karl Otto Freiherr von Aretin, Karl Härter (eds.), 45–57, Mainz: F. Steiner Verlag, 1990.

22 Hyman 1991, 15ff.

The introduction of legal equality in Alsace, a region with traditions of diversity, was thus rather successful in the first years of the French Revolution. Germanophone Protestants and Jews became aware that the new discourses of "equality" could be a means of legitimizing their longstanding claims for emancipation in a new and more efficient way. At that time, revolutionary "equality" seemed to be open for specific social and cultural groups with formerly distinct rights and culture. It was only later, in the course of the radicalization of the revolution, that the "unity" of the early years was lost and that Protestants, German-speakers, and Jews were attacked violently and excluded from the realm of the revolution.

III Equality by exclusion – the case of *Saint-Domingue*

Saint-Domingue, a French colony in the Caribbean Antilles since 1697, had a "diverse" society in a double sense. It was not only an island with enormous differences between social groups ranging from rich, noble planter aristocrats on the one hand, to slaves of African origin on the other, but also a society of a kind that was entirely different from the one in the French motherland. In fact, the whole attraction of the colonial projects in the Caribbean was based on the fact that political and social structures existed there that were unthinkable in Europe. Slave-based plantations provided a base for huge economic profits that were impossible to gain within Europe.[23]

With a certain degree of generalization, one can say that the society of *Saint-Domingue* on the eve of the French Revolution was composed of four major groups: at the top of the social pyramid were the *grands blancs*, rich owners of big plantations, often of aristocratic origin, often mobile between the colony and the motherland. Beneath them were the so called *petits blancs*, who had only modest or no property. The *hommes de couleur* were descendants of racially mixed couples; they were free, and many of them became owners of plantations themselves and employed slaves to labor them. Some of the *hommes de couleur* were wealthier than some of the *petits blancs*, but due to the color of their skin, their social status was precarious. Slaves of African origin constituted the vast majority of *Saint-Domingue*'s population. On the eve of the Revolution, almost every second slave had been born in Africa. Their living and working conditions

23 Oliver Gliech, *Saint-Domingue und die Französische Revolution. Das Ende der weißen Herrschaft in einer karibischen Plantagenwirtschaft*, Vienna: Böhlau, 2011, 205–208. Pierre Pluchon, *Histoire de la colonisation française*, vol. 1, Paris: Fayard, 1991, 369–431.

depended largely on their master, the plantation they served on, and their specific task. Employment in the house or in an agricultural industry like refinery was better than in the fields; domestic servants, foremen, and coachmen fared better than the rest of the slaves.[24]

All of these groups had particular rights, some of which one finds difficult to call "privileges" in this context. Since the 17th century, there had been a growing colonial legislation, most of which was issued by the King and the *Ministère de la marine* that was in charge of the colonies. Some of these legal regulations gained high symbolic, but also economic and political, value. This holds true for the *Exclusif colonial*, the trade monopoly between colony and motherland,[25] and the *Code Noir* of 1685, which provided specific legislation for slaves and their masters.[26]

In 1789, the ambitious project of a new constitution granting equal rights for all posed a major challenge to the specificities of colonial society.[27] From the first days of the revolution on, many of the different groups in *Saint-Domingue* felt that it was crucial to participate in the process of defining equality. The first three groups to do so were the *grands blancs*, the *petits blancs*, and the *hommes de couleur*. The driving forces of their interventions were, of course, as diverse as their social situations. But all three of them were able to organize lobby work and to have an influence in the National Assembly in Versailles and Paris.

---

24 In 1789, the population of *Saint-Domingue* rose to approximately 560,000 people, of which 500,000 were slaves of African Origin, 30,000 whites of different social status, and 30,000 *hommes de couleur*, Gliech 2011, 55.

25 Manuel Covo, L'Assemblée constituante face à l'Exclusif colonial, in *Les colonies, la Révolution française, la loi*, Frédéric Régent, Pierre Boulle (eds.), 69–92, Rennes: Presses Universitaires de Rennes, 2014.

26 Louis Sala-Molins, *Le Code Noir ou le calvaire de Canaan*, Paris: Presses Universitaires de France, 2007.

27 Jean Tarrade, Les colonies et les principes de 1789. Les Assemblées révolutionnaires face au problème de l'esclavage, *Revue française d'Histoire d'outre-mer* 76 (1979): 9–34. Yann-Arzel Durelle-Marc, Sur la question coloniale durant la Constituante (1789–1791): l'idéal liberal à l'épreuve des colonies, in *Les colonies, la Révolution française, la loi*, Frédéric Régent, Pierre Boulle (eds.), 51–68, Rennes: Presses Universitaires de Rennes, 2014. Yves Benot, *La Révolution française et la fin des colonies 1789–1794*, Paris: La découverte, 2004. William Max Nelson, Colonizing France. Revolutionary Regeneration and the First French Empire, in *The French Revolution in Global Perspective*, Suzanne Desan, Lynn Hunt, William Max Nelson (eds.), 73–85, Ithaca, London: Cornell University Press, 2013. Lynn Hunt, The French Revolution in Global Context, in *The Age of Revolutions in Global Context c. 1760–1840*, David Armitage, Sanjay Subrahmanyam (eds.), 20–37, Houndmills: Palgrave McMillan, 2010. Christopher Alan Bayly, *The Birth of the Modern World 1780–1914*, Oxford: Blackwell, 2004.

The "big whites" were organized in a Parisian association known as the *Club Massiac*. They were successful in claiming seats in the National Assembly, which from July, 1789 on gave them, as officially recognized deputies of their home island, the opportunity to defend the status quo in the colony. These representatives insisted that *Saint-Domingue* could by no means be integrated in the realm of constitutional equality. For them, the plantation society needed a constitution of its own – while staying a French colony under the command of Louis XVI.

The "small whites" chose a much more radical stance by pushing not only toward a separate Domingan constitution, but also toward the independence of the island altogether. By following the example of the United States, they hoped to be able to free themselves not only of the dominance of the metropolis, but also of the hegemony of the "big whites", and to become the elite of a new independent Caribbean State. Even though less well connected in Paris, the "small whites" found a base for their initiatives in the newly created colonial assemblies on the island that had no counterpart in the French continental system of administration.

The *hommes de couleur* also lobbied in the National Assembly. Their organization was called the *Société des colons américains* and their political interventions went in yet another direction: they wanted *Saint-Domingue* to become an integral part of France and to submit it entirely to the new constitution, thus hoping to become full citizens in the new order. Even though the Assembly received a deputation of the *hommes de couleur*,[28] it did not fulfill their demands. The free people of color, unlike the planters, were not granted any seats in the early assembly.

At the beginning of the Revolution, the free men of color were thus the only group to argue for "equality" in the sense of the constitutional texts. Their claim to equality had limits though: the *hommes de couleur* did *not* lobby for citizen's rights for slaves. Actually, even though there was some isolated unrest on Santo Domingan plantations already, the slaves did not enter the political scene before 1791. The question of freedom and even citizenship for slaves was discussed, most of all by the Parisian members of the abolitionist *Société des amis des noirs*,[29] who tried to mobilize the National Assembly for the rights of slaves and worked against the interventions of the "big whites"; but abolition did not have the

28 Erick Noël, Les libres de couleur dans le jeu politique in France en 1789: Origines, implications, devenir, in *Les colonies, la Révolution française, la loi*, Frédéric Régent, Pierre Boulle (eds.), 41–50, Rennes: Presses Universitaires de Rennes, 2014.

29 Marcel Dorigny, Bernard Gainot, *La Société des Amis des Noirs*, Paris: Éditions UNESCO/EDICEF, 1998.

slightest chance of becoming a mainstream revolutionary goal in the early years of the Revolution.

In response to the controversial initiatives by groups from *Saint-Domingue* and other colonies, the National Assembly established a *comité des colonies* in order to prepare a parliamentary decision on the relation between the motherland and the colonies. A first committee was founded as early as September 1789, after a heated debate on the *Exclusif colonial* and a first preliminary parliamentary decision that the colonies were "*exemptés de la loi* [exempted from the law]" until a general decision on their future had been made. The committee finished its work in November 1789. But its rather liberal report, which also touched on the delicate question of slavery, was never read to the Assembly, where the majority of deputies were convinced that the new regime should by no means put at risk the enormous income that the colonies meant for the French economy.

A second committee, founded at the beginning of March 1790, was chaired by Antoine Barnave. Its composition was yet another victory for the Club Massiac. Barnave, who beforehand had vociferously fought for a liberal understanding of the rights of man, quickly allied himself with the representatives of the colonial elites, which yielded him the nickname *Monsieur double visage* ("Mister Double Face"). Accordingly, the results of the committee's deliberations, which were read in a report to the Assembly on March 8, 1790, were not very surprising.

In the preamble, the authors of the text distanced themselves from too broad an interpretation of "equality". They stated that the legislators, even though they wanted the colonies to profit from the regeneration that the French Empire had undergone, never had the intention to submit the peripheries of the realm to a law that "could be incompatible with the particular local customs".[30] The committee's proposal specifies that the question of the colonial constitution should not be treated by the National Assembly, but be laid in the hands of colonial assemblies to be elected by the island's citizens. Nevertheless, their idea of the autonomy of the colonies was limited. The committee claimed that the colonial constitution was to be approved by the National Assembly and had to be ratified by the King, just like every other law of the Kingdom. Finally, the report underlined that the system of commerce between colony and motherland should not undergo any modifications. It was only later, by the additional decree of 13 May 1791, that the National Assembly accorded the colonial assemblies the right to decide about the "status of persons" on the island. This was meant to reassure

30 "*qui pourroient être incompatibles avec leurs convenances locales & particulières.*" (*Décret de l'assemblée nationale concernant les colonies, du 8 mars 1790*, Paris: Imprimerie nationale, 1790, 2).

the white colonists that the national government would not alter the institution of slavery.

The assembly applauded the proposal of March 1790 enthusiastically and adopted it unanimously as law on the very day of its first reading. The adversaries of slavery and advocates of the rights of man, like Count Mirabeau, did not intervene in the discussion.[31] But even though they did not raise their voices as on previous occasions, the *amis des noirs* must have felt that, on that day, the National Assembly passed a law that conflicted with the idea of equality, that renewed particular legislation, and that was moreover an infraction of the principles of popular sovereignty and *volonté générale*. The decree created a tension between the sovereignty of the colonial assembly and of the National Assembly, because it was Paris that fixed the procedure of colonial administration and that controlled the outcomes of the political will on the island.

This became even clearer when, on March 28, 1790, the Assembly detailed its former decree in an *Instruction adressée par l'Assemblée nationale à la Colonie de Saint-Domingue*. The instruction designated the active citizens as all those who were over 25 years old, owners of real estate, and taxpayers. This regulation did not mention the free men of color, but it could be interpreted as including them, while excluding the majority of Santo Domingans, the slaves. The instruction confirmed that all the decisions of the colonial assembly were only provisional until they were confirmed by the National Assembly and ratified by the King. The latter was declared the single and only holder of sovereignty, represented in the colony by a governor.

When the March decree and the instruction were published and applied on the island of *Saint-Domingue*, they almost immediately led to serious conflicts. The most radical of opponents were the *hommes de couleur*. They had been satisfied at first, as they saw it as a legitimate claim that the new legislation provided them with voting rights for the new colonial assemblies. But the Governor of *Saint-Domingue* read this paragraph of the decree differently, and thus triggered armed resistance by the colored citizens, who felt deprived of their equal rights. From this moment on, *Saint-Domingue* gradually slipped into civil war. Soon the slaves would enter the political scene, claiming revolutionary equality just as it was proclaimed in the solemn declarations of the National Assembly. Despite all kinds of political and military manoeuvers, which included the abolition of slavery in 1794, the spiral of violence and unrest could not be brought to a halt. In 1804, the French colonizers were beaten and expelled from

31 Marcel Dorigny (ed.), *Les Bières flottantes des négriers, un discours non prononcé sur l'abolition de la traite des Noirs*, Saint-Étienne: Publication de l'université de Saint-Étienne, 1999.

the island. *Saint-Domingue* was declared independent. A former officer of the army of slaves, Jean-Jacques Dessalines, became the first Emperor of the newly founded state of Haiti.

IV Conclusion

This article has analyzed the contradictions between revolutionary discourses and practices concerning legal "equality". Even though "equality" was solemnly declared a cornerstone of the new revolutionary order, the political realization of this idea posed a serious problem to the French legislators of the early years of the Revolution. This becomes particularly obvious when one looks at the margins of the national and the imperial realm of France.

The reasons for the gap between ideas and practice lay first of all in the specific eighteenth-century idea of "equality" that only in theory meant a harmonization of social and cultural diversity. First, the meritocratic understanding of the idea of "equality" did not allow for a general, unstructured application; second, it seems obvious that the historical actors made a clear distinction between citizens or humans on the one hand, and slaves on the other, who even after the Revolution deserved only a minimum of protection, but no rights; third, revolutionary politics were shaped by pragmatism: revolutionary principles were important, but – in a context of a state close to bankruptcy – only as long as they did not put slavery, a most important source of income, at risk.

It moreover seems that "equality" in the ranks of the National Assembly and on the local level was understood as a new field of discourse in which particular interests could be negotiated. Citizens (and noncitizens) of France very quickly learned to use the new language of liberty and equality to defend or even extend their rights. This also meant that, in the political debates, "equality" was defined in many different ways. When an Alsatian Protestant used the word, it meant: citizenship, political participation, and, most of all, an end to discrimination against his faith. When a planter from *Saint-Domingue* used the same concept, he was referring to more autonomy for the colonial elites of the island. This meant that, at the top and on the bottom of society, equality in the end did not mean equal rights for all, but rather the introduction of a new form of legal diversity. The French revolutionary discourse and practices thus continued a more general dilemma of universalism and colonial exclusion that had haunted European Empires ever since the beginning of Enlightenment.[32]

References

de Baecque, Antoine (ed.), *L'an I des droits des l'homme*, Paris: CNRS, 1988.
Baker, Keith Michael, Constitution, in *Critical Dictionary of the French Revolution*, by François Furet, Mona Ozouf (eds.), vol. 2, 4474–479, Cambridge, Mass.: Harvard University Press, 1989.
Bayly, Christopher Alan, *The Birth of the Modern World 1780–1914*, Oxford: Blackwell, 2004.
Bell, David A., Nation Building and Cultural Particularism in Eighteenth-Century France: The Case of Alsace. *Eighteenth–Century Studies* 21:4 (1988): 472–490.
Benot, Yves, *La Révolution française et la fin des colonies 1789–1794*, Paris: La découverte, 2004.
Bock, Gisela, *Women in European History*, Oxford: Blackwell, 2002.
Bossenga, Gail, *The Politics of Privilege. Old Regime and Revolution in Lille*, Cambridge: Cambridge University Press, 1991.
Courrier de Versailles à Paris, et de Paris à Versailles, no. 30 of Aug. 6, 1789.
Covo, Manuel, L'Assemblée constituante face à l'Exclusif colonial, in *Les colonies, la Révolution française, la loi*, Frédéric Régent, Pierre Boulle (eds.), 69–92, Rennes: Presses Universitaires de Rennes, 2014.
Dann, Otto, Gleichheit, in *Geschichtliche Grundbegriffe*, vol. 2, 1014–1018, Stuttgart: Klett–Cotta, 1975.
Décret de l'assemblée nationale concernant les colonies, du 8 mars 1790, Paris: Imprimerie nationale, 1790.
Dorigny, Marcel (ed.), *Les Bières flottantes des négriers, un discours non prononcé sur l'abolition de la traite des Noirs*, Saint-Étienne: Publication de l'université de Saint-Étienne, 1999.
Dorigny, Marcel, Bernard Gainot, *La Société des Amis des Noirs*, Paris: Éditions UNESCO/ EDICEF, 1998.
Durelle-Marc, Yann-Arzel, Sur la question coloniale durant la Constituante (1789–1791): l'idéal liberal à l'épreuve des colonies, in *Les colonies, la Révolution française, la loi*, Frédéric Régent, Pierre Boulle (eds.), 51–68, Rennes: Presses Universitaires de Rennes, 2014.
Duverger, Maurice, *Les constitutions de la France*, Paris: Univ. de France, 1993.
Fauré, Christine (ed.), *Les declarations des droits de l'homme de 1789*, Paris: Payot & Rivage, 1988.
Fitzsimmons, Michael, *The Remaking of France. The National Assembly and the Constitution of 1791*, Cambridge: Cambridge University Press, 1994.

32 Klemens Kaps, Zwischen Emanzipation und Exklusion: Fortschrittsdenken und die Wahrnehmung kultureller Differenz in der europäischen Aufklärung, in *Europa als Weltregion. Zentrum, Modell oder Provinz?* (=Edition Weltregionen, vol. 23), Thomas Ertl, Andrea Komlosy, Hans-Jürgen Puhle (eds.), 66–79, Wien (New Academic Press) 2014.

Ford, Francis L., *Strasbourg in Transition 1648–1789*, Cambridge, Mass.: Harvard University Press, 1958.
Furet, François, Halévi, Ran, *La Monarchie républicaine. La constitution de 1791*, Paris: Fayard, 1996.
Gauchet, Marcel, *La Révolution des droits de l'homme*, Paris: Gallimard, 1989.
Gliech, Oliver, *Saint-Domingue und die Französische Revolution. Das Ende der weißen Herrschaft in einer karibischen Plantagenwirtschaft*, Vienna: Böhlau, 2011.
Godechot, Jacques (ed.), *Les constitutions de la France depuis 1789*, Paris: Flammarion, 1995.
Higonnet, Patrice, *Goodness beyond Virtue: Jacobins during the French Revolution*, Cambridge, Mass.: Harvard University Press, 1998.
Hufton, Olwen, *Women and the Limits of Citizenship in the French Revolution*, Toronto: University of Toronto Press, 1992.
Hunt, Lynn, The French Revolution in Global Context, in *The Age of Revolutions in Global Context c. 1760–1840*, David Armitage, Sanjay Subrahmanyam (eds.), 20–37, Houndmills: Palgrave McMillan, 2010.
Hyman, Paula, *The Emancipation of the Jews of Alsace*, New Haven, London: Yale University Press, 1991.
Kaps, Klemens, Zwischen Emanzipation und Exklusion: Fortschrittsdenken und die Wahrnehmung kultureller Differenz in der europäischen Aufklärung, in *Europa als Weltregion. Zentrum, Modell oder Provinz?* (=Edition Weltregionen, vol. 23), Thomas Ertl, Andrea Komlosy, Hans-Jürgen Puhle (eds.), 66–79, Wien (New Academic Press) 2014.
Lévy, Paul, *Histoire linguistique d'Alsace et de Lorraine*, vol. 1, Paris, Les belles lettres, 1928.
Lyons, Martyn, Politics and Patois: The Linguistic Policy of the French Revolution. *Australian Journal of French Studies* 18 (1981): 264–281.
Markoff, John, *The Abolition of Feudalism. Peasants, Lords, and Legislators in the French Revolution*, University Park: Pennsylvania State University Press, 1996.
Nelson, William Max, Colonizing France. Revolutionary Regeneration and the First French Empire, in *The French Revolution in Global Perspective*, Suzanne Desan, Lynn Hunt, William Max Nelson (eds.), 73–85, Ithaca, London: Cornell University Press, 2013.
Noël, Erick, Les libres de couleur dans le jeu politique in France en 1789: Origines, implications, devenir, in *Les colonies, la Révolution française, la loi*, Frédéric Régent, Pierre Boulle (eds.), 41–50, Rennes: Presses Universitaires de Rennes, 2014.
Ozouf, Mona, Equality, in *Critical Dictionnary of the French Revolution*, François Furet, Mona Ozouf (eds.), 669–683, Cambridge: Harvard University Press, 1989.
Pelzer, Erich, Sprachpolitik und Propaganda in Straßburg während der Französischen Revolution, in *Revolution und konservatives Beharren. Das alte Reich und die Französische Revolution*, Karl Otto Freiherr von Aretin, Karl Härter (eds.), 45–57, Mainz: F. Steiner Verlag, 1990.
Pluchon, Pierre, *Histoire de la colonisation française*, vol. 1, Paris: Fayard, 1991.
Rapport, Michael, *Nationality and citizenship in revolutionary France, the treatment of foreigners 1789–1799*, New York, Oxford: Oxford University Press, 2000.
Raynaud, Philippe, La declaration des droits de l'homme, in *The French Revolution and the Creation of Modern Political Culture*, Colin Lucas (ed.), 139–160, Oxford: Pergamon Press, 1988.
Rétat, Pierre, Citoyen, sujet, civisme, in *Handbuch politisch-sozialer Grundbegriffe in Frankreich 1680–1820*, Rolf Reichardt, Eberhard Schmitt (eds.), 75–105, Munich: Oldenbourg, 1988.

Richet, Denis, L'esprit de la constitution 1789–1791, in *The French Revolution and the Creation of Modern Political Culture*, Colin Lucas (ed.), vol. 2, 63–68, Oxford: Pergamon Press, 1987.
Robinson, J. H., (ed.), *Readings in European History*, vol. 2, Boston: Ginn, 1906.
Sala-Molins, Louis, *Le Code Noir ou le calvaire de Canaan*, Paris: Presses Universitaires de France, 2007.
Schmale, Wolfgang, Constitution, constitutionnel, in *Handbuch politisch-sozialer Grundbegriffe in Frankreich 1680–1820*, Rolf Reichardt, Eberhard Schmitt (eds.), vol. 12, 31–64, Munich: Oldenbourg, 1992.
Schönpflug, Daniel, *Der Weg in die Terreur. Radikalisierung und Konflikte im Straßburger Jakobinerclub 1790–1795*, Munich: Oldenbourg, 2002.
Sewell, William H., Le citoyen / la citoyenne: Activity, Passivity, and the Revolutionary Concept of Citizenship, in *The French Revolution and the Creation of Modern Political Culture*, Colin Lucas (ed.), 105–123, Oxford: Pergamon Press, 1988.
Sieyès, Emmanuel, *Essai sur les privileges*, s.l. 1788.
Singham, Shanti Marie, Betwixt Cattle and Men: Jews, Blacks, and Women, and the Declaration of the Rights of Man, in *The French Idea of Freedom. The Old Regime and the Declaration of Rights of 1789*, Dale van Kley (ed.), 114–153, Stanford: Stanford University Press, 1994.
Sittler, Lucien, *L'Alsace terre d'histoire*, Strasbourg: Alsatia, 1988.
Streicher, Jean Claude, Fischer, Georges, Blèze, Pierre, *Histoire des alsaciens*, vol. 1 + 2, Paris: Nathan, 1979.
Tarrade, Jean, Les colonies et les principes de 1789. Les Assemblées révolutionnaires face au problème de l'esclavage, *Revue française d'Histoire d'outre-mer* 76 (1979): 9–34.
de Tocqueville, Alexis, *The Old Regime and the Revolution*, New York: Harper, 1858.
Vogler, Bernhard, Les protestants et la Révolution. *Revue d'Alsace* 116 (1989/90): 197–205.
Wahnich, Sophie, *L'impossible citoyen. L'étranger dans le discours de la Révolution française*, Paris: Albin Michel, 1997.

Contributors

Ali Anooshahr is Associate Professor of History at the University of California, Davis. He focuses on the history of the Persianate world, with a particular focus on the Indo-Persian intellectual history (especially historiography) on which he has published a number of articles. His forthcoming book entitled *Turkestan and the Rise of Eurasian Empires* investigates the treatment of Turco-Mongol identity and tradition in Persian chronicles of the early sixteenth century.

Blain Auer is Professor of the Study of Islam in South Asia at the University of Lausanne in the Department of South Asian Languages and Civilizations. He specializes in Perso-Islamic history and culture in the context of premodern South Asia. His book titled *Symbols of Authority in Medieval Islam: History, Religion, and Muslim Legitimacy in the Delhi Sultanate*, was published by I.B. Tauris in 2012.

Thomas Ertl is Professor of Economic and Social History of the Middle Ages at the University of Vienna. His fields of research include transcultural entanglement and comparison. One result of this interest is an edited book titled *Handling Diversity. Comparative Perspectives on Medieval and Early-Modern India and Europe*, published by Sage Publications in 2013.

Sumit Guha is Professor of History at the University of Texas at Austin. He studies the social, economic and intellectual history of Southern Asia through the past millennium. His most recent book is *Beyond Caste: Identity and Power in South Asia, Past and Present*, published by E.J. Brill worldwide and Permanent Black for India. He is presently completing a history of Indian historical memory over c.1500-1900.

Karl Härter is a legal historian and research group leader at the Max-Planck-Institute for European Legal History, Frankfurt/M. and teaches early modern and modern history at the University of Darmstadt. His research interests and publications concern early modern and modern legal, political and constitutional history with a focus on the history of public and penal law, crime and criminal justice.

Mia Korpiola is a legal historian working on various aspects of Swedish and Finnish legal history from the Middle Ages to modernity. Her publications include an edited book on the Svea Court of Appeal in the early modern period and another on regional variation in matrimonial law and custom in later medieval and sixteenth-century Europe.

Gijs Kruijtzer is a historian of the early modern period and teaches colonial and global history at Leiden University. His publications include a monograph on identity in seventeenth-century India and articles on visual representations across boundaries. He currently researches justifications for the transgression of divine law, comparing the Persian world and Europe.

Corinne Lefèvre is a Research Fellow at the CNRS (National Center for Scientific Research) and the CEIAS (Center for Indian and South Asian Studies). She specializes in the political and cultural history of the Mughal empire (16th-18th c.). She recently edited (with Ines G. Županov and Jorge Flores) *Cosmopolitismes en Asie du Sud. Sources, itinéraires, langues (xvie-xviiie siècles)* published by Editions de l'EHESS in 2015.

Sanjog Rupakheti is an Assistant Professor of history at College of the Holy Cross, Worcester, MA. His research interests include modernity, law, caste and gender relations. His forthcoming book, *The Making of a Himalayan Kingdom: Family, Law, and Power in Nepal*, examines a socio-political history of the creation of the Nepali state within the comparative context of late eighteenth and mid nineteenth century South Asia.

Daniel Schönpflug teaches 18th and 19th century history at the Freie Universität of Berlin and is Academic Coordinator at the Wissenschaftskolleg zu Berlin. His fields of research include the history of the French Revolution, of royal marriages and of modern terrorism. He currently finishes a book project on the experiences and visions of the era immediately following the First World War.

Index